Understanding Global Politics

KEVIN BLOOR

ii

E-INTERNATIONAL RELATIONS PUBLISHING

E-International Relations
Bristol, England
2022

ISBN: 978-1-910814-61-1

Production: Michael Tang
Cover Image: Alba_alioth/Shutterstock

A catalogue record for this book is available from the British Library.

E-International Relations

Editor-in-Chief and Publisher: Stephen McGlinchey
Editor: Kieran O'Meara
Editorial Assistance: Franny Klatt, Adeleke Olumide Ogunnoiki, Farah Saleem Düzakman.

E-International Relations is the world's leading International Relations website. Our daily publications feature expert articles, reviews and interviews – as well as student learning resources. The website is run by a non-profit organisation based in Bristol, England and staffed by an all-volunteer team of students and academics. In addition to our website content, E-International Relations publishes a range of books. As E-International Relations is committed to open access in the fullest sense, free electronic versions of our books, including this one, are available on our website.

Find out more at https://www.e-ir.info/

About the author

Kevin Bloor is an author, Principal Examiner and teacher. He has over twenty years of experience in the social sciences and is the author of several texts and educational resources such as *The Definitive Guide to Political Ideologies* and *Understanding Political Theory* and *Sociology: Theories, Theorists and Concepts*. He holds a BA in Politics and International Relations and an MA in International Relations, both from Staffordshire University, and an MPhil in Government from Manchester University. He maintains the personal website https://www.kevinbloor.com/

To my wife, Melanie for all your love and support.

Contents

Introduction

The structure of this book is based on a popular A-Level Politics course, taken by students typically aged 16–18 in the United Kingdom's national curriculum system. While it serves as a guide for students and instructors, it also seeks to go beyond the basic requirements of preparing for the examination by discussing theoretical perspectives that lie largely outside the restrictions of the syllabus and exploring case studies that cast light on the forces that shape the politics of our world. In that sense, this book is both a guide to an A-Level student and/or a starting point for any reader looking to get to grips with the fundamentals of how the world works – including as preparation for embarking on an International Relations degree at university. The book seeks to offer a comprehensive guide for all those with an interest in a constantly evolving subject matter

Tour of the book

• Each chapter is split into headed sections that allow you to break up the information and gradually see how the content fits together as you read it through.
• To help you use the book effectively, and to lock in the information for revision purposes, each chapter ends with a 'Key Terms' box and 'Key Points' box.
• There is an extensive glossary and a list of commonly used abbreviations towards the back of the book that you may wish to consult as you read through each chapter.
• A set of resources specially made to accompany this book is available from kevinbloor.com under supporting resources / global politics: https://www.kevinbloor.com/supporting-resources/#1620731679567-bb11b767-28b5

About the Chapters

The opening chapter offers an exploration of the two dominant paradigms within the academic discipline of International Relations – realism and liberalism – and how they debate elements such as human nature. It is via these notions that the subject matter can be better understood. The two main theoretical perspectives will be subject to a critique, highlighting the strengths and weaknesses of each. It should be noted that there are various concepts covered in the opening chapter unique to these two theoretical approaches alone. It will also consider several prominent divisions within the debate. The two dominant theories in the context of global politics are then applied to events since the turn of the century. The opening section ends with a discussion of alternatives from outside of the realism/liberalism dichotomy. These include constructivism, critical theory, feminism, postcolonialism and world systems theory. Each of these perspectives lights a candle upon our theoretical understanding of global politics and shines a light on the flaws inherent within the mainstream accounts.

Chapter two considers the relationship between the state and globalisation. The primary focus throughout is the role of the state and the broader significance of globalisation. It also identifies the characteristics that define the nation-state, national sovereignty and the concept of interdependence. There will be an evaluation of globalisation alongside its implications. Most notably, globalisation may have potentially altered how we might contextualise the state. It could even spell the death-knell of the nation-state, although it has also been claimed that globalisation has contributed towards a resurgence in the state. The chapter ends with an examination of the ways and extent to which globalisation seeks to resolve issues such as conflict prevention.

The book next considers how global governance shapes global politics. The establishment of international institutions that resemble a quasi-legislature, executive and judiciary provides a workable basis for the practice of global governance. Chapter three begins with an outline of the development of the United Nations (UN). It then moves to an assessment of the significance, and the changing role, of the North Atlantic Treaty Organisation (NATO). The institutions that lie at the very heart of the 'Washington Consensus' are examined before we move onto how the institutions of global governance such as the World Trade Organization (WTO), the G7 (formerly the G8) and the G20 operate. This lays the groundwork for an application towards transnational issues and problems.

Chapter four then applies the concept of global governance towards the protection of human rights and the environment. The chapter begins with an examination of attempts to uphold the universality of human rights. Humanitarian intervention is placed within a broader context of international law, judicial institutions and the continued significance of national sovereignty. This inevitably opens up a discussion of selective intervention, Western hypocrisy and other recent developments. We then examine the role, significance and impact of those measures implemented to address climate change. The manner in which the institutions of global governance deal with this existential threat is of vital importance towards contemporary international relations. The chapter concludes with an examination of the extent to which institutions of global governance address and resolve pressing global issues.

The focus of the book then shifts towards a consideration of power and developments. It begins with a detailed analysis of power and its importance. The aim of Chapter five is to place contemporary developments within the context of power and polarity. This requires a consideration of concepts such as unilateralism, hegemony and mutually assured destruction. The various systems of government are outlined and identified. In theoretical terms, there is a detailed evaluation of the liberal prescription for a better world and an application of the changing nature of power towards the Middle East.

Chapter six, the final chapter in the book, examines the magnitude of regionalism as a force that shapes global politics. This chapter analyses the reasons for regional integration, evaluates the relationship with globalisation and outlines the development of regional organisations. The chapter's primary focus will centre on the EU and consider the organisation's significance as an actor on the global stage, before concluding with the ways and extent to which regionalism attempts to resolve contemporary issues.

Getting started with Global Politics

If there is one quote that encapsulates politics, we need to look no further than a remark by Ernest Benn (1875–1954) – 'politics is the art of looking for trouble, finding it everywhere, diagnosing it incorrectly and applying the wrong remedies'. Politicians have an uncanny ability to find trouble, misunderstand the problem and apply an incorrect response. One of the repeated political failures is a reluctance to interpret a situation from an alternative perspective. Many conflicts could have been prevented by adopting this mindset. If there is one theme that occurs time and time again throughout this book, it is surely found in that wise observation from Benn.

My interest in global politics was forged during the turbulence of the Cold War. The battle of ideologies marked an epic struggle for the future of mankind. Like others of my generation, I had a ring-side seat to a seemingly new chapter of history. That which had been such a dominant feature of my formative years (such as the prospect of nuclear annihilation) changed overnight. The fall of the Berlin Wall in 1989 felt like the end of the ideological contest between Capitalism and Soviet Communism. The social experiment of creating a new utopia appeared to have failed its people, or at least that was the dominant narrative I was presented with. It was a time in which the news presented in 'The West' was coloured by a heady sense of optimism. The war was over, capitalism was in the ascendancy and democracy was spreading its reach throughout the world. In the words of an often cited and heavily contested theorist of the time, we had reached 'The end of history' (Fukuyama 1992). Liberal democracy emerged victorious, and the future seemed to be tinged with freedom and happiness. By the time the liberal 'democratic peace thesis' was presented to me during an undergraduate lecture, the correlation between the spread of liberal democracy and peace made perfect sense. How times have changed. That optimism has since been decimated by populism, pandemics and protectionism – and that is without leaving the letter 'p'. The world seems to be a much darker place now, and it is to that reality we must all now face.

The unmistakable drift away from liberal democracy is a prescient reminder that there are no final victories in politics. The liberal optimism that characterised the early 1990s has been buried under the weight of history. There are several developments within international relations that have overturned the optimism of that time. The rise of the self-styled 'strong man', the existential threat posed by Covid-19, the poisonous character of tribal politics and the prospect of a trade war now shape the contours of the debate. The concepts and theories that captured the zeitgeist of a previous era must be reassessed for the modern world.

Such a dramatic turnaround reminds us that there is always the potential for events to overturn cosy assumptions. Equally, there are no final defeats in politics. For instance, the rise of populist politicians has witnessed a revival in nationalist (and even quasi-fascist) sentiment. The contest of ideas is an ever-present feature of the political arena, and this clash of ideas has the capacity to reinvent itself from one era to the next. Borrowing language from Economics, there is an inherent competition between international actors over scarce resources. Inevitably, this will shape the behaviour of states and non-state actors. Equally, the dynamics of a 'glocal' (a portmanteau of 'global' and 'local') commons often generate some level of cooperation and coexistence. Frankly, nothing is deterministic in the political realm.

In seeking to identify which theories and concepts are appropriate to an explanation of the world today, there have at least been some welcome developments. We have for instance seen a sustained challenge to the Eurocentric worldview that captured the zeitgeist at the end of the Cold War. A number of theoretical perspectives have exposed the limitations of this approach. Schools of thought within International Relations and the wider Social Sciences such as constructivism, critical theory and postcolonialism all offer valuable insights into the unconscious bias that can overshadow our understanding, alongside offering a different means of interpretation. The greater the number of perspectives available for application, the more likely we can escape the confines of a dominant mindset.

Another valuable lesson concerns the changes within the hierarchy of states. There is no permanent power status within international relations; nor is there a permanency of 'polarity' (the distribution of power). At any given time, a number of states are in ascendancy, whilst others are invariably in decline. The so-called 'unipolar moment', where the United States (US) was the only global superpower after the collapse of the Soviet Union in 1991, has changed dramatically.

A further misconception that has been exposed with the passage of time is the actual importance of states. Global politics was (and to some degree still is) presented as a contest between states, and to understand global politics demands a state-centric perspective. With the benefit of hindsight, who could have predicted that multinational corporations such as Apple or Alphabet (the parent company of Google) would take annual revenues greater than the gross domestic product (GDP) of nation-states? Part of the reason is that most of us carry around with us a realist mind map from our initial awareness of history (see Chapter one). With the passage of time, this has been shown to be a misconception, one of several within the field and an issue I feel needs addressing.

In order to properly comprehend the subject, there are a number of misconceptions that need highlighting before we can fully explore what makes up global politics. Firstly, the academic discipline of International Relations offers far more than just a Western-centric (or sometimes called 'Eurocentric') account of history (see McGlinchey 2022). There is a surprisingly rich variety of perspectives to consider when seeking the means to interpret global politics. For instance, there is an on-going debate between realists and liberals in terms of understanding how the global system operates. Having said this, it is difficult to entirely escape Western-centric assumptions. It should also be acknowledged that Western-centric assumptions undoubtedly casts valuable light on the practice of humanitarian intervention and what constitutes a rogue state.

Secondly, the subject could never be fully understood through one particular prism. In reality, there are various contesting perspectives and each one offers something unique. Each of the major theoretical narratives (notably realism and liberalism) offers a cogent and at times convincing account of International Relations. Realism is often depicted as reflecting three Ss –

statism, survival and self-help (Dunne and Schmidt, 2020) – and provides a conventional framework for interpreting global politics. In contrast, liberalism offers a very different set of assumptions and prescriptions. The two main paradigms have been updated in recent years to reflect recent developments, and whilst this has stimulated greater interest in the two main paradigms, there are other more developed theories that demand consideration. This will be expanded upon in Chapter one with reference to constructivism, critical theory, feminism, postcolonialism and world systems theory. Each of these perspectives takes us further away from the Western-centric prism that still casts a degree of influence over the subject matter.

Another notable misconception within the field is that of 'American exceptionalism' (Chomsky 1991). This is an entirely unconvincing social construct and an extremely unhelpful one. Although the importance of the United States in global politics is undeniable, the notion that one country is somehow exceptional does not survive close scrutiny. American exceptionalism is however of some importance in terms of explaining America's role as a 'hegemon' (a dominant state within international relations), which at times can also result in the US adopting the role of a so-called 'world policeman'. There also seems to be a mindset amongst policymakers in the US that other countries must simply follow the American normative prescription of life, liberty and the pursuit of happiness. It should also be noted that any argument which matches the worldview of American policymakers (such as Fukuyama's 'End of History' thesis) is adopted more quickly than those that appear to challenge it.

Another intellectually fashionable comment that may have outlived its usefulness is that all 'truth' is relative. This is a key element within the postmodernist perspective. It is based on the notion that there are several versions of 'truth', and all have a certain degree of validity. Politics therefore consists of comparing different versions of the 'truth'. However, there are some truths relevant to the subject matter that can be said to be absolute and undeniable. Without these, it would surely be impossible to construct any understanding of the subject matter. We need some fixed points in order to navigate the stormy seas of global politics and see through instances of 'fake/false news'.

There are of course other misconceptions that do little to advance our understanding. For instance, the argument that 'Americans are from Mars, and Europeans are from Venus' is overly simplistic and now somewhat dated (Kagan 2004). In reality, the United States is a bastion of both hard power and soft power (see Chapter five). In contrast, the European Union (EU) has expanded its military capacity in recent years. The description of the latter as a civilian actor has been overtaken by events. Once again, we are reminded how events can overturn long-held assumptions.

This book is aimed at those with an interest in cultivating a clearer understanding of global politics. It will hopefully bring together those who are interested in the changing dynamics of the international system with those who seek to comprehend the often-bewildering pace of change in the world around them. Above all, it is aimed at those who recognise that in global politics the last page is never truly written. We therefore need a theoretical and conceptual framework in order to ground us in stormy waters. It is only through a better awareness that we can hope to offer any lasting improvement to the world we inhabit. The significance of global politics is, and will surely always remain, a constant feature of our lives.

Anyone with the slightest curiosity about the forces that shape the world around them will hopefully take away something valuable from these pages. There is always much to be gained from the study of global issues, human rights, protection of the environment, humanitarian intervention, international cooperation and conflict prevention – and as far as the will to understand global politics goes, there will never be a better time than the present.

Finally, regarding the use of the core term 'International Relations' in this book: It is capitalised when referring to the named discipline that is taught and studied at universities. However, the same term is often used in the lowercase 'international relations' when referring to the non-academic everyday interactions of people (for economic, political or other reasons) on the global political stage. The term 'global politics' is therefore interchangeable with lowercase 'international relations' and is also used in this book as a reference to a section of the A-Level course (Global Politics) on which this book is primarily designed to accompany.

1

Theories of Global Politics

This opening chapter offers an exploration of the two dominant and contesting paradigms within International Relations: 'realism' and 'liberalism'. We will consider the main ideas of both theories and how they offer a contrasting perspective on aspects of International Relations. The strengths and limitations of realism and liberalism will be considered. Concepts covered in this chapter entail the balance of power, complex interdependence, the cobweb model, the society of states, the billiard-ball model and the security dilemma. This section also considers several prominent theorists from the binary debate, alongside certain theoretical divisions within each school of thought. The chapter leads towards an evaluation of realism and liberalism in the context of global politics since the turn of the century and concludes with a discussion of alternative theories outside of the realism/liberalism dichotomy prior to laying out some key terminology and points of the chapter.

The Key Qualities of Realism

The chief qualities of realism that will be discussed individually are as follows:

- Sovereign states as the primary actor of global politics
- The balance of power
- The importance of international anarchy
- The inevitability of war
- The security dilemma

Sovereign States as the Primary Actors of Global Politics

The realist school of thought claims that states are the main actors and key agents within global politics. Whilst non-state actors are of some relevance, they pale into insignificance when compared to states. For instance, the actions of a state can be detrimental to the interests of non-state actors (such as a trade embargo upon companies from another country). In a more dramatic sense, it is only the state that can launch a military operation. A handful of states even possess the ability to press the nuclear button and bring devastation to the planet.

The realist conception of the state is rooted in the traditions of the Westphalian system. The 1648 Treaty of Westphalia laid down the principle that every state is sovereign over its designated territory, and that this should overlap with common cultural, linguistic, religious and historical norms – what we call 'The Nation'. As a theoretical concept, the nation-state can be thought of as a sovereign state in which most of its members share a common language, history and culture. In essence, sovereignty can be defined as the authority of a state to govern itself. The principle therefore applies equally for a small state like Tuvalu alongside powerful ones such as members of the G7.

The Westphalian system is thus based upon the notion of non-intervention. As sovereign states, intervention by an external power is contrary to the United Nations Charter as 'nothing should authorise intervention in matters essentially within the domestic jurisdiction of any state' (United Nations 1945). However, in practice, the doctrine of non-intervention is routinely violated for a number of reasons. These can range from military aggression to humanitarian intervention. Intervention in the domestic affairs of a sovereign state also undermines the Westphalian notion that each state should have equal recognition under international law. It could also be argued that the only means by which non-intervention can ever be completely guaranteed is the possession of nuclear weapons, acting as a deterrent to intervention.

The Balance of Power

The balance of power is both a theoretical concept and a pragmatic means to protect the existence of the state. The concept is built upon the assumption that states can only secure their survival by preventing other states (or alliances) from bettering their military dominance and power basis.

In a world governed by 'Realpolitik', military aggression is countered by an equilibrium of power between rival coalitions. When a country is under threat, it can gain safety and security by adopting a policy of either 'balancing' or 'band-wagoning'. Let's unpack these terms. The former refers to states allying themselves against a threat to their territorial existence, such as the Warsaw Pact in response to the North Atlantic Treaty Organisation (NATO). In contrast, band-wagoning consists of aligning with a stronger power (such as the special relationship between the United Kingdom (UK) and the US).

Other strategies associated with the balance of power principle include 'buck-passing' and 'chain-ganging'. The former refers to the refusal amongst nation-states to confront a growing threat in the hope that another state will act as a necessary deterrent. One of the most famous historical examples was the policy of appeasement adopted by the major powers of Western Europe in the face of Nazi expansionism. In doing so, the European Powers effectively passed the buck to the Soviet Union – 'buck-passing'. 'Chain-ganging' however is a term used to describe the probability of inter-state conflict due to multi-state alliances. The agreed principles of such alliances are usually centred upon a mutual defence clause, such as Article 5 of the NATO Charter. Inevitably, the consequence of such an arrangement is an elevated possibility of triggering war, as with the notion of Mutually Assured Destruction (MAD) during the Cold War.

In a system built upon self-help, structural realists, such as the noted thinker Kenneth Waltz (1979), predict that a balance of power will always emerge even in the absence of a conscious attempt to maintain equilibrium. In an anarchic system, alliances will form against those who pose a threat of some kind regardless of its intentions. In contrast, classical realists emphasise the deliberate role played by state leaders and diplomats in the maintenance of a balance of power. The Balance of Power must therefore be constructed in some manner via international law and diplomatic agreements. It is important to note that, despite such differences, all realists view the balance of power as a fundamental aspect of international relations, being the outcome of human behaviour and/or the cause of state behaviour.

International Anarchy and its Implications

Anarchy is a Greek term meaning without rules or without a ruler. Within an anarchic system, sovereign states must ultimately focus their energies upon the search for stability and order, given that there is no sovereign entity higher than the state – i.e., the social condition between states is ruler-less and thus depends on their cooperative capacities. This leads them towards the pursuit of strategies such as the aforementioned balance of power within the boundaries of a particular type of polarity and structural order.

Amongst realists, there is an acceptance that anarchy is prevalent within the global system. Due to the absence of an overarching authority (such as a federated world government), sovereign states can only secure their own survival via maintaining some form of equilibrium. States must hence forge a chain of informal understandings with other units that maintain a system of cooperation. This equilibrium of anarchical self-help reveals itself to be rooted in norms and rules that can increase levels of trust and reciprocity between states.

Although the international system lacks a world government, there is a system of global governance to impose a semblance of structural formality. The obvious example of this is the United Nations (UN). Created in the aftermath of the Second World War, the UN implements international law agreed upon between states out of their condition of mutual anarchy, and as such, maintains peace and stability. There are also a number of judicial organisations such as the International Criminal Court and the International Court of Justice. However, effective measures from international organisations require the support of powerful states.

According to the neorealist school of thought, foreign policy decisions and the behaviours of states are shaped by the structure of the international system. The anarchic character of the global commons encourages rival states to build up their military arsenal, for example, which lead to a 'Security Dilemma' – as discussed below. In some cases, this can lead to the development of a nuclear capability (as in the arms race between India and Pakistan). The development of nuclear capability can often result in a negative cycle of regional tensions. Given the tensions between certain states, power can in essence become an end in itself as a result of the anarchic condition these states find themselves in.

Another consequence of an anarchic system is that powerful countries such as China and the United States act in a manner that would potentially result in condemnation if performed by less powerful states. There are obvious double standards in the response of the international community that are reinforced by the lack of an overarching authority at the international level, where such double standards are thus unaccountable. It would be unlikely that a state or organisation would impose sanctions on the United States for sponsoring terrorism, but the threat is often used against 'rogue' states, such as Iran – illustrating this point. The perspective taken upon an anarchic system may depend upon the relative power of the state itself. For larger states, anarchy may well be viewed as an opportunity to pursue their own interest and to act in a unilateral manner. There are few more prescient illustrations of this point than the campaign pledge from US President Donald Trump to construct a large wall along the Mexican border, naturally, without the consent of Mexico. By contrast, less powerful states may view the anarchic system as one that necessitates forging an alliance with others. It is hardly surprising to note that the most enthusiastic supporters of deeper European integration have been smaller states like Luxembourg.

The Inevitability of War

In ideological terms, the realist view of human nature derives from a conservative perspective. The mindset (or ideology) of conservatism adopts a very different view to the liberal perspective. According to conservatives, humans are driven by primordial instincts centred upon survival. Inevitably, this is reflected in the realm of international relations. Having said this, it is important to note that conservatism and realism exist with a degree of symbiosis. Not all conservatives are realists, and to be a realist does not necessarily make someone a conservative.

The classical realist conception owes a great deal to the theory of Niccolò Machiavelli. His pessimistic outlook on human nature and his classically republican commitment to realpolitik both hold a natural affinity with the realist perspective. Machiavelli is also a figure very much rooted within practical experience due to his preference for pragmatism. For instance, his most famous work *The Prince* provides a guidebook to those who practice the art of statecraft. To be an effective leader, a politician must be able to utilise every advantage to their disposal possible and keep fortune on their side for the benefit of the political community they serve.

Machiavelli further contends that it is impossible to be a good prince whilst always being a morally good person. To be good in the spiritual sense is to be considered weak in the eyes of others. Ultimately, it is fear of the consequences that keeps people in check – rather than piety or meekness. For a statesman, it is better to be feared than loved, but not feared alone. Indeed, to act in a Christian way with every decision would be very dangerous for any statesman. As a Prince, therefore, it is necessary to learn how *not* to be good (Machiavelli 2008, 53).

According to the realist conception, International Relations is characterised by a Machiavellian world devoid of morality. In such an environment, it is better for a state (and its leader) to be feared on the basis of hard power. Sovereign states have no choice but to face the world as it is and act accordingly. Even when a powerful state pursues a policy of upholding liberal values, these can only be secured via actions devoid of morality. There are few better examples of this argument than the United States. In promoting capitalism, the US has engaged repeatedly in Machiavellian policies. Although something of a simplification, the realist conception of International Relations can be described as 'the end justifies the means'. Having said this, there is a degree of division within realism as to the inevitability of war. According to the classical strand of thought, the cause of war is human nature, following the thought of classical thinkers such as Thomas Hobbes (2017) or Hans Morgenthau (1948). However, structural realists emphasise the importance of an anarchic system.

The Security Dilemma

According to the theorists Nicholas Wheeler and Ken Booth (2007), the term can be defined as a situation in which the military preparations of one state creates an unresolvable uncertainty in the mind of another. The search for security for one state is very often another state's source of insecurity. Other states must ask themselves if those military preparations are designed to enhance that country's security, or if they are designed to secure an advantage.

According to the realist outlook, states are naturally suspicious of other states, given the self-help system. The security dilemma contributes to a spiral of insecurity, especially evident in those scenarios in which two or more states are implacable rivals. In a hypothetical case of the Middle East, a military build-up by Israel or Iran would be viewed in a hostile light by surrounding states and as such increase tensions and the possibility of 'flash points' that could spark a conflict. The historical conflict within the region makes the security dilemma and the spiral of insecurity virtually inevitable. In the words of Michael Howard (2000, 1) 'war, armed conflict between organised political groups, has been the universal norm in human history'.

Following on from this point, some form of military escalation (or exercise) may do little to enhance the security of the state that engaged in that action. Ironically, its position may actually become more insecure in that it may provoke neighbouring states to militarise out of fear. The security dilemma can also be applied to an organisation. From the perspective of policymakers in Russia, the expansion of NATO towards Russian territory appears to be an offensive strategy. Whilst member states of the organisation might view their enhanced military capacity as strengthening their security, it is also likely to provoke anxiety within the Russian Federation – as seen in 2014 with the emergence of the conflict in Crimea and Eastern Ukraine.

The dependent factor is often the perspective taken of another country. In a system in which mutual trust exists, military operations by one country may provoke little or no concern amongst others. This may be due to a habit of cooperation between those states. A military build-up by the United States will cause little concern amongst the governments of its natural allies. In contrast, even the prospect of American military involvement may cause considerable anxiety amongst policymakers in Beijing.

A related point to consider here is the role of propaganda. Traditionally, governments have used propaganda in order to identify and exaggerate an external threat. This can lead to the public having a distorted perception of the outside world. The significance of propaganda is more overt in the case of a closed society such as North Korea. The regime in Pyongyang blames interference by the United States for every misfortune faced by the country. Anti-Washington propaganda is also a feature of the Tehran-based regime in Iran.

The spiral of insecurity caused by the security dilemma can at times take on a force of its own. On 26 September 1983, the world came very close to an all-out nuclear war. It was a time of heightened tension between the two military superpowers after the Soviet Union had shot down a Korean airliner. Although not widely known within the West, the world was saved by the calmness of Duty Officer Stanislav Petrov. His system reported that missiles had been launched by the United States. Luckily, he judged the reports to be a false alarm and therefore disobeyed orders given to him by Soviet military protocol (Aksenov 2013). His quick thinking prevented an erroneous retaliation on the US and its NATO allies. This isolated example serves to underline the sheer magnitude of the security dilemma. Now that the principles of realism have been discussed, we shall turn our attention to the qualities of the liberal perspective.

The Key Qualities of Liberalism

The chief qualities of liberalism that will be discussed individually are as follows:

- The significance of morality and an optimism concerning human nature
- Harmony and balance within the international system
- Complex interdependence
- Global governance
- The importance and growth of international institutions

The Significance of Morality and Optimism Concerning Human Nature

First and foremost, liberalism adopts a normative approach to international relations. The discourse of liberalism is embedded with norms and values that seek to establish a better world. Whereas realists are primarily concerned with the world as it is, liberals focus on how the world ought to be. From this basic starting-point, the whole tone and language of liberalism differs dramatically from the realist perspective.

Secondly, liberal theorists seek to make the world a better place. This is based upon progress towards a more peaceful and prosperous environment grounded on global governance, respect for human rights and the spread of liberal values. These objectives are underpinned by an increasingly optimistic view of human nature. Whereas realists take a Machiavellian view, the liberal outlook flows from an assumption that human beings are rational entities who can recognise and respond to shared interests. Extending this practically, such a perspective produces a world of cooperation as opposed to that of a Hobbesian 'State of Nature'.

The fundamental mission of liberalism concerns 'the bonds of perpetual peace', in the words of the enlightenment philosopher Immanuel Kant (1991). Theorists from the liberal viewpoint believe that an international system grounded on free trade, democratic accountability and dispute-resolving institutions provides the most effective means towards securing a lasting peace between states – forging a world that is governed by rationalism as opposed to passion.

As a normative theoretical perspective, the worldview of liberalism gravitates towards that of morality. It is both necessary and desirable to create a system in which liberal norms and values are fostered amongst nations. Unlike rogue and dictatorial regimes such as North Korea, liberal democracies must always take into account the wishes of their electorate. This acts as a significant motivational factor in the need to avoid warfare and pursue diplomatic means.

Liberalism is therefore based upon three interrelated principles. Firstly, it is a body of theory that attempts to reject the power politics highlighted within the realist perspective. Secondly, it is a belief-system which claims that the recognition of mutual benefits shapes international cooperation. Finally, it seeks to create a system of global governance in order to influence and adjudicate the policy decisions of states and non-state actors. Unlike realists, the liberal perspective has greater faith in the ability of international organisations to maintain an effective level of global governance. For instance, international law provides a forum in which states can identify and pursue their mutual interests. These principles, thus, push for a peace based upon rational behaviour and mutual cooperation.

The Possibility of Harmony and Balance

Liberalism contends that international institutions maintain a system of harmony and balance amongst states. Military and political conflict can be reduced with a combination of international institutions combined with a complex system of 'interdependence'. According to liberals, mutual dependence provides the key towards a degree of equilibrium within international relations. Harmony can therefore be created through an emphasis upon liberal values.

Following on from this, there are three main theories to consider. Firstly, 'the democratic peace thesis', which suggests that the spread of democratic values can establish a better world. In a democracy, leaders have an electoral incentive to avoid military conflict. Elected leaders will always seek to avoid war whenever humanly possible due to the financial and human costs involved. Amongst liberal democracies, warfare is very much the last resort after all reasoning has failed. The democratic peace theory has a lengthy tradition amongst liberal scholars dating back to the Enlightenment and is continually a topic of discussion even today (Placek, 2012).

Equally, 'commercial peace theory' also has a lengthy pedigree within International Relations. Associated with free-market economists such as Richard Cobden (1903) and David Ricardo (1817), it is a body of thought which claims that free trade has a pacifying impact on the international system. Countries that trade with one another have an overwhelming economic reason to maintain those trading links. In a contemporary twist to this argument, Thomas Friedman (2000) points out that no two countries with a McDonalds have ever gone to war. Known as 'the Golden Arches theory of international relations', Friedman observed that: 'countries with middle-classes large enough to sustain a McDonald's have reached a level of prosperity and global integration that makes warmongering risky and unpalatable to its people' (1996).

The third element to consider is the 'institutional peace theory'. Unlike the other two theoretical models, the emphasis here is upon the beneficial role played by forums such as the UN, the World Bank and the EU. International institutions seek to generate a habit of cooperation amongst sovereign states. Following from this, institutions can also provide a means by which bilateral disputes can be resolved in a non-violent manner. Furthermore, institutions ensure that states interact with one another in a relatively transparent manner and thereby uphold the norms of global governance. Given the right mix of economic and institutional factors, states will maintain a harmonious system in order to maximise prosperity and minimise conflict. As a conclusion, it could hardly be more at odds with the realist paradigm, at least without a deeper investigation of the manner in which they may hold similarities; a subject that is discussed later.

Complex Interdependence

The term 'complex interdependence' is associated with the ground-breaking work of Robert Keohane and Joseph Nye (1977). When '*Power and Interdependence*' was first published during the late-1970s, it offered a robust intellectual challenge to the realist paradigm. Their work seemed to capture an era of détente between the two superpowers and growing calls for a new international economic order that included developing countries. It remains a seminal text in the liberal perspective on International Relations. Nonetheless, what does the term indicate?

Complex interdependence consists of four interrelated elements. First of all, there are important linkages between states and non-state actors that shape global politics. Secondly, the international agenda exhibits none of the realist differentiation between low and high politics. The former relates to economic, cultural and social affairs whilst high politics centres on that which is essential to the survival of the state. Thirdly, there is a recognition of multiple channels for interaction amongst actors across national boundaries. Finally, there has been a marked decline in the effectiveness of military force as a tool of statecraft. In a system characterised by complex interdependence, there are multiple channels of interaction between societies. The existence of a global civil society has brought about a decline in the reliance upon military force and power politics. Even the most powerful military states no longer rely upon the fire and fury of their military arsenal. The web of linkages that connect states together, that lead to their condition of mutual cooperation and dependency – this is the condition of complex interdependence.

In a world of complex interdependence, 'soft power' will gradually replace the use of hard power. According to Joseph Nye (2004, ix), soft power relates to: 'the ability to get what you want through attraction rather than coercion ... it arises from the attractiveness of a country's culture, political ideals and policies.' States could thereby achieve their objectives via non-military means such as diplomacy and cooperation. Due to a system of complex interdependence, military force or coercion is no longer a common feature of international relations. Nye (2012) also adds that 'the best propaganda is not propaganda.' In other words, the most effective use of propaganda is via persuasion rather than force; to make others want what you want. This aids the creation of a normatively interconnected, pacified, world.

It should also be noted that multiple channels of interaction are present within a system centred upon complex interdependence. Informal ties between governmental elites and non-governmental elites exist alongside regular and routine communication amongst transnational organisations. These arenas of multiple channels are often summarised as inter-state, trans-governmental and transnational relations. These links generate a shared mindset, interest, and a habit of cooperation. In doing so, the concept of complex interdependence contends that we have moved beyond the boundaries imposed via the realist paradigm, of states out for themselves alone.

Global Governance

Global governance is a movement towards political cooperation amongst transnational actors with the aim of negotiating solutions that affect more than one state or region. There are several institutions that function within a system of global governance. This being said, global governance is not a unified system which can be observed precisely because there is no single overarching sovereign world government – as explained above when discussing the concept of anarchy within the realist framework.

In terms of a definition, James Rosenau (1995) claims that the term governance denotes the regulation of interdependent relations in the absence of an overarching political authority. Others have suggested that global governance refers to the management of global processes in the absence of a 'cosmocracy'. The term is widely applied to a shared political authority that leads towards a single government or state with global jurisdiction (Skolimowski 2003). Either way, global governance entails concrete and co-operative problem-solving arrangements on either a formal or informal basis. Such definitions are flexible enough to apply whether participation is bilateral, regional or international.

By its very nature, global governance entails a number of states and international organisations. That said, a powerful state or institution may take on a prominent role and drive the process forward. In the case of tensions within the Middle East, the United States has long sought to establish stability in an area of clear economic and strategic importance. Russia also plays an interventionist role within the region and both countries are members of the Middle East Quartet (alongside the EU and the UN).

The term global governance has gained greater prominence in the contemporary era given the trend towards globalisation. It is a relatively broad term that encompasses the process of designating laws, rules and regulations within the global commons. The need for global governance is almost certain to increase as globalisation becomes embedded further within the field of International Relations and global social relations as a whole.

The post-Cold War world of the 1990s instigated a renewed attempt to establish a systemic form of global governance. The end of the Cold War shifted the goalposts of international relations beyond the somewhat narrow confines of US-USSR 'bipolarity' – the international power structure that forms around two major poles of power - and the balance of power between two monolithic spheres of influence. Perhaps the most obvious illustration of this trend is the growing salience of environmental issues. This can also be identified in the context of a more conventional political realm. Naturally, this poses a number of interrelated challenges. Building a responsible and effective global governance requires the establishment of democratic legitimacy amongst important stakeholders. However, obtaining the required level of legitimacy demands a complete rethink of the Westphalian system due to its emphasis on state sovereignty. The purpose, remit and scope of international institutions would also have to be transformed entirely. Sovereignty is ultimately a concept that embeds the status quo, placing ultimate decision-making power in the hands of the state; emphasising a certain statism. Above all, the relationship between the state and global institutions would require recalibration. For instance, sovereignty would have to be shared or pooled, whereby ultimate decision-making power is disseminated amongst a plethora of international bodies.

Global governance has also encroached upon the realm of high politics. For instance, almost every sovereign state is a signatory to the 1968 Nuclear Non-proliferation Treaty (NPT). More countries are party to the NPT than any comparable agreement. Adherence to the NPT is a testimony to the ability of sovereign states to protect the shared global commons. However, it is also the case that a handful of nuclear states have either not signed (or simply withdrawn from) the Treaty – North Korea, India, Israel and Pakistan. This is a significant problem as this condition of exclusive dissent adds to the perception of instability within the regions these states cohabit. Whilst multilateral agreements can, and do, play a crucial role in global governance, it is also important to note their limitations.

The War on Terror'is another interesting case study to consider in regards to global governance. This term was used repeatedly by the Bush administration in order to justify intervention in Afghanistan and Iraq. Firstly, the nature of the threat is transnational. Secondly, international security and cooperation is largely driven by Washington on the basis of their hegemonic status. Partly because of this, attempts to prevent the spread of global terrorism lack the institutional support compatible with its overall importance.

For all the high-minded rhetoric of global governance, there are three notable gaps to highlight. The first of these is the jurisdictional gap between the growing need for global governance and the lack of appropriate authority to take action. Secondly, the incentive gap relates to the factors that motivate cooperation. Although globalisation does enhance the incentive to co-operate with one another, this clearly does not occur in every situation. For example, there was very little cooperation during the early stages of the COVID-19 pandemic. Finally, the participation gap refers to the fact that international cooperation remains primarily the affair of governments. This inevitably means the marginalisation of civil society groups such as pressure groups and non-profit organisations, even when international in scope and reach, or at least their secondary placement in relation to the significance of state actors.

Arguably the most optimistic objective for those who seek global governance is the formation of a global constitution. According to Gustavo Marin and Pierre Calame (Marin and Calame 2005), a global constitution would act as 'the common reference for establishing the order of rights and duties applicable to UN agencies and to the other multilateral institutions.' One of the conditions for building democratic governance is the development of platforms for citizen dialogue on the legal formulation of global governance and the harmonisation of objectives. Furthermore, a global constitution must clearly express a limited number of objectives in order to remain pragmatic and applicable globally. Such a constitution could guide the common action of UN agencies and multilateral institutions. The specific role of each of these would be subordinate to the pursuit of such objectives. In order to achieve this, citizens must be persuaded by tangible benefits to their own standard of living.

As with much else within the subject matter, the significance of the phrase 'global governance' is a contested one. Despite the continued process of globalisation, realists tend to downplay its importance. Institutions remain relatively weak within an anarchic international system. However, liberals contend that the term has gained increasing significance. The noted academic David Held even claimed that global governance has changed the parameters of debate surrounding sovereignty. Here it was argued that we have now moved beyond classical sovereignty, in the Westphalian sense of the phrase, to a mode of sovereignty that is internationalised (Held et al. 1999; Held and McGrew 2002).

The Impact and Growth of International Organisations

It is widely accepted that a correlation exists between the number of international organisations and the process of globalisation. The impact of those institutions has also increased alongside an expansion in their scope and scale. For instance, there was a rapid increase in the number of peacekeeping operations launched by the UN shortly after the end of the Cold War. Between 1989 and 1994, the Security Council authorised 20 new operations and an increase in the number of peacekeepers from 11,000 to 75,000 (United Nations Peacekeeping 2021). There have also been a number of international organisations created since the 1990s, such as the International Criminal Court (ICC), the African Union (AU) or the Southern

Common Market (MERCOSUR), all formed to deal with the growth of a truly global politics.

In terms of regional integration, the European Union is perhaps the clearest example of an organisation expanding its influence on global affairs. Since the 1990s, the EU has more than doubled its membership. Consistent with the process of deeper integration, twenty-seven sovereign states have willingly chosen to pool their resources within an institution that contains supranational institutions. From a continent with a devastating history of warfare and rampant nationalism, this is a major achievement. In the contemporary era, the European Union holds considerable elements of soft power with over 140 diplomatic embassies throughout the world. The Single European Market is the largest of its kind, and the EU continues to adopt a greater burden in terms of global governance as its power (both hard and soft) grows.

The effectiveness of international organisations depends upon several factors, some of which may be interrelated. Arguably the most important dilemma is the tension between the liberal values embedded within such institutions and the concept of national sovereignty. For such institutions to be effective, they must transcend the barriers posed by national sovereignty. However, many of the most powerful states are reluctant to accept the authority of international organisations when it conflicts with their own narrowly defined national interests. For instance, the five permanent members of the UN Security Council (P5) sometimes flout the rules of international institutions in the absence of any effective sanction. It is also common for a superpower to simply ignore international condemnation. Illustrating this, since 1992, the UN General Assembly has passed an annual resolution condemning the American embargo against Cuba, yet this has amounted to little in the way of US response. Under successive administrations, the United States has also brushed aside criticism from Amnesty International (2020) for its treatment of 'enemy combatants' in facilities such as the infamous Guantanamo Bay Detention Camp.

Another problem to consider is the level of legitimacy held by several institutions. Reliant upon soft power, such organisations can only persuade rather than coerce. As such, the presence of international organisations needs to be seen as legitimate by the parties involved in order to be effective. For instance, between 1999 and 2006 peacekeeping troops were welcomed in Sierra Leone and contributed to stabilising the country. By contrast, the 'blue helmets' (UN Peacekeepers) sent to Somalia in 1992 and 1993 conspicuously failed to secure peace because rival groups did not view the involvement of the UN as legitimate. In the oft-used phrase, there was no peace for the peacekeepers to keep. As such, the perceived legitimacy of international institutions is key to their successful functioning in achieving their objectives.

The efficacy of international institutions is further limited by the lack of political will to address vested and powerful economic interests. In regards to the Washington Consensus, international institutions have proved incapable of addressing the problems associated with multinational companies. The role of the World Trade Organisation (WTO) and the World Bank may have been complicit in the growing economic strength of technology giants known by the acronym FAANGs (Facebook, Apple, Amazon, Netflix and Google). A similar critique is applicable when addressing the threat posed by environmental degradation and human rights violations.

A further inherent weakness with institutions is that they are often reactive. For instance, the UN Security Council (UNSC) first discussed the Covid-19 pandemic some three months after the issue arose in the Wuhan province of China (Nature 2020). International institutions have also been slow to act when faced with humanitarian disasters. In the case of Sudan, repeated human rights violations in the region of Darfur were either downplayed or simply ignored for many years, leading to what is now considered to be a genocide.

On a more prosaic note, such institutions often lack the necessary funding to be an effective actor on the international stage. It is often problematic to gain funding in the first place. For instance, the United States is in considerable financial arrears with the United Nations. As the largest contributor (around a fifth of the total budget), this is clearly a major problem. Donald Trump even withdrew American funding to the WHO for its inability to deal effectively with the Chinese government in relation to the Covid-19 pandemic.

There are also problems specific to particular organisations. For instance, the effectiveness of the UN is undermined by the difficulties posed by representativeness. The General Assembly operates on the democratic principle of one vote for each member state. However, this distorts representativeness and results in a loss of credibility. Rather than exercising the capacity to influence, the UN General Assembly (UNGA) effectively passes the buck to powerful countries. Thus, each organisation holds equally unique and distinct problems.

The 'alter-globalisation' academic Joseph Stiglitz (2015) argues that the need for international institutions has never been so great, but trust in them has never been so low. This is indeed a salient point. Those of a reformist outlook argue that improved global governance demands more powerful institutions, consensus-building and heightened levels of accountability. However, this first requires a level of engagement and cooperation from national governments.

The Divisions Between Realism and Liberalism

The main distinction between realism and liberalism concerns human nature, power, security, the likelihood of conflict, and the importance of institutions and states. We will now consider each element in turn, beginning with their different views of human nature.

Human Nature

Liberalism is built upon the assumption that individuals are rational entities whose behaviour is shaped by their own best interests. Like individuals, nation-states are able to identify areas of shared benefit such as trade and mutual security. States are also able to rationalise that their interests are best served by the avoidance of warfare. This can be achieved via cooperation with other states, pooling sovereignty within a regional organisation or by conforming to the norms and conventions of international relations.

The realist perspective however is based upon a very different set of assumptions. Unlike liberals, realists generally hold a more pessimistic view of human nature. As with individuals, the relationship between nation-states is characterised by power politics. In an anarchic system, it is simply impossible to completely trust another state. There is always the possibility that a state (or even a group of states) will ignore international diplomacy and cooperation. For instance, during the 1930s, military expansion by Nazi Germany took place without an effective system of prevention from the League of Nations. All realists, whether classically or structurally inclined, would concur with the slogan 'to ensure peace, you must prepare for war.' According to the realist position, liberals are far too naïve about (a) the potential for cooperation amongst sovereign states, and (b) how national interest undermines common interest.

Perhaps the first-ever document to outline the realist position on International Relations was Sun Tzu's *Art of War*. The ancient Chinese military strategist considered each aspect of warfare from laying plans to the use of spies. There are several arguments put forward by Sun Tzu, but perhaps the most useful is that 'war is a thing of pretence' (Tzu 2010, 10), of deception, alongside that 'the supreme art of war is to subdue the enemy without fighting' and that we should know our enemies and ourselves (Tzu 2010, 20). When using force, the aggressor must also appear inactive. When they are near, they must seek to make the enemy believe they are far away (and vice versa). Many a battle has been won or lost without fighting, and his observations have been adopted by other guides to statecraft.

The realist perspective also owes a great deal to the influence of the seventeenth century philosopher Thomas Hobbes. According to Hobbes (2017, 80), the relationships that govern human nature are characterised by 'a perpetual and restless desire for power after power that ceaseth only in death.' In an anarchic system, states must ensure their survival against the threat of military action. In the eyes of a realist, this can only be achieved via the balance of power. Forging alliances on this basis acts as a check upon potential aggression from a hostile state. In the realist conception of international relations, states must at all times acknowledge that 'the enemy of my enemy is my friend'.

In contrast, there is an unmistakable streak of idealism that runs through the liberal perspective. Liberalism is built upon an assumption that we *should* be optimistic about human nature and its capacity to make the right decisions. Whilst realists view human nature as fixed and immutable, liberals contend that human nature is perfectible. This enables social progress based upon democracy, free trade and effective institutions. In a system of complex independence and global governance, foreign policy decisions can actually make the world a more peaceful and prosperous place. In order to support this argument, research into globalisation has shown that we are living in the most peaceful era in history (Pinker 2011).

Power

In relation to power, the language of liberalism is normative whereas realists are cynical. The former emphasises the possibility of conflict-resolution by international institutions, whilst realism is grounded upon a more hard-headed assessment. For realists, states must ensure their survival through self-help alone within an anarchic system of international relations. This can only be achieved via an emphasis upon hard power such as military hardware and economic inducements.

Within foreign policy discourse, in order to distinguish between realists and liberals, the terms 'hawks' and 'doves' are sometimes used. Hawks focus upon a realist worldview whilst doves adopt a more liberal and idealistic tone. This distinction enables us to categorise the interests and actions of various bureaucracies within government. For instance, in the US, there is often a tension between the hawkish approach of the Department of Defense and the diplomatic approach of the Department of State. Symbolically, as the chief foreign policy actor of the United States, the presidential seal contains both an olive branch and a quiver of arrows.

Another area of division between liberals and realists in the contemporary era concerns their grasp of how power operates. To neoliberals, the process of globalisation has transformed the manner in which power is exercised. In the early 1990s, Joseph Nye applied the concept of soft power which consists of the ability to attract rather than coerce. Soft power entails the utilisation of culture and political values in order to persuade. The mobilisation of soft power enables one country to get other countries to want what it wants without the threat of coercion. The term soft power is emblematic of the assumptions that govern the liberal perspective.

In contrast, neorealists claim that globalisation has not changed the fundamentals of global politics. In an article entitled '*Back to the Future*', John J. Mearsheimer (1990) challenged the prevalent liberal argument of the time that the end of the Cold War would lead to a more peaceful world. Instead, Mearsheimer (1995, 9) observed that cooperation would still be: 'constrained by the dominating logic of security competition, which no amount of cooperation can eliminate'. According to the neorealist outlook, the end of the Cold War era would result in the return of traditional balance of power concerns. Talk of a peace dividend was therefore nothing more than a false dawn. According to realists, physical force will always trump persuasion.

Order and Security

Alongside human nature and power, there are also a number of divisions between these two grand narratives in relation to order and security. Realists contend that the focus must be upon preventing another state (or alliance) from securing sufficient military resources to impose its will upon others. The state system is governed by Darwinian principles in which the strong exploit the weak. The emphasis within the realist perspective is therefore upon high politics (such as warfare and national security). For realists, order can only be secured via an equilibrium of power. It is a self-help system with no overarching world government to impose an effective sanction.

Liberalism however asserts that order is borne out of multiple interactions of governance. Stability within a global system of governance stems from laws and behavioural norms between states and non-state actors. Liberalism seeks to ensure a more orderly system via the democratic peace theory, the commercial peace theory and the institutional peace theory. Taken together, they provide the means by which liberal values of peace, prosperity and progress can be achieved.

The distinction between these two seemingly polar opposites emerges from unproven and untestable assumptions. When it comes to order and security, realism describes the world as it really is (or as opponents point out, the way that realists choose to see it). By contrast, the language of liberalism is notably more progressive. There is a shared hope amongst liberals that the world can (and should) be improved via a system of global governance and the spread of commerce and democratic norms. There is also a tendency amongst liberals to highlight the importance of transnational linkages and mutual dependence.

Given the contestable character of theoretical assumptions, there are clearly problems with both grand theories of international relations. For instance, the realist roadmap contributes towards the security dilemma which can spiral out-of-control and lead to yet further conflict. There is also disagreement within the perspective itself over which system of polarity is most likely to ensure an equilibrium of power. Equally, the liberal mindset can be criticised for its excessive and misplaced faith in the ability of democracy and capitalism to ensure peace and stability. In addition, international institutions are themselves greatly constrained by the realist outlook adopted by member states.

The Likelihood of Conflict

Under the realist paradigm, conflict between states is inevitable. The world only has a limited number of resources available – and in the absence of an effective world government, states are locked in a Darwinian struggle for survival. In order to support the realist position, the likelihood of conflict is usually greater when a state (or region) holds valuable resources. In the case of oil, the Middle East has been a source of geo-political tension. Realists would claim that Washington has sought to intervene in the region via a deliberate strategy of 'divide and rule' amongst Arab states in order to aid Israel. The high-profile attempt at peace under the Trump administration recognised Israeli settlements on occupied Palestinian territory, established Jerusalem as the undivided capital, and recognised the Jordan valley as part of the Israeli state. The bias shown towards Israel by the Trump administration forms part of a clear and lengthy narrative of American engagement in the Middle East.

Although the realist stance has been modernised over time, its main tenants can be traced back to the Athenian historian Thucydides. His work considered the conflict between the oligarchs that ruled Sparta against the more democratic Athenians. In the specific context of conflict, an understanding of the realist paradigm is outlined further in contributions ranging from Hobbes to Machiavelli – who were keen readers of Thucydides, and in Hobbes' case is credited with the first translation of Thucydides into English (Skinner 2002). Whilst the international system can at times drift towards a more peaceful equilibrium, such phases are merely temporary. In the words of the neorealist Kenneth Waltz (1959, 232) 'wars occur because there is nothing to prevent them from occurring.' It is an observation of particular relevance towards his neorealist '*Theory of International Politics*' (1979) as it marked the same year that the era of détente came to an abrupt end. The Soviet invasion of Afghanistan in December 1979 is widely seen as marking the end of a general thaw in the Cold War that characterised the 1970s period of 'détente'.

Liberals, however, believe that states are rational entities who seek to avoid the financial cost and economic disruption caused by warfare. Even in regions of the world with a lengthy history of tension, states do co-operate on a regular basis. Once again, this could be readily applied to the Middle East. There have been several attempts at reconciling peace between traditionally warring neighbours. This has usually entailed a two-state solution to the Palestinian-Israeli conflict.

As one would expect, both the realist and liberal positions have been subject to criticism. Realists have been charged with imposing 'truths' which turn into a self-fulfilling prophecy. This prevents the possibility of creating a more peaceful world in which swords turn into ploughshares. There are few better illustrations of this point than the security dilemma. Equally, it must surely be observed that the supposed stability of MAD brought the world to the brink of disaster during the Cuban Missile Crisis in 1962. The First World War could also be seen to expose the inherent flaws with the realist assumption that alliances lead to order and stability.

Liberals however have long been accused of overestimating the ability of states to recognise shared interests and acting rationally upon them. They may also have placed too much faith in the efficacy of international organisations to ensure cooperation. During the late-1980s, Joseph Grieco (1988) identified two barriers towards cooperation. The first is simply that of cheating. In the absence of effective sanctions, it is often possible for one (or more) states to cheat the system. The second barrier concerns the relative gains secured by another state. According to Grieco, 'absolute gains' refers to those situations in which states are able to increase their power and influence. This makes cooperation relatively straight-forward. However, states are also concerned with relative gains. The likelihood of states accepting international co-operative efforts is greatly undermined when participants see others as gaining more from the arrangement. In an unpredictable world of rivalries and a hierarchy of states, the issue of relative gains offers a thoughtful critique of the liberal mindset.

The Impact of International Organisations and the Significance of States

Perhaps the most important point of departure to consider is their conception of how the international system operates. According to realists, domestic politics ends at the water's edge. Relations between states operate according to the 'billiard-ball analogy'. In this analogy states are like billiard balls: they are self-contained and their reaction to an exogenous force from another self-contained unit coming into conflict with it is calculable, reinforcing the notion of a self-help system. International organisations designed to ensure peace and cooperation are largely irrelevant to a realist outlook on International Relations. The most significant actors are (and will always be) states. In contrast, liberal theorists such as Keohane and Nye view the world as a cobweb of interactions. As a consequence of globalisation, states have been permeated – making the billiard-ball conception redundant. Some theorists even predict the end of the nation-state due to the dynamics of globalisation (Ohmae 1995).

It is important to note that there are strands of thought within both of these paradigms. Most notably, there has been a perceptible shift in the focus of realist thinking. Neorealists claim that international actors shape the behaviour of states. As such, international organisations do have some impact upon the behaviour of states. Unlike classical realists such as Hans Morgenthau, neorealists stipulate that structure determines behaviour. According to Kenneth Waltz, the interaction of sovereign states can therefore be explained via pressures exerted upon them by the anarchic structure of the global system. Inevitably, this imposes a constraint upon their choices.

From a shared perspective, Graham Allison (2017) claims that national security concerns can no longer be resolved by a strategy of unilateralism. Global pandemics, terrorism and climate crisis require a multilateral approach from a plurality of organisations and institutions. It may also be necessary to forge partnerships with non-state actors. The attention of international relations has therefore shifted towards a multitude of actors, although states retain primary importance for a variety of reasons, such as their monopoly upon the legitimate use of political violence.

Although there are clear areas of overlap between them, the main distinction is that classical realism claims that warfare is caused by human nature, whilst neorealism stipulates that the dynamics of an anarchic system determines the behaviour of diplomats, leading them to seek structural security and power for their nation state in a self-help system. Warfare is therefore the result of an anarchic system rather than merely the primordial desire to dominate others.

Another area of dispute between realism and liberalism is the importance attached to the role of institutions. Viewed from the realist lens, institutions are relatively insignificant when compared to states. Moreover, institutions are largely constrained by the interests and interplay of states. Organisations tasked with global governance ultimately rely upon states for funding and support. Without a major state playing a key role, the actions of various institutions are unlikely to achieve peace and cooperation. The realist perspective adopts a much more conservative outlook in regards to human nature. Our behaviour is fixed and immutable, and institutional change based upon high-minded rhetoric does little to change that. The ill-fated experience of the European Union in the Balkans conflicts of the 1990s offers a stark illustration of this argument. Early talk was of a European problem requiring a European solution, but it took the military might of the United States and NATO to bring stability to the former Yugoslavia and end the genocidal activity that thinkers such as Mary Kaldor (2013) have labelled as 'New Wars', typical of the contemporary world.

Liberals however view institutions as having a crucial role to play in terms of facilitating cooperation and ensuring peace. Regarding the significance of states, one of the most influential liberal thinkers is the English philosopher John Locke (1967) who claims that civil government can remedy the anarchic state of nature. People are more likely to act rationally when a government is in place because there are laws and consequences to abide by. Locke's dictum (1967, 324) 'without laws, man has no freedom' has been adopted by liberals in terms of creating a method of global governance. In the contemporary era, the purpose of international institutions should be to serve as a mediator to inter-state problems. In a world characterised by complex interdependence, actors are mutually dependent and therefore have a rational interest in maintaining economic ties and peaceful cooperation. The role of international organisations is to maintain this system and ensure that rules are adhered to. In contrast, having states deal with economic and political disputes would be much more costly and uncertain. Ultimately, it is better for states to rely upon international institutions to resolve problems.

On a final note, liberalism tends to gain momentum amongst scholars of International Relations after the perceived failure of the international system to avoid the outbreak of war. As an ideology, liberalism first emerged from the Thirty Years War. The conflict was brought to an end via the Treaty of Westphalia, in 1648, which in turn shaped political thinking behind the concept of state sovereignty and the social contract. Liberalism also gained greater prominence as a result of the horrors of the First World War, and to a lesser extent as a reaction against the prospect of nuclear armageddon at the height of the Cold War. Realism however benefits from its traditional predominance within International Relations theory. Most of us probably carry a realist mind-map around to a certain extent, and that invariably makes the perspective slightly more convincing.

Anarchy and The Theory of International Society

There is much that divides liberals from realists within the contested arena of International Relations. However, there is one thing they both accept – the international system is anarchic. Although the term anarchy is associated with disorder and chaos, this would be misleading. In the specific context of international relations, anarchy implies the lack of a supreme authority. In absentia of a world government, there is no higher body in which states can go to resolve disputes. However, there are certain rules and conventions similar to any social structure. This is widely described as thus being an 'international society' or a 'society of states' (Bull 2012; 1966).

In terms of a definition, Chris Brown and Kirsten Ainley describe a society of states, an 'international society', as a 'norm-governed relationship whose members accept that they have ... limited responsibilities towards one another and the society as a whole' (Brown and Ainley 2009). As with all relationships, there are certain rights and duties to observe. For instance, the right to self-determination entails a duty to respect the national sovereignty of another state. The obligations that fall upon states are also outlined within the United Nations' responsibility to protect (R2P).

The society of states theory begins with the realist argument that an international system emerges the moment two or more states have a sufficient level of interaction. The theorist Hedley Bull (2012, 9) describes that an international system is formed 'when two or more [states] have sufficient contact between them, and...sufficient impact on one another's decisions to cause them to behave as part of a whole.' He also observes that states share a limited degree of common interest within this system of power politics. For instance, the fear of unrestricted violence leads towards the development of certain rules and conventions. A society of states, in contrast to an international system, thereby exists when a group of states establish diplomatic procedures for the conduct of their relations – i.e., it exists in the emergence of common norms, values, interest and principles that are reproduced and upheld by state behaviours within said society. Even within an anarchical order, a society must have rules and restraints upon the use of coercion and the sanctity of agreements. Simply put, in this condition, obligation and responsibilities remain. Without these elements, there would be no such thing as even the thinnest society (of states).

The rules that govern the society of states are contained within a set of institutions that reflect accepted behavioural patterns. Since these rules are clearly not binding in a manner comparable to domestic politics, the emphasis upon norms holds particular relevance towards our understanding. In the society of states, there are norms that govern the conduct of warfare and the recognition of sovereignty. Crucially, this argument is applicable from both a realist *and* liberal perspective.

The 'English school' of IR, as the 'society of states' or 'International Society' approach as it has come to be known, adopts a non-deterministic nature of anarchy that draws upon the normative element of liberalism, alongside the power-centric statist focus of realism. It is a body of thought built upon the assumption that a society of states emerges from the ideas that shape an anarchic system. The English school is commonly divided into two main wings: pluralists and solidarists. The former claims that the diversity of humankind is contained within a society that facilitates the greatest possible independence for states. Pluralists such as Robert Jackson (2000) or James Mayall (1990; 2000) contend that states must be able to express their own conception of 'the good life'. Solidarists however argue that the society of states should be limited towards the promotion of human rights and a cosmopolitan outlook. According to figures such as Nicholas Wheeler (2000), humanitarian intervention should take precedence over the Westphalian concept of non-intervention in domestic affairs.

The Absence of Overarching Authority

According to classical realists, states are the primary actors within the international system. Ultimately, states can only rely upon themselves for security. They have no choice but to accept the doctrine of self-help within an anarchic system. The fundamental motive for the behaviour of states is simply one of survival.

From this basic starting-point, the interaction of states becomes clear. States are forced to take into account the threat posed by others within the anarchic order. Security can also be viewed in zero-sum terms. In other words, enhancing security means a decline in security for another state. As such, an increase in the security of one state can lead to a decrease in the security of others (especially neighbouring states). The system is therefore competitive and, as the classical theorist Hans Morgenthau (1948, 13) once observed, 'international politics is a struggle for power. Whatever the ultimate aims of international politics, power is always the immediate aim.'

Not surprisingly, the realist conception of power is firmly centred on military terms. This can be viewed through the prism of either offensive realism (in which a state seeks to become a dominating hegemonic power) or defensive realism (in which states forge alliances based upon the balance of power for security). A sovereign state may therefore enhance its security on the basis of seeking dominance over other rivals, or via siding with others in order to balance the threat of another state (or group of states) (Waltz 1979). Either way, the realist paradigm is centred upon military capabilities. It also places an emphasis upon the economic dimension of hard power. This may entail the use (or threat) of economic sanctions.

In an article entitled '*Anarchy and the Limits of Cooperation*', Joseph Grieco (1988, 485) argued that 'international anarchy fosters competition and conflict among states and inhibits their willingness to co-operate even when they share common interests.' This is an insightful quote to consider when seeking to identify the realist position on the significance of anarchy. Grieco emphasises the assumption shared by all realists that states can never entirely trust another state. There are several implications to consider here. According to Robert Jervis (1978), states can never be fully aware of the intentions of others. The build-up of military resources by one state could therefore be (mis)interpreted as an aggressive act. This particular view is more likely when it leads to a relative gain for another state. In this scenario, an arms race on a regional or international scale is virtually inevitable.

The security dilemma might also force states to form new alliances or strengthen existing ones. According to Glenn H. Snyder (2007), there are two reasons that an alliance will form. Firstly, a state dissatisfied with its current level of security will form an alliance in order to bolster its own national security. In addition, a state will decide to secure an alliance when it has doubts about the reliability of an existing ally. The French President Charles de Gaulle once raised this quandary in regards to American assistance during the Cold War, with his provocative question 'would Washington risk Philadelphia for Paris?'.

Finally, realists claim that the security dilemma necessitates a reliance upon the balance of power. There are two concepts to consider (e.g. 'chain-ganging' and 'buck-passing'). In a multipolar world, national security is interconnected with other members of an alliance. When an ally decides to participate in warfare, it drags its partners into warfare. If one member marches, the others must follow. If the partner does not participate, it will endanger the security of its allies. In regards to buck-passing, states might choose to avoid confronting an emerging threat. It is hoped that other states will balance each other out, or engage in a war of annihilation. In doing so, they are acting as a 'free-rider' on the military capacity of others. They are therefore able to gain the benefits of a military alliance without bearing any of the costs.

Neorealism emerged during the 1970s as an attempt to rectify some of the conceptual limitations of the classical approach. Neorealists would argue that their perspective is not based on interpretivism; what makes them different from Classical Realists is that they are not interpretivists but positivists – they focus on structure due to their engagement with political science methods and the measurement of power by quantitative means. Neorealism is most closely associated with the influential theorist Kenneth Waltz. Whilst classical realists such as Morgenthau attribute the dynamics of power politics to human nature, neorealists emphasise that state behaviour is influenced by the overarching structure of the anarchic system. From a shared perspective, John Herz (1976, 10) reminds us that global politics is a struggle for power 'even in the absence of aggressivity or similar factors.' As is abundantly clear, the tone of the realist perspective is one which lacks optimism.

Cooperation From Common Norms, Rules and Obligations

Liberalism offers a very different interpretation of the anarchic international system. According to liberals, anarchy can be mitigated via institutions, democracy and interdependence. It is therefore both possible and necessary that institutions are created to bolster levels of trust and provide for a system of behavioural reciprocity amongst states. Liberals advocate a better world via three related models discussed above (the democratic peace thesis, commercial peace theory and the institutional peace theory). All three are based firmly upon the desirability of liberal-democratic values, central of which are those such as free trade.

Liberalism asserts that the combination of democracy, free-market economics and global governance will greatly reduce the likelihood of conflict. According to liberal theorists such as Norman Angell (1909), Leonard Woolf (1916, 1922) or Thomas Friedman (2005), democratic capitalist states are highly reluctant to fight one another due to the financial cost involved, and as such increased trade reduces the likelihood of war. To engage in warfare would be highly disruptive to trading links with other states. As rational enlightened actors, states fully recognise that warfare is emphatically not in their interests.

The liberal view of the national interest differs significantly from the realist conception. Whereas the latter is focused upon the high politics of security matters, the liberal view is somewhat broader. For instance, the interests of the state can be identified from an economic and even cultural angle. These multiple ties bind us all together on a variety of levels. Either way, it is an argument that moves beyond the narrow security concerns put forward by the realist model of behaviour.

The implications of the liberal perspective are stark. Peaceful existence between states is entirely possible even in the absence of an overarching sovereign. States have mutual interests and in cases when a dispute arises, international institutions can offer a channel for mediation between them. The potential conflict is therefore mitigated by the actions of various international organisations (the apex of which is the UN).

The liberal perspective of power, broadly, is clearly very different in character to that of realism. Whereas the latter is focused upon 'hard power', liberal theorists claim that states can pursue their objectives via 'soft power', by, as Nye (2004, 6) claims: 'getting others to want the outcomes you want'. Liberalism thereby rejects the realist view that power is secured via the threat of military action. Rather than focus upon the three S's (survival, self-help and statism), liberals argue that shared values generate mutual dependence. In doing so, the prospect of military conflict is considerably weakened. As Norman Angell (1909, 137) points out: 'we cannot ensure the stability of the present system by the political or military preponderance of our nation or alliance by imposing its will on a rival.'

As with realism, the main tenets of liberalism have been adapted to reflect the complexities of the contemporary era. Neoliberalism emerged as a response to the neorealist argument that institutions are simply unable to mitigate the constraining effects of anarchy, yet mirroring its scientific and positivist approach to International Relations. Even with the absence of an absolute sovereign, cooperation between states can (and does) emerge on the basis of trust and reciprocity.

According to neoliberals, such as Robert Keohane, the effects of the anarchic system are distorted by the realist prism. Time and time again, states are more concerned with absolute gains rather than relative gains. This argument holds major consequences for our understanding of the behaviour of states. The logical conclusion of the realist worldview is that anarchy necessitates a focus upon survival and self-help. In contrast, the neoliberal perspective emphasises cooperation between states based upon mutual interests.

The most important contribution from this perspective is that of Neoliberal institutionalism. This branch of theory prescribes a mediator role for international institutions such as the WTO and the UN. As a means to achieve cooperation, such institutions help to govern the international system. These institutions endorse multilateralism as a means of promoting peace and prosperity. The dynamics of inter-state relations are thereby governed by an alphabet soup of institutions. Although some regions are more integrated than others, the process of integration and mutual dependence provides a means whereby states co-operate in a non-military fashion. Due to globalisation, we are witnessing an increase in the role and significance of intergovernmental and even supranational institutions. As an aside, neoliberal institutionalists recognise that cooperation is difficult to achieve when leaders perceive there to be no areas of mutual interest between them.

The distinction between neoliberalism and neorealism is particularly stark when we consider the vexed issue of security. Neorealists (and realists broadly) assume that security is a competitive and relative concept. Neoliberals (and liberals broadly) however adopt an entirely different conclusion. Rather than a zero-sum game, states can enhance their own security by engaging in cooperation with other states. Crucially, this does not mean that the security of other states is in any way compromised, thereby allowing states to move beyond the potentially destructive spiral of insecurity known as the security dilemma.

To What Extent Do Realism and Liberalism Explain Twenty-First Century Developments in Global Politics?

When seeking to evaluate realism, the obvious starting point is the state system that emerged from the 1648 Treaty of Westphalia. The Westphalian system is built upon several interrelated elements. Firstly, each state holds exclusive sovereignty over its territorial boundaries. The UN Charter (United Nations, 1945) declares that 'nothing should authorise intervention in matters essentially within the domestic jurisdiction of any state.' Secondly, each state is entitled to have its sovereignty respected by other states. International law centres upon an assumption that all states should be treated equally regardless of their size or relative power. Intervention from another state would therefore be illegal unless expressly authorised on humanitarian grounds. States can also act in accordance with the notion of self-defence.

Realism is also based upon the assertion that states are the most important actors within International Relations. Although realists concede that non-state actors hold some significance, global politics is conducted primarily at the state level. Following on from this, states are analogous to a billiard-ball. In theoretical terms, states are unitary actors and their internal politics are irrelevant to their behaviour on the international stage. In the realist conception, domestic politics ends at the water's edge, and beyond is the realm of international politics. Theorists within the realist tradition centre their attention firmly upon the interaction of states. In contrast, liberal theorists adopt a cobweb model towards their understanding of the subject matter, a web-like nexus of connectivity between actors on different levels but with the state still firmly in a position of primacy.

In terms of the distinction between high politics and low politics, classical realism emphasises the importance of those matters essential to the very survival of the state. In an anarchic system, the state must ensure its survival and therefore engage in policies that fall under the remit of high politics (such as maintaining a nuclear deterrent). In contrast, the liberal perspective views low politics as a fundamental element of International Relations. For instance, no realist would ever claim that the capitalist peace theory offers a convincing explanation of international relations. The liberal emphasis on the salience of democracy and institutions is also rejected by state-centric realism.

The function of any theoretical perspective is to enable us to better understand the world around us. In regards to events since the turn of the century, the realist perspective offers a persuasive and coherent account. For instance, the sovereignty of the state has been reasserted in recent years. Powerful countries such as China and the United States have pursued their own national interests with considerable vigour. The reassertion of state sovereignty perhaps shows that the impact of globalisation has been exaggerated and misunderstood by liberals.

It should also be noted that the world remains one in which conflict and warfare are central towards our understanding. The realist emphasis upon warfare underlines on-going conflict throughout the world, i.e., that war is, has been, and will continue to be an ever-present part of human dynamics. In historical terms, some of these conflicts have been significant. For instance, until 2021 the United States was engaged in the longest military conflict in its history, in Afghanistan. The liberal assumptions that underpin the democratic peace theory have been shown to be somewhat optimistic. Whilst inter-state warfare is less common, the incidence of civil war has continued to be a marked feature of international relations. There have also been sporadic acts of terrorism (most notably on 11 September 2001) and concerted attempts to create a caliphate amongst Islamic extremists at different localities around the globe. Over the last two decades, the battle against Islamic extremism has dominated national politics in several countries. Realism also provides a convincing and clear framework for understanding outbreaks of ethnic cleansing against minority groups (such as Christians in Iran) and genocide (such as against Iraqi Yazidis by ISIS). The Chinese government has also been accused of genocide against Uyghur Muslims (Newlines Institute 2021; Amnesty International 2021). Unlike liberals, realism fully recognises the existence of conflict and hatred within international relations.

The discourse of realism also provides a convincing account of relations between competing states and alliances. The realpolitik concerns of states are clearly evident in regards to the relations between the West and Russia, especially following the 2014 annexation of Crimea. The security dilemma, and the associated spiral of insecurity, also offer an explanation of relations between rival states. The politics of the Middle East lends itself towards the language of realism, given the justification for conflict and political manoeuvres taken in the 'national interest'. For instance, Israel employed a narrative of national defence in terms of tensions with Palestinians in both 2014 and 2021.

Although there have been some attempts at peace, the continued tension between Israel and many of its Arab neighbours can be clearly understood through the realist lens. The normative and optimistic tone of the liberal outlook doesn't translate well to the long-standing conflict between Israel and Arab States within the region. The realist perspective also highlights the conduct and broader significance of proxy wars between Iran and Saudi Arabia.

However, the realist perspective falls short in its account of certain aspects of global politics. There are several aspects to this critique. Of these, perhaps the most insightful is the tendency to reduce global politics towards a negative view of human nature. The subject matter is arguably far more complex than the framework offered by thinkers such as Hobbes and Machiavelli would have us think. There are habits of cooperation, patterns of behaviour and systems of mutual dependence within global politics that realists always downplay. Since the year 2000, the international community has managed to make some progress towards a more peaceful and progressive world. For instance, the International Criminal Court was established in 2002 and the UN Human Rights Council was created in 2006. These institutions have since provided a rigid apparatus for dealing with global justice, interdependence and cooperation in the name of common interest.

Secondly, the realist perspective seems particularly unconvincing in the context of regional integration. The fact that countries throughout the world have transferred sovereignty to various organisations sits uncomfortably with the emphasis upon the three Ss (statism, self-help and survival). Even the transfer of sovereignty towards supranational institutions within the EU has provided a template for other regions in the world (such as ASEAN). Moreover, the African Economic Community is committed to deeper economic integration by the year 2023. In addition, the realist preoccupation with hard power offers a less than convincing description of the contemporary era.

On a final note, the myopic focus upon the Westphalian system is also flawed. Indeed, the whole concept of sovereignty could be described as a Eurocentric construct designed to serve the powerful whilst marginalising the periphery. The Westphalian rhetoric of non-intervention and equality amongst nations hides the exploitative character of neoimperialism. As the former diplomat Stephen Krasner (1999) points out, talk of absolute sovereignty for many countries is little more than 'organised hypocrisy'.

Liberalism adopts a very different approach to their understanding of International Relations. First and foremost, the whole tone of liberalism is more normative and optimistic. This enables us to better comprehend the growing emphasis within the international community upon protection of the global commons and the salience of human rights. Liberalism also casts light upon soft power, the importance of low politics and mutual dependence.

This normative narrative leads us towards a better understanding of how the world has made progress towards peace and prosperity in recent years. Since the turn of the century, democratic values have spread throughout many parts of the world. Liberals claim that there is a degree of causation between the spread of liberal values and a more stable and peaceful system. The counter argument would suggest that only a slight correlation exists between the two variables. It is therefore difficult to properly ascertain if the expansion in the number of people living in a democratic system has contributed towards the bonds of perpetual peace.

The capitalist peace theory also presents certain flaws when applied to real-life events. The liberal perspective advocates free trade as a means by which to establish a more peaceful international system. This is based upon the innate view amongst liberals that free trade creates the circumstances by which warfare can be largely avoided. Once again, there is a great deal of evidence to support the golden arches argument of Thomas Friedman. According to liberals, the realist standpoint misses the significance of commerce as a contributor towards global peace.

The institutional peace theory is another central element of the liberal prescription for a better world. Liberals argue that international institutions have a positive impact upon cooperation between state and non-state actors. Liberalism also seeks to go beyond the narrow focus upon state sovereignty towards establishing a system of global governance. Interactions between states are shaped by the rules, conventions and sanctions that derive from international institutions. In the contemporary era, it must be recognised that the actions of states are governed in a direct and indirect manner by the system of global governance. For example, the existence of a global governance may prevent states from engaging in warfare against neighbouring rivals.

In each of these three areas, liberalism enables us to better comprehend the world of global politics. Most notably, liberalism helps to explain why states that trade with one another are less likely to engage in warfare. There is a clear economic and political benefit in maintaining a constructive relationship. To take one example, the rivalry between China and the United States since the turn of the century has not yet stepped over into outright conflict. Part of the reason can be found in the mutual economic benefits established between Beijing and Washington.

Liberalism also assists our understanding of international law. Liberal values concerning the universal character of human rights are upheld via a number of institutions. There is also a legal process that is broadly followed when the international community considers humanitarian intervention (such as Libya in 2011). Despite the G77 (and China) rejecting the concept of humanitarian intervention at the turn of the century, intervention on humanitarian grounds has been implemented on several occasions.

Another important point to consider is that global governance enables states to manage disputes and thereby avoid a deadly and disruptive path to warfare. Having said this, global governance still suffers from three gaps (jurisdictional, incentive and participation). For instance, there have been several criticisms levied against bias shown by the International Criminal Court. Equally, global governance failed to prevent the world's hegemonic power from unauthorised military engagement in Iraq, in 2003. The hard-headed approach of realism enables us to properly comprehend the motivation behind the intervention (such as achieving regime change, gaining access to oil, and out of security concerns for national interest). The realist outlook also helps us understand how and why powerful states often ignore international law so as not to limit their individual interests.

Whilst the realist account may be more persuasive in terms of power and developments, and the continued importance of the state; it is somewhat less relevant towards an understanding of global governance. According to the realist outlook, states are the most important actors within International Relations. The growing significance of non-state actors and international institutions is far more likely to be recognised via the liberal perspective. Moreover, the liberal perspective offers a particularly persuasive description of globalisation.

Another crucial point of departure of the two main theoretical perspectives concerns their understanding of human nature. Realism is fundamentally conservative in its outlook on human nature. According to their outlook, we must adopt a pessimistic view about the capacity of humanity for improvement. Liberals however are notably more optimistic about human nature, with humans intrinsically holding rational capabilities that forge a will to mutual interest and cooperation. Since the year 2000, there is evidence to support both sides of the argument. The realist discourse enables us to comprehend the fact that global spending on defence increased from 1.14 trillion US dollars in 2001 to 1.92 trillion US dollars in 2019 (Szmigiera 2021). The pessimistic outlook of realism also casts light upon the continued threat of terrorism, the actions of rogue states and the threats posed by failed states. Equally, the liberal perspective emphasises the centrality of low politics and the dynamics of mutual dependence.

It is also worth noting here that dramatic events such as 9/11 can be used to support both perspectives. To the liberal perspective, the terrorist attack on the American mainland underlines the significance of globalisation. The multiple atrocities were committed by citizens of Saudi Arabia, the United Arab Emirates, Lebanon and Egypt. Moreover, the response from the international community in Iraq brought together troops from Poland to Mongolia (Beehner 2007). Equally, the terrorist acts of 9/11 underscore the continued relevance of the realist paradigm. As the analytic philosopher John Gray dramatically declared at the time: 'the era of globalisation is over' (Gray 2001). The causes and consequences of other historic events since the turn of the century (such as the financial crisis and the coronavirus outbreak) can also be understood from either perspective with the interrelation.

For all their differences, both liberalism and realism provide a useful framework for seeking to comprehend International Relations. As the political scientist Robert Cox (1981) rightly points out, they can both be described as problem-solving theories offering a blueprint for dealing with cooperation and security. When seeking to properly assess these two contrasting outlooks, it is important to recognise their similarities. It is also important to acknowledge where the similarity ends. No theoretical perspective is entirely watertight, and theoretical debate is a constant feature of International Relations.

Alternative Theories of International Politics

Constructivism

Outside of the dichotomy between realism and liberalism, there are a wide number of contesting theories available to broaden our palate. Of these, constructivism is arguably the most vibrant of the alternative perspectives (Katzenstein 1996; McNamara 1999). Unlike the pessimism of realists and the optimistic tone that characterises liberalism, constructivism claims that concepts used within International Relations are socially constructed. These include power politics, state sovereignty and the absence of a 'cosmocracy' (defined as a world government with a single state or polity).

Arguably the best-known contribution within constructivism derives from Alexander Wendt (1992). In an article entitled 'Anarchy is what states make of it' Wendt offered a thought-provoking critique of the 'neo-neo' debate between neorealism and neoliberalism. In highlighting the centrality of the social construct, he offers a pathway in which we might move beyond the limitations posed by the two dominant paradigms. According to Wendt, concepts within International Relations are formed via an ongoing process of social practice and interaction. The identities and interests of purposive actors are constructed by these dynamic forces. States can therefore have a multitude of identities socially constructed via interaction with other actors. Identities are representations of an actor's comprehension of who they are, which in turn signals their interests to others. It is the construction of these identities and interests that should be placed at the forefront of our understanding of the subject matter.

Following on from this, another important element of the constructivist school of thought is their robust intellectual challenge to neorealism. According to constructivists, the behaviour of actors is governed by their identities and interests rather than the structure of the international system. States and non-state actors have the scope to attach different meanings to different things. They are not trapped within a realist prism in which behaviour is determined solely by the need to protect themselves in the absence of a global government. The structural determinism that, according to neorealists, means that states can only rely on themselves for survival is merely a construct established by social practice. Crucially, Wendt argues that anarchy is not objectively a self-help system. It only compels states to self-help if they conform to neorealist assumptions surrounding security as a relative concept. Instead, it is entirely possible for states to adopt an alternative conception of security on the basis of cooperation. States could thereby maximise their own security without any adverse impact on the security of others. Neorealists are also flawed in their belief that meanings are unchangeable. Indeed, concepts and conventions are capable of being transformed by human practice, out of agency. This enables states to escape the debilitating consequences of the security dilemma.

The primary insight offered by constructivists is the capacity for transformation. Interests and identities are always in a state of flux. As such, we can move beyond the blunt dichotomy of realism - liberalism and the inherent materialism of both. Constructivists seek to comprehend interests, norms and identities in order to explain the international system. For instance, the World Bank is influential in terms of attitudes adopted by the international community towards the eradication of poverty. It is a mindset consistent with the Washington Consensus of privatisation, marketisation and deregulation. Changes in the nature of social interaction between states can thereby bring about a sustained and lasting change within international relations. For instance, the relationship between the two superpowers may be improved by the interests and identities of the two leaders.

It should also be noted that constructivism is not entirely inconsistent with either liberalism or realism. It is possible to offer a synergy of realism and constructivism – such as Jennifer Sterling-Folker's analysis of American unilateralism (2008). That said, constructivism offers a perspective that is widely thought of as distinct from the realist-liberal debate. Most notably, the focus on how language and rhetoric construct the social reality of the international system offers a more optimistic view of international relations than realism. We should therefore focus on the identities and interests of actors within the system itself as interests are constructed through social interaction (Finnemore 1996).

Critical Theory

As the term itself implies, critical theory offers a critique of mainstream International Relations (Cox 1981). This is primarily achieved via the lens of positivism and post-positivism. The former can be thought of as a scientific approach towards a study of the subject matter. Positivism is built on the assumption that the social sciences should replicate the methodology employed within the natural sciences. In doing so, knowledge can be verified on a scientific and causal basis. Within International Relations, the positivist approach is characterised by the Marxist (and neo-Marxist), neorealist and neoliberal perspectives. This particular approach has a lengthy history within the subject matter. For instance, in utilising the socio-economic and political thought of Karl Marx and his 'Scientific Socialism', the Marxist perspective offers a critique of capitalism that may be empirically discernible. Post-positivism however refers to those theories that reject the epistemological basis of positivism. For instance, the study of ethnicity casts valuable insight towards the subject matter (such as stateless nations). Unlike the predominant metanarratives, the focus of post-positivism centres on how power is experienced. Post-positivism also claims that discourse can never be entirely free of power concerns. Post-positivist critiques stem from a number of sources (such as post-structuralism and post-colonialism). Of these, the post-colonial approach, which is discussed below, is the most important contributor towards contemporary understandings of global politics.

One of the most insightful contributions from the field of critical theory is the famous observation from Robert Cox (1981, 128) that 'theory is always for someone and for some purpose'. Dominant ideologies and actors can therefore be said to serve a particular purpose within international relations. For instance, the Washington Consensus plays a key role in upholding the inequities of the global economic system. As a branch of critical theory, post-colonialism seeks to redress this imbalance via a focus on the persistence of colonialism and prejudice within political discourse. For instance, the term 'developing countries' is constructed via measurement to a Western-centric standard. This inevitably downplays the quality of life within countries outside of 'the West'.

Regarding the post-positivist element, critical theory does not attempt to create an overarching grand narrative. Critical theory is not a general theory of International Relations in the manner of either realism or liberalism. Instead, it is a method of analysis that allows for useful insights into existing theories and our conventional understanding of the subject; locating the site of both the powerful and 'the oppressed' or 'subaltern'.

On the plus side, critical theory could be praised for raising awareness of the impact of Eurocentric exclusivity in relation to the frameworks and concepts the discipline examines and employs. For example, the widespread assumption that the Cold War provided stability on the basis of mutually assured destruction ignores the devastation caused by proxy wars outside of North America and Europe. On a final note, the most salient contribution of all from critical theory is to point out that metanarratives have proved unworkable.

Feminism

In the field of International Relations, the feminist perspective may be said to offer a critique of patriarchy and a prescription for a gynocentric interpretation of social issues. In the field of International Relations, the primary focus of feminist theory has been on the role and importance of gender as a social construct. Feminist theory has also sought to highlight the negative consequences of the mindset created from the mainstream (or malestream) approach. For example, Carol Cohn points out that the overtly masculine mindset of the defence establishment has served to separate war from human emotion (1987). This narrative serves the interests of patriarchy at the expense of the female experience.

In terms of gender as a social construct, Charlotte Hooper offers an excellent insight into the relationship between power and masculinity. For instance, Hooper (1999) observes that masculine identities are perpetuated by how the subject is practised. A certain view of masculinity predominates within International Relations because men compose the vast majority of scholars within the field. Borrowing language from the constructivist approach, she claims that masculine identities have been socially constructed over time. International Relations often presents a contrast between hegemonic masculinity and a subordinate feminine approach.

One of the most important contributions from the feminist theory of International Relations is that of anti-militarism. The anti-militarism of the feminist approach is couched within an understanding of how masculinity is imposed within malestream literature. Masculine identity is commonly assigned to strength and rational behaviour, whereas feminine identity is associated with weakness and irrational behaviour. In this deliberately engendered paradigm, the act of disarmament can only be perceived as one of emasculation. As a consequence, the build-up of military weapons becomes normalised (Cohn and Ruddick 2004). Theorists such as Cynthia Enloe (2004) have also sought to raise consciousness as to how a gendered lens offers an explanation of International Relations. In terms of applying feminist theory to the subject matter, Parashar (2013) observes that men are portrayed as the sole actors in wartime. In contrast, women are routinely characterised as grieving widows and mothers, selfless nurses and anti-war activists. Yet, this is not exclusively the case. Feminist scholars also seek to explain why sexual violence against women is so prevalent during wartime.

In terms of the various strands of feminist thought, the impact of liberal feminism has been the most notable. Liberal feminists have engaged with the conventional decision-making process and campaigned effectively for an inclusive approach towards policymaking. For example, the language of 'lived reality' and equal opportunities has shaped strategies implemented by agencies of the United Nations. Liberal feminism has also impacted on the formation of foreign policy from countries such as Sweden, France, Mexico and Canada. The principal focus has been in terms of foreign aid and women's empowerment. For instance, in 2017 Canada launched its foreign assistance programme entitled 'Canada's feminist international assistance policy'. Canada's budget for foreign aid supports initiatives that assist women in the Global South. Such policies are consistent with the UN's Sustainable Development Goals (SDGs) (notably the focus on gender equality). The policy stems from the notion of gender mainstreaming. Gender is therefore placed at the forefront of foreign policy initiatives.

The feminist perspective has also offered a valuable analysis of how gender, as a social construct, impacts the subordination of the female and 'the feminine'. Women face a significantly greater level of criticism for their actions, and a myopic focus on their appearance. These factors combine to place women at a major disadvantage. Female politicians and issues of greater relevance towards women are effectively marginalised within the political realm. In recent years, the level of misogynistic hate expressed on social media platforms acts as a particularly salient barrier towards women entering public life. In doing so, the predominant status of masculinity is reinforced. It also underlines that patriarchy has the ability to reproduce itself from one generation to the next.

The feminist perspective has paid considerable attention towards the importance of discourse within academia. There are a wide number of concepts that could be analysed here such as intersectionality, heterosexism and hegemonic masculinity. The feminist perspective has therefore expanded our terminology within the subject matter via a focus on how gender serves to maintain the subordination of women. It is the 'personal as political' mantra that opens up much of the vibrancy and relevance of feminist theory. This slogan seeks to highlight the political significance of the personal realm on women's lives. For instance, poststructural feminism casts light upon the public / private dichotomy within political discourse. Notably, Judith Butler (1990) challenges the assumptions that lie behind our understanding of gender identity. In her study into gender performativity, Butler (1988) points out that gender is something we both physically and linguistically act out in our daily lives, rather than something we are objectively born into. The traditional understanding of gender and sex is geared towards the assumption that sex is biological and natural, whereas gender can be seen instead as a social construct – a product of norms and linguistic speech acts. Gender can therefore be (re)constructed in order to shatter patriarchy and facilitate a more representative society.

Postcolonialism

Postcolonialism centres on the persistence of colonial forms of power and the existence of racial prejudice and discrimination. Postcolonialism therefore seeks to highlight the pernicious impact of racial stereotypes within International Relations. For instance, 'the white man's burden' is a narrative that denies the non-white perspective any level of validity or agency (Easterly 2007; Wintle 2020).

Arguably the main contribution from the postcolonial perspective is in terms of its robust challenge to the Eurocentrism that prevails within the discipline. Postcolonial thinkers such as Edward Said (1978) claim that mainstream theory is built on the assumption that the Western enlightenment project is superior to all others. The dominance of the Western approach is further upheld via a construction of 'the other' as irrational and backward. The bias within mainstream International Relations is readily identifiable both within state-centric realism and the progressive tone of liberalism. Moreover, the historical context of global politics is characterised by a Western-centric (mis) understanding. There is much veracity to the often made comment that the domineering power writes history.

The postcolonial school of thought has also taken aim at geographical parochialism and cultural chauvinism. In terms of the former, the widespread portrayal of the Cold War as an era of stability wilfully ignores the devastation caused in the developing world. Postcolonialism also seeks to expose the parochial assumptions that underpin conventional thinking, such as the belief that enlightenment thinking is superior, progressive and universal and a concurrent cultural insensitivity to those perspectives that fall outside of these paradigms.

A clear illustration of cultural chauvinism is the construction of race. The 'white man's burden' was a fundamental ideological element of colonialism and may help to comprehend contemporary concepts such as humanitarian intervention (Ayoob 2004). The debate is often framed in a manner that more developed countries are saving less developed countries. It does not take much effort to identify a degree of racial stereotyping at work here.

As one of the leading proponents of the post-colonial perspective, Edward Said considers the political importance of Western dominance over knowledge. On the basis that knowledge equates to power, Said claims that ultimate power is dominance over our means of establishing knowledge, drawing on thinkers such as Michel Foucault and Antonio Gramsci. The framing of an academic discipline will invariably match the vested interests of the powerful. Much of the literature within the field of international relations seeks to uphold and reinforce the status quo. In his book '*Orientalism*', Said (1978) points out that the ability to frame debate is held by those in the West. The manner in which an argument or debate is framed will have a considerable impact on the eventual result. He also points out that the Western-centric understanding of the Eastern world contains culturally inaccurate representations. As such, orientalism is contained within an imperialist mindset. Said also argues that those subject to imperialism are viewed from a colonial perspective.

Another prominent figure within the postcolonial tradition is Frantz Fanon (1963). Based on a psychoanalytical approach, Fanon claims that the colonial subject is locked into the oppressors' gaze. The colonial subject is therefore unable to reconcile its own self-image with the image projected back by the imperialist power. It is also the case that the coloniser's identity is shaken by the realisation that our common humanity is denied by the political impact of colonial discourse. In common with other theorists of the post-colonial approach, Fanon reminds us that discourse is never neutral. Instead, it is a deliberate attempt to uphold existing power structures.

World Systems Theory

World systems theory emphasises the global system as our unit of analysis (Wallerstein 1979). As with all theories, it is built upon a number of assumptions. First and foremost, the world systems theory claims that the global economic system is an exploitative one. As a theoretical framework, it therefore adopts an entirely different set of assumptions to a free-market approach. The unregulated marketplace has long been championed by classical economists and (more importantly) the powerful institutions that uphold the Washington Consensus. However, the world systems theory suggests that the global economy is structured in order to serve and reproduce conditions that are beneficial to the interests of economically dominant states alone. The global system is, thus, deliberately designed to extract the maximum profit from people and other resources found at the very margins of globalisation.

The world systems perspective stipulates that a division of labour exists within the global economy, forming a discernible structural relation between states of domination and dependence. In the world systems perspective, there are three kinds of states: 'Core', 'Semi-Peripheral' and 'Peripheral'. The former consists of those states that specialise in high-skill sectors of the economy whilst peripheral states are those that concentrate on the low-skill sectors of the world economy (with semi-peripheral somewhere in between). Marking a clear distinction between the core and the periphery, it claims that the 'rules of the game' are heavily rigged in favour of the core. Countries at the periphery are therefore unable to progress in the same manner as those that have already developed and modernised. For instance, countries within the core control wages and monopolise the production of manufacturing goods. It is therefore impossible for less economically developed countries to progress in the same manner as those in the core. It is therefore necessary to reject the assumptions that drive modernisation theory (Rostow 1971).

The third aspect of world systems theory is the insights offered into the process of globalisation. According to Immanuel Wallerstein (1974), we need to consider the world system as a whole rather than via the perspective of individual states. Our focus should be upon the global system rather than the nation-state. Moreover, multinational corporations are significant actors within International Relations. The movement of global capital underlines the porous nature of state boundaries. In order to comprehend the reasons why some nations are wealthy, and others are not, we need to comprehend the considerable power of economic institutions and corporations.

In terms of its positives, world systems theory could be said to capture the dynamics and exploitation of the global economy. Core countries are driven by a competitive need to extract profit from those less powerful, and it is this search for profit that shapes the boundaries and contours of international relations. Those at the core are continually identifying and exploring new methods of gaining profit from those at the periphery. This can only lead to an inequitable global trading system. Another major strength of world systems theory is that it offers a relatively convincing framework towards understanding how a fundamental economic concept (the division of labour) can be applied on a global level. It is also sufficiently nuanced to recognise that three different zones could apply to the same country (such as the emerging economies). It even claims that a semi-peripheral zone may exist that resembles the core within urban centres, whereas the level of rural poverty is comparable to countries within the periphery. Moreover, countries can be upwardly or downwardly mobile within the system. There are several clear and cogent illustrations of these movements, most notably the BRICS (a grouping between Brazil, Russia, India, China and South Africa), that teeter between the semi-periphery and the core.

As with other theoretical perspectives, world systems theory has been subject to criticism. Firstly, it could be argued that the causes of underdevelopment are more complex than those identified by Wallerstein. Economic reductionism ignores other salient factors ranging from corruption to ethnic tensions. The global economic system may have little actual impact on the day-to-day lives of those living in the periphery. This is particularly notable in a failed (or failing) state. The power vacuum may be filled by religious fundamentalists or a self-serving elite. It could also be claimed that the world systems theory ignores the fact that some regions throughout the world remain relatively unaffected by global capitalism. In addition, the division between the three sections is vague and problematic to delineate. Whilst this does not in itself undermine the persuasiveness of the entire perspective, it does expose an undoubted flaw.

Conclusion

This opening chapter sought to examine the two main theoretical paradigms within the subject matter and in the context of salient issues. Realism and liberalism offer contesting assumptions for scholars to consider. As with all theoretical perspectives, there are positives and negatives to weigh up. There is also a specific language used by both, and internal divisions to highlight. Each perspective offers a cogent explanation of events in global politics since the year 2000. Following this, an understanding of realism and liberalism would have been incomplete without some reflection on alternative theoretical perspectives, prior to a discussion concerning the concept of the nation-state and globalisation.

BOX 1.1 – KEY TERMS FROM CHAPTER ONE

Realism

Whilst there are two main strands of realism within International Relations (Classical Realism and Neorealism) there are a number of common themes readily identifiable to both. First and foremost, the international system is characterised by self-help and each nation-state must therefore ensure its own security within the anarchic system. Secondly, the system of international relations is dominated by interactions between nation-states. Furthermore, the realist perspective argues that nation-states are in a battle for survival, a battle dominated by the power of national interest.

Liberalism

The emphasis within liberalism is upon seeking harmony amongst nation-states. According to liberals, the nation-state is a rational entity that seeks to identify shared areas of interest with other comparable countries. Unlike realists, liberals adopt an optimistic view of human nature. Their optimistic outlook upon human nature leads towards a number of normative assumptions centred upon democratic peace theory, soft power and the economic peace theory.

International anarchy

In the specific context of International Relations, anarchy refers to the lack of a supreme authority. Although the term anarchy is often associated with chaos, this would be misleading. Given the absence of a world government, there is no authority in which states can contact as an arbitrator of disputes or as an enforcer of international law. Although some states are more dominant than others, the global system is basically leaderless.

The Security dilemma

The security dilemma is a recurring theme within the theory and practice of International Relations. It describes a situation in which actions that intend to increase the security of one state can lead to other states responding with similar measures, producing increased tensions and the potential for conflict. The security dilemma reflects a Hobbesian understanding of International Relations.

Complex interdependence

Complex interdependence is a theory that depicts mutual dependence as the norm. In a world characterised by globalisation, events in one part of the world invariably affect others. International actors inhabit a system of mutual dependence in which isolation and self-sufficiency are frankly implausible. The concept of complex interdependence is a manifestation of the liberal perspective on International Relations.

Global governance

Global governance depicts moves towards political integration amongst transnational actors aimed at negotiating a response to problems affecting more than one state or region. Developments towards a system of global governance have occurred in an incremental (and often irreversible) process. There are few arenas of international relations that are untouched by global governance, and the salience of global governance has increased as a consequence of globalisation.

The anarchical society and the society of states

This theory suggests that the states of the world can be members of a society despite the anarchic nature of the international system. Within an anarchical society, there exists a society of states grounded upon shared interests and underpinned by the need to ensure the survival of the state. Unlike domestic law, international law operates largely on the basis of consent from sovereign states.

BOX 1.2 – KEY POINTS FOR CHAPTER ONE

1. The two dominant perspectives within International Relations are liberalism and realism.

2. Liberals and realists offer contesting views on:
   *   Human nature
   *   The salience of the nation state
   *   The means to ensure stability
   *   The best means and ends of exercising power
   *   The significance of international institutions.

3. Neoliberalism and neorealism have emerged in order to better interpret recent developments in combination with scientific and positivist methods (as opposed to interpretivist methods).

4. International politics functions through an anarchic system, due to the absence of a sovereign entity above the state that can make ultimate decisions about global issues.

5. Liberalism and realism have offered relatively convincing explanations of events since the turn of the century.

6. Neoliberalism and neorealism have emerged in order to better interpret recent developments.

7. There are some similarities between liberalism and realism.

8. There are a number of other theories of International Relations that are of interest.

2

The State and Globalisation

This chapter provides an overview of the role and significance of the state and globalisation. It seeks to outline the characteristics of the nation-state, national sovereignty and interdependence. The advantages and disadvantages of globalisation will be considered alongside its implications. The process of globalisation has potentially altered how we should understand the role of the state within International Relations. Given the contested nature of the subject matter, this is part of a broader theoretical debate between the two dominant paradigms of International Relations. The chapter ends with an examination of the ways and extent to which globalisation seeks to address and resolve issues within contemporary world politics.

The Nation-State and National Sovereignty

The Nation-State

A nation-state is both a legal and theoretical concept. In a legal sense, a nation-state is an entity in which the majority of its citizens share the same national culture and identity. A nation can be defined as a community of people united by a common language, history or culture inhabiting a particular territorial area. In terms of the state, the sociologist Max Weber (1994) argued that the state has a monopoly on the legitimate use of coercion within a given political entity. In a *de facto* sense, a nation-state can therefore be defined as a political community bound together via citizenship and nationality. Members of nation-states are considered citizens, and such a consideration includes the attachment of rights and obligations.

In terms of the latter, a nation-state is a theoretical ideal in which national and cultural boundaries match up with territorial ones. A nation-state is therefore based on the belief that the nation should be able to define its own borders and thereby exercise control over them. The term is common within political discourse and the idea of a nation-state continues to shape independence movements. Throughout the world, independence movements seek to form their own nation-state, and as such ascertain the dominant mode of sovereign self-determination.

In an era characterised by globalisation, nation-states find it increasingly difficult to protect their borders from external threats posed by non-state actors that operate in the space between states, such as international terrorists. Nation-states can also find themselves relatively powerless against the dynamics of a global financial system. Unsurprisingly, many informed commentators contend that the Westphalian era is in decline due to the wide-ranging impact of globalisation. That said, citizens of a nation-state often hold a deep emotional attachment to their nation, following the ascendance of nationalism and national identity from the Romantic period onwards (Carr 1945). National identity offers a sense of comfort in a world of rapid and sometimes bewildering social change, and globalisation may have led to a revival in nationalism. Indeed, there are several populist parties, figures and movements, such as Fidesz in Hungary, The Law and Justice Party (PiS) in Poland, The United Kingdom Independence Party (UKIP) in the UK, Geert Wilders' Dutch Freedom Party, or even ex-President Donald Trump that gain support based on opposition towards globalisation and the so called 'liberal elite'.

It is also worth noting the distinction between a nation and the state. Crucially, the state is an objective reality, defined whereby a single faction holds a legitimate monopoly of violence and thus bureaucratically administers a defined territory, whereas the nation is a construct. The UK is a state, whereas British identity is difficult to adequately describe in any meaningful sense. In global terms, political tension is surely inevitable when there are numerous nations living alongside each other in any given territory, particularly when there is a substantial minority to accommodate. Equally, conflict may arise when divergence exists between the dominant nation and other national groups with opposing cultural traditions. In the world's most populous democracy, India, Hindus are the majority religious group. However, there are more Muslims residing in India than there are in the Islamic Republic of Pakistan. Indian society seeks to accommodate non-Hindu religious groups via an official policy of secularism.

The nation-state is also an instrument by which a nation may serve its collective interest. To establish an effective and functioning society, the nation-state may seek to coerce oppositional forces. As such, one of the outcomes of nationalism is the rhetorical construct of 'terrorists' against those who pose a threat to national identity. The nation-state may therefore be a counter against terrorist groups utilising what James Kiras calls the 'weapon of the weak' (Baylis, et al. 2019).

In order to more properly comprehend the meaning of a 'nation-state', a useful comparison can be made with other types of states. For instance, a 'multinational state' is one in which no singular ethnic group is dominant. These are sometimes referred to as 'multicultural states' depending upon the level of assimilation amongst ethnic groups. This may consist of an official recognition from the national government (as in the case of Canada). There are also entities that differ in size to a nation-state. For instance, the city-states of pre-unification Italy were much smaller than a nation-state and were usually dominated by a single ethnic group. In contrast, an empire is composed of several countries under a single monarch or system of government. At its peak, the British Empire was the largest in history with almost one in four of the world's people living under its dominion. A colonised homogenous nation within an imperial system is not a sovereign state, and as such, cannot be thought of as a nation-state.

A contrast can also be made between a nation-state and a confederation with a league of sovereign groups (e.g. Switzerland is a confederation that consists of twenty-six cantons under a common government). From a similar perspective, a federation is a political entity that contains partially self-governing regions under a central government. This is often designed to reflect ethnic diversity. For instance, the federation of Bosnia and Herzegovina is delineated along ethnic lines. Two of the most powerful countries in the world (the United States and Russia) are also classed as federations.

Any understanding of a nation-state also requires an examination of the actual meaning of a nation. For instance, the UK consists of at least four separate nations. England, Scotland and Wales are distinct nations within a unitary political system centred upon the sovereignty of the Westminster parliament. Northern Ireland is a far less cohesive nation due to a sectarian division between an Ulster-British culture and an Irish culture.

In essence, a nation is a constructed entity in which people are bound together by a common language, religion, historical narrative and cultural traditions. It is grounded in a palpable yet intangible sense of national identity and belonging. The historian Benedict Anderson (1983) provides a useful insight here with his phrase 'imagined communities'. For him, a nation is a social construct imagined by those who perceive themselves to be members of that group. An imagined community is distinct to an 'actual' community because it is not based upon everyday interaction amongst its members, but upon the perceived and constructed linkages between those members. It is inherently constructed and bound up with sentimental appeals to kinship with others.

A nation is often confused and conflated with the notion of a nation-state, but this is often misleading. A nation is an intangible entity based upon a collective identity, whereas a nation-state is a territorial construct in which the boundaries of a nation overlap with that of the state. The nation-state is, importantly, also a legal concept based upon the principle that each nation-state is sovereign over its defined territory.

A stateless nation consists of an ethnic or identity group that does not possess its own nation-state. Stateless nations are either dispersed across several states (such as the Yoruba people in sub-Saharan Africa) or form the majority population of a province within a larger state (such as the Catalans and the Basques). There are also stateless nations with some history of statehood. For example, the Tibetan government-in-exile asserts that Tibet is an independent state under unlawful occupation from the People's Republic of China. There are other nations that were always stateless due to domination by another state. For instance, Israeli occupation of Palestinian land is now the longest in modern history.

There are also a number of ethnic (and religious / linguistic) groups who were once a stateless nation that later forged a nation-state (such as the nations of the Balkans that constituted the former Yugoslavia in 1946). There are also situations in which members of a stateless nation may become citizens of the country they reside in despite their oppression. Members of a stateless nation invariably group together to demand greater autonomy or full independence. There are varying degrees of autonomy available such as devolution, full fiscal autonomy and full sovereign independence.

As a case study, 'Kurdistan' presents an interesting example. The Kurdish nation covers four states and Kurds have faced sustained discrimination from the official authorities. Most dramatically, the Kurdish people were gassed by the Saddam Hussein regime during the Iran-Iraq war, and now face discrimination from the Turkish authorities. The Kurdish nation seeks to establish control of northern Syria in addition to its autonomous entity within the Republic of Iraq. Demands for independence are championed by the Kurdistan Workers' Party (PKK).

National Sovereignty

National sovereignty refers to the ability of the state to impose a system of government upon its citizens. In Weberian language, the modern state is defined by its monopoly over the legitimate use of coercion or force within that given political entity. For realists in particular, this is the very essence of national sovereignty and an unmistakable reminder of its importance.

Under international law, a state is said to be sovereign over a territorial area. International law (following the 1933 Montevideo Convention on Rights and Duties of States) defines a sovereign state as one with a permanent population, a clearly defined geographical scope, a single government and diplomatic recognition from other states. To illustrate the point, there are a number of states that are not recognised as such within the international community. For instance, the Turkish-occupied region of Cyprus is only recognised by the government in Ankara. An unrecognised state cannot engage in diplomatic relations with other sovereign states, and therefore lacks one of the essential characteristics of statehood.

The concept of national sovereignty also refers to the authority exercised by a governing body without interference from external sources or organisations – known as 'external sovereignty'. In a theoretical sense, sovereignty is absolute. In practice, this is never the case as even dominant states are subject to international laws and conventions. In an increasingly interconnected system, the potential for outside interference is a constant feature. Indeed, the Russian and Chinese authorities have proved particularly adept at cyberwarfare.

Any proper understanding of national sovereignty requires a sharp distinction between *de facto* and *de jure* sovereignty. Sovereignty in a *de facto* sense means the ability to act in a certain manner, as the ultimate decision-making power over a defined territory. The latter, *de jure* sovereignty, merely refers to the technical and legal ultimate decision-making power of an actor or agent. The terms political sovereignty and legal sovereignty are also used here. It should be relatively clear that *de facto* (or political) sovereignty is of greater importance than *de jure* (or legal) sovereignty. The Republic of China (commonly known as Taiwan) holds *de facto* sovereignty but is not universally recognised by other states. For instance, the United States does not support full national independence for Taiwan although it does favour Taiwan's membership in various international forums.

In a practical sense, a state is subject to a degree of influence from more powerful states. Whilst the UK is able to determine its own foreign policy, decisions are shaped to a considerable extent by its special relationship with the US. Given its relative power, the UK is unlikely to act in a manner contrary to its strategic and military ties with Washington. On a more straight-forward point, colonies are neither *de facto* or *de jure* sovereign, with ultimate decisions being made by the colonial power.

From a theoretical standpoint, it has been argued that we have reached a post-Westphalian epoch in which the concept of sovereignty and the nation-state can no longer be sustained. This argument has grown due to the process of globalisation. The phrase post-Westphalian has also gained in salience from usage by prominent political figures and academics (Kreuder-Sonnen and Zangl 2015).

One of the more obvious consequences of the post-Westphalian system is the increased reliance upon humanitarian intervention in order to maintain liberal values. Military intervention from a US-led alliance has been implemented in several parts of the world (such as in Iraq 1991 and 2003, and Afghanistan in 2001). Humanitarian intervention within a failed state may even be coordinated by regional powers. Since 2015, the Saudi-led 'Arab coalition' has offered military assistance to the internally recognised government in Yemen. Humanitarian intervention underlines the extent of global governance within the contemporary era.

From the opposing angle, notions of state sovereignty and non-intervention remain relevant towards our understanding of global politics. There are a number of conflicts in which international organisations (and powerful states) choose not to directly intervene. From a realist interpretation, the dependent factor is the relative standing of the country in question. In the post-Westphalian world, it can sometimes be advantageous for a country to be of little economic or strategic interest to the outside world. In contrast, those with valuable resources (notably hard commodities such as oil or metals) are always more likely to attract intervention from outside forces out of their own policy of self-interest.

Globalisation

The Process of Globalisation as a Complex Web of Interconnectedness

Globalisation can be defined as a complex web of mutual dependence within a multitude of areas (economic, social and political). Globalisation has been driven by a number of interlinked factors such as technological development, economic integration and the movement of people. In terms of theoretical perspectives, the trend towards globalisation is perhaps best outlined via 'the cobweb model'.

In an era characterised by globalisation, the velocity of events has been profound. Events in one part of the world can have an immediate and lasting impact upon another. Technological developments in communication tie the world together in ways unimaginable to previous generations. In the words of the cultural theorist Marshall McLuhan (1964), we inhabit a 'global village' in which the world is getting smaller. Some have even depicted globalisation as concomitant with the death of distance (Cairncross 1997). Either way, globalisation is built upon an intricate web of communication within the political, cultural and economic sphere over the course of the second half of the last century.

If there was to be but one word that summarises the phenomenon of globalisation, it would be that of *interconnectedness*. Globalisation is ultimately a process that generates deeper and wider levels of interaction and integration amongst a plurality of actors (such as Non-Governmental Organisations (NGOs), Multinational Corporations or Companies (MNCs), and states). In an ever-more interconnected world system, transnational networks surmount traditional boundaries and make them largely irrelevant.

Globalisation is conventionally divided into three areas: economic, political and cultural. In each of these areas, the extent to which the world is connected is stark and seems unlikely to be reversed in the foreseeable future. In terms of economic globalisation, the world is analogous to a global marketplace. Local and national economies are embedded within a worldwide market, with the forces of supply and demand transcending national borders. For instance, in commercials for the Hongkong and Shanghai Banking Corporation Ltd. (HSBC) a child attempting to sell or market a homemade product outside their home will take multiple currencies. Such a scenario, no matter how unrealistic, would not have been conceivable prior to globalisation. The spread of economic interdependence has been facilitated by deregulation and technological developments. A clear illustration of this was the 2008 financial crisis and credit crunch. Instigated by a complex relation between deregulation, investment into 'subprime' mortgage bonds, issuing cheap mortgages, and a lack of consideration for systemic risk by banks in the US, the financial contagion affected virtually all parts of the global economy. The interconnectivity of the markets could no longer be denied by even the staunchest of globalisation sceptics.

In political terms, globalisation has called into question the continued relevance of the Westphalian conception of the nation-state. Traditionally, the principle of national sovereignty lay at the very heart of international relations. Due to the interconnectedness of the global system, nation-states have little choice but to work together to deal with cross-border issues such as terrorism, security and the movement of refugees, to name but three. In an era characterised by globalisation, even the most powerful states co-operate with other actors to achieve their aims, and this has been made absolutely clear with the increased relevance of International Organisations at both the global (the UN, NATO, ICC, etc.) and regional (EU, AU, ASEAN, etc.) levels where such interconnectivity, cooperation and common interest is made manifest.

In order to underline this argument, it seems fittingly ironic that the process of integration has gone further and deeper amongst the European states that gave birth to the nation-state through the Treaty of Westphalia in 1648 than any other. Since the Treaty of Rome in 1957, the European Union has formed a set of intergovernmental and supranational institutions. States that once went to war against one another for extended periods of time chose to pool (or share) their sovereignty over certain areas of governance. There are few clearer illustrations of interconnectedness in the political realm than within the EU. On the international stage, the EU repeatedly employs its considerable soft power in an effective manner. In a highly symbolic move, the EU was awarded the Nobel peace prize in 2012 for its role in continually stabilising the region and transforming Europe from a continent of war to one of peace and cooperation.

In a cultural sense, the Internet has brought people together like never before. We are able to connect with others in a manner inconceivable just a couple of decades ago. The statistics are truly staggering here. If Facebook were a country, it would be the largest in the world on the basis of population (Taylor 2016). In addition, the number of monthly users of Twitter now exceeds the entire population of the United States (Statista Research Department 2021). Such unprecedented levels of communication generate yet further interdependence within the economic and political realm. For instance, initial protests in 2011 against the Tunisian regime spread via the use of social media to five other countries, causing the overturning of several long-standing regimes – the effects of which are still observable in Libya and Syria today. This international event is known today as 'The Arab Spring'.

All three elements of globalisation interconnect and overlap in some manner. An understanding of economic globalisation inevitably entails a cultural and political context. For instance, the increased salience of the global marketplace comes with a sense of cultural imperialism. Equally, the growing success of companies from certain countries underlines shifts in the power balance within global politics (such as the continued rise of China).

The Impact of Globalisation on the State System

The political scientist David Held (Held, et al.. 1999, 2) argues that globalisation consists of the 'widening, deepening and speeding up of worldwide interconnectedness in all aspects of contemporary social life.' The process itself permeates all facets of international relations including the state system, the economic and the everyday. In order to properly comprehend the meaning of interconnectedness and interdependence, it is first necessary to define the terms.

In the context of globalisation, interconnectedness entails two related elements. The first is the loosening of international borders to facilitate the flow of goods, services and people. Secondly, institutions have either been created or modified to accommodate the new normal. In doing so, globalisation can be said to have created a global village in which we are all connected in some manner. For instance, technological developments enable us to share images and ideas on an immediate and far-reaching basis.

Mutual dependence is perhaps most overtly expressed within the realm of economic globalisation. In terms of the positives, countries that might have once engaged in warfare now have a strong financial incentive to avoid such a scenario. Despite the hyped-up rhetoric of a 'trade war' between the US and China, neither side has any rational interest in implementing complete protectionism. The liberal perspective refers to this as the 'capitalist peace theory' (Gartzke 2007), or sometimes the 'Commercial Peace Theory'. On the downside, economic instability in one region of the world can have a damaging impact upon others, as discussed in relation to the 2008 global financial crisis. Despite some limited level of state regulation, transactions worth trillions of US dollars occur outside of any meaningful government control.

Another area in which interconnectedness holds major implications relates to humanitarian intervention. The normative element of liberalism tends to provide a basis for humanitarian intervention. However, realists remind us that humanitarian and strategic considerations are often meshed together. As such, humanitarian intervention in an era of globalisation can be justified on grounds of self-interest. In some regions of the world, intervention is a useful means of preventing regional instability, which can also affect neighbouring regions. States also have a rational interest in adopting a highly selective definition of humanitarian intervention. For instance, authoritarian regimes that violate human rights are highly unlikely to experience outside interference from a strategic ally.

Globalisation demands that we rethink our conventional view of world politics. As Professor Anthony McGrew (2016, 29) points out 'the sovereign power and authority of national governments...is being transformed but not necessarily eroded' in the twenty-first century. Illustrating this, globalisation has turned traditional assumptions on their head (such as the dichotomy between the domestic and external sphere of politics). 'Power politics', in the established sense of the phrase, also needs to be reconfigured to recognise the importance of economic ties. Due to interconnectedness and mutual dependence, a multitude of actors play an increasingly important role within global affairs. Globalisation has also brought with it an expanded vocabulary of International Relations with terms such as complex interdependence, soft power, global governance, and so the list could go on.

According to liberal theorists like Robert Keohane, interconnectedness and mutual dependence will contribute towards the establishment of a more peaceful world order. As states tend to maximise their own perceived interests, they each have a stake in maintaining the global economic system. The dynamics of globalisation enable states to escape the straight jacket imposed upon them by the Westphalian conception of the sovereign state. Naturally, these normative assumptions about globalisation are not universal. The realist perspective takes a less optimistic view of globalisation. Despite an undeniable degree of connections and interdependence, the state system remains anarchic and states must always ensure their own survival, at least for Realists. Conflict between (and within) states therefore continues to be a feature of contemporary international relations.

The Challenge of Globalisation to State Control Over Citizens

The process of globalisation makes it more difficult for the state to perform the fundamental function of maintaining social order within its borders. There are several cogent illustrations of this point. Most notably, the formation of a shared space between like-minded individuals and organisations undermines the ability of the state to claim a monopoly on the legitimate use of force. When faced with demand for radical change, the legitimacy of the existing regime can buckle under severe strain from the momentum of transnational movements (as witnessed during the Arab Spring).

In the twenty-first century, politics is increasingly conducted on a cross-border level. As people make meaningful and lasting connections on this basis, their loyalty to the state is greatly weakened. This is a particular problem within failed states such as Libya. After forty-two years of Muammar Gaddafi as 'Brotherly Leader and Guide of the Revolution of Libya', in 2011 the demise of Gaddafi's regime caused the emergence of a power vacuum that led to a NATO-led coalition intervening via the installation of a no-fly zone and the assistance of the United Nations (UNSMIL). This was all the more important due to the oil reserves in the country, leading to a number of critics claiming intervention arose out of national interest (Campbell, 2013). However, this cross-border phenomenon also presents a problem for those states with well-established and clearly defined territorial borders. A number of closely connected movements calling for greater regional autonomy makes it much more problematic for the central government to uphold the law.

Globalisation has also made it more difficult for the state to control the movement of goods, services and people within its own borders. The dynamics of globalisation are shaped primarily by the forces of demand and supply, whilst governments are somewhat marginal to the process. In EU countries, for example, the member states must uphold the four freedoms (including the free movement of labour and capital). In the Global South, the state is in a particularly weak position in relation to the demands made by multinational companies. The former is in need of jobs and investment, whilst multinationals are in a position to provide.

Having acknowledged this, the state also retains its importance. The agents of the state remain the most important elements in the maintenance of law and order. The implementation of social order requires a fully functioning government with an effective state apparatus. The state also remains a relevant institution due in part to the public's reaction against the process of globalisation. In countries throughout the world, there has been a resurgence in nationalist feeling via self-styled 'strong men' to deal with the dangers posed by globalisation (such as terrorism and uncontrolled immigration). This is an observation that readily applies to the United States (Trump), Brazil (Bolsonaro), Russia (Putin), India (Modi), Hungary (Orban) and the Philippines (Duterte), alongside many others.

From an academic standpoint, Professor Steve Smith (Baylis et al.. 2019) argues there is a clear paradox at work here. In one sense, the public wants governments to protect them from the chill winds of globalisation. This approach necessitates policies such as increased military spending and tougher border restrictions. Equally, the process of globalisation makes the maintenance of stability and order considerably harder to achieve in practice. Either way, globalisation can be said to have changed how the state exerts control and influence over its citizens.

On the Development of International Law Alongside Globalisation

The impact of globalisation on international law is contested. From one angle, it could be argued that it represents a profound alteration in the behaviour of states. International law is arguably more effective than ever before due to the interdependence fostered by globalisation. These developments have embedded certain norms of behaviour that emphasise diplomacy, cooperation and the maintenance of liberal norms.

In order to support this argument, there has undoubtedly been a major expansion in the scope and efficacy of international law since the 1990s. Tyrants that would at one time have escaped trial by international jurisdiction due to their strategic importance to a Cold War ally are more likely to be held to account for their crimes. Most have welcomed such developments as a positive outcome of globalisation.

From the opposing angle, globalisation has done little to alter the fundamental basis of international law. All too often, international law is merely a servant of the most powerful. For instance, international law undoubtedly has a Western-centric bias towards universal human rights. This often provides a fig-leaf to advance American interests (such as the invasion of an oil-rich country). There are also clear double standards at work that underline the extent to which international law serves as a tool of powerful states. For instance, the United States has never been a member of the International Criminal Court. This may in part reflect the hegemonic power held by Washington.

In theoretical terms, the realist perspective has long viewed international law as ineffective. According to Hans Morgenthau (1948, 21) states are 'continuously preparing for, actively involved in, or recovering from organised violence in the form of war.' The trend towards globalisation has done nothing whatsoever to change this long-standing observation about the anarchic system of international relations. Frankly, the only obligation to behave in accordance with international law are in those rare occasions when the threat of sanctions is both credible and potentially effective. In the case of the US-led invasion of Iraq, this was emphatically not the case.

As one would expect, the liberal perspective takes a more positive view of international law. The creation of a more just system of international relations requires international law. In contrast to the realist paradigm, international law is considered important because it sets the boundaries of acceptable behaviour. It confers legitimacy towards humanitarian intervention and offers redress of grievance for sovereign states. The achievements of international law should therefore be recognised and built upon.

No understanding of international law would be complete without marking out the distinction between *jus ad bellum* and *jus in bello* that are central to the legal discussion of 'Just War'. The former relates to laws that specify when a state is justified in the use of military force, i.e., the condition on which a war may be considered 'just'. There are two main provisions to consider. Under Chapter 7 Article 42 of the UN Charter, the Security Council may authorise military action in order to ensure peace. This tends to occur for peacekeeping missions in failed states such as Sierra Leone (1999–2006), Bosnia (1992–1995) and Somalia (1992–1995). Under Article 51, states can also use military force as a legitimate means of self-defence against an armed attack. In addition, Article 2(4) calls on member states to respect the sovereignty and territorial integrity of an independent state.

Jus in bello, however, refers to the conduct of warfare, i.e. what sort of action is 'just' during warfare. For instance, the use of chemical weapons is prohibited under international law. The treatment of captured military personnel, medical staff and non-military civilians is covered under four separate Geneva Conventions. Whilst there is considerable evidence to suggest that states adhere to the principles of *jus ad bellum* and *jus in bello*, powerful states have ignored these fundamental tenets of international law. During the Iraq war, for instance, the US-led coalition failed to gain full authorisation from the UN Security Council prior to the invasion of Iraq. The treatment of 'enemy combatants' at Guantanamo Bay is also a clear violation of what should constitute the just conduct of warfare.

Humanitarian and Forcible Intervention in a Globalised World

Humanitarian intervention can be defined as the use or threat of force with the express goal of bringing the violation of human rights to an end in a specific locality. Non-military forms of intervention may also be included – such as the provision of aid and the imposition of diplomatic sanctions. There is often an absence of consent from the host state, although a functioning government might be lacking in the case of a failed (or failing) state. Humanitarian intervention often occurs in response to a scenario that does not pose a direct threat to the strategic interests of states involved in the intervention.

There is of course an unyielding tension between the Westphalian principle of state sovereignty and the use of humanitarian intervention. The concept of non-interference in the affairs of a sovereign state is a central feature of international law. Article 2(7) of the UN Charter clearly states that nothing shall authorise intervention in matters essentially within the domestic jurisdiction of any state. Yet, having said this, the UN Charter facilitates the use of force in order to establish peace and stability in Article 51. There is also a degree of consensus over the essential characteristics of humanitarian intervention. According to the UN Office for the Coordination of Humanitarian Affairs, there are four principles that provide the foundation for humanitarian action: humanity, neutrality, impartiality and independence.

Humanitarian intervention can at times bring together an unlikely alliance of hard-headed realists and idealistic liberals. The former may support intervention in order to rid the world of a geopolitical threat to regional or national security whereas the latter tend to support intervention in order to uphold universal human rights and to seek justice. There are several illustrations in which both realists and liberals could comfortably identify some degree of justification. One of these examples would be NATO's intervention within Kosovo in 1999.

The background to humanitarian intervention in Kosovo is one of Serbian nationalism, ethnic cleansing and genocide. In the aftermath of the Bosnian war (1992-1995), Yugoslav forces sought to eradicate the Albanian population in Kosovo. The Kosovo Liberation Army was formed as a reaction to human rights abuses by Serbian forces in Kosovo and the region broadly, abuses which were denied by the then Serbian President Slobodan Milošević, such as the Srebrenica Massacre in 1995 where over eight-thousand Bosnian Muslims were murdered by the Serbian aligned army. After diplomatic attempts to end the killing, NATO sought to intervene on behalf of Kosovan Albanians. Although the Security Council failed to authorise intervention, NATO engaged in a campaign of air strikes in an attempt to defeat Serbian forces. The short-lived Kosovo war was fought between the Federal Republic of Yugoslavia and the Kosovo Albanian rebels. The war was brought to an end via a peace treaty that ensured the withdrawal of Yugoslav and Serb forces in order to provide space for an international presence. According to official estimates, almost 1.5 million Kosovo Albanians were forced to leave their homes.

Another revealing case study to consider here is the multi-state NATO-led 2011 coalition in Libya. Unlike Kosovo, the military organisation gained official authorisation for humanitarian intervention in order to protect civilians in the midst of the civil war that broke out at the start of the Arab Spring. The UN Security Council was committed to the clear and achievable aims of bringing an immediate ceasefire to the civil war in the failed state (including an end to crimes against humanity in terms of attacks against civilians). The Libyan intervention was part of a broader attempt by NATO to reinvent itself in a post-Cold War era. It was a largely successful intervention partly due to the lack of an effective response from the Gaddafi regime. NATO countries managed to utilise their military hardware in terms of enforcing a no-fly zone, a naval blockade and an arms embargo.

In a strictly legal sense, Chapter 7 of the UN Charter allows the Security Council to take action in those situations where there is a 'threat to the peace, breach of the peace or act of aggression' (United Nations, 1945). The exact meaning of what constitutes a 'threat' has been broadened since the end of the Cold War, which has led to the authorisation of force in situations that at one time would have been considered either an internal conflict or one firmly within a superpower's sphere of influence.

On pragmatic grounds, humanitarian intervention can be justified in order to prevent genocide. The 1948 Convention of the Prevention and Punishment of Genocide defines the term as those acts 'committed with the intent to destroy, in whole or in part, a national ethnic, racial or religious group.' If this definition is met, those states and organisations tasked with the mobilisation of resources face a number of practical dilemmas. Perhaps the most important of these is how to avoid further instability within the country affected. Examples of *jus post bellum* to consider include political reconstruction, financial reparations and restraining conquest. Another additional concern is how to construct an effective strategy on the ground in terms of gaining public trust.

In regards to global governance, gaining authorisation from the UN Security Council can at times be problematic. In order for action to be effective, the five permanent members need to adopt unanimity. Given the moral dilemma posed by potential intervention, agreement can at times be difficult to achieve. For instance, in November 2002, Washington interpreted UN Resolution 1441 as a justification for intervention against the Iraqi regime. Although the resolution was passed on a unanimous basis, at least three of the permanent five voiced grave doubts about the wisdom of military intervention. In other situations, a member of the permanent five has used their veto powers to prevent any planned intervention on humanitarian grounds (such as the Syrian Civil War).

The 'Responsibility to Protect' (R2P) also bears some relevance towards our comprehension of humanitarian intervention. Endorsed in 2005 by General Secretary Kofi Annan as official policy of the UN, R2P is a global political commitment to recognise the obligations that arise from the concept of sovereignty. R2P is therefore based on an understanding that sovereignty imposes a positive duty upon the state to protect those housed within its borders. When a state fails to do this, the responsibility shifts towards the international community. The responsibility to protect entails three stages (to prevent, to reach and to rebuild). Supporters claim that the doctrine of R2P will, in time, replace the right to intervene. The international community has a duty to intervene when a state has failed to meet its obligations. R2P has also been praised for its reliance upon non-military measures, and for changing the contours of the debate over humanitarian intervention.

The Debate Between Hyper-globalisers, Globalisation Sceptics and Trans-formationalists

When considering the theoretical debate concerning globalisation, the obvious starting-point is the dichotomy between the two main theoretical perspectives discussed in the previous chapter – i.e. realism and liberalism. As a conventional starting-point, realism stipulates that globalisation has done little to change the fundamental conduct of international relations. The

Westphalian system may have changed, but it's far from buried. It is also possible for the major powers to impose economic protectionism and exercise populist language. From a less dramatic perspective, the decision to leave the European Union by the UK also demonstrates the continued relevance of national sovereignty within the contemporary era. In time, globalisation itself may perhaps be viewed as a passing fad.

The traditional theoretical opponent of realism is that of liberalism. Liberals claim that globalisation represents an irreversible and profound change in the dynamics of international relations. There are two aspects to consider here. The first is a direct challenge to the realist paradigm. Liberals point out that the borders of states are now more porous than ever before. The sovereignty of states has been compromised beyond recognition and the billiard-ball analogy now looks one-dimensional. Whilst realists cling to an out-dated statism, we now have a disaggregated state in which various agencies pursue their own departmental interests. The second is the prescriptive element of globalisation. Liberalism is built upon the assumption that human nature is perfectible. Institutions can therefore provide for an effective system of global governance as an extension of this will to perfect our human condition, and eradicating war is part of this process. Liberal thinkers undoubtedly have a more optimistic outlook than their realist counterparts.

Outside of the liberal-realist debate are a number of other theoretical perspectives that hold a perspective on globalisation at their centre. Three of these will be discussed, namely: Hyper-globalisers, Globalisation Sceptics, and Transformationalists. Each will be addressed in turn. As the term implies, hyper-globalists such as Kenichi Ohmae (1995) predict that globalisation represents the gradual demise of the sovereign state. Governments around the world can no longer manage their own domestic affairs as international interdependence has become a fact affecting both domestic and foreign affairs. Instead, governments must negotiate with non-state actors in order to achieve their aims. This is shown most dramatically within the economic sphere.

Globalisation Sceptics however stipulate that the hyper-globalist argument is little more than 'globaloney' (Veseth 2006). The sceptical position proclaims that there is nothing inherently new in the current mania for globalisation. Far from being a profound transformation in global politics, the process of globalisation occurs in waves and there is little to stop the tide turning against globalisation (an argument supported by the rise of populism). In recent years, there have been a number of 'strong men' who have sought to present themselves as opponents of globalisation. Alongside this, Stephen Krasner (1999) adds that states and geopolitics remain the principal agents and forces that shape world politics.

The sceptical argument is supported by patterns of global trade. The most significant trading links are concentrated within the relatively wealthier economies. Trading links are also increasingly formalised on a regional rather than truly global basis. From a more sceptical position, Justin Rosenberg depicts the term globalisation as a 'conceptual folly' which acts as a self-serving myth (2000). Globalisation is only meaningful for the rich and powerful. For the majority of people, the term is largely without substance. This is an argument that seems pertinent to the Global South (sometimes called the 'majority world' because the majority of the earth's population inhabit developing countries).

Transformationalists such as David Held and Anthony McGrew (2002) claim that both hyper-globalists and sceptics exaggerate their arguments. Transformationalists seek a half-way position between these two polar opposites. Whilst they accept that globalisation has undermined traditional notions of International Relations (such as the distinction between the domestic and the external), predictions about the demise of the nation-state are premature. Given its position within the broader debate concerning globalisation, it could be said to offer the best of both worlds. It also helps us escape the blunt dichotomy of the realist-liberal debate.

Debates Concerning the Impact of Globalisation: The Pros and Cons

The Impact of Globalisation

When seeking to evaluate the impact of globalisation, there are a number of clear advantages worth highlighting. Perhaps the most obvious benefit of globalisation exists within the economic sphere. Globalisation entails free movement of goods, services and, to a more limited extent, people. The world economy is often analogous to a marketplace in which prices are determined by the forces of demand and supply, often just referred to as 'market forces'. This helps to ensure that scarce resources are allocated in an effective manner. Economists such as those from the Chicago school (Friedman 1980) argue that free trade creates wealth and opportunities that benefit everyone. The impact of 'trickle-down economics' can be seen most dramatically in China. As a result of free-market reforms, China has witnessed the largest number of people lifted out of poverty in world history. However, it is important to remember that the efficacy of 'trickle-down economics' is heavily contested by economists also.

Secondly, globalisation facilitates a shared global social space forged by a heightened sense of cross-border solidarity. This shared social space is most evident in transnational movements supportive of democratic values, such as freedom of assembly. During the early 2000s a wave of peaceful protests engulfed authoritarian regimes in the former Soviet Union, for example, prompted by the spread of values from such a global social space. The demand for change was characterised by a series of colour revolutions during the noughties. Calls for democratic reform spread from Yugoslavia (2000) to Georgia (2003), Ukraine (2004) and Lebanon (2005). A similar phenomenon also occurred some years later during the Arab Spring, beginning in Tunisia in December 2010.

Thirdly, the technological dimension of globalisation prevents authoritarian systems acting in a manner that seeks to suppress dissent within their own borders – at least theoretically. Images of human rights violations can now be uploaded and disseminated at the click of a button. For instance, during the Umbrella Revolution in Hong Kong, protestors shared pictures of the police using tear gas against them. This led to even more people joining the movement. Non-governmental organisations, pressure groups and civil society expose the treatment of dissidents in a manner scarcely imaginable in previous generations.

In the political realm, globalisation enables states to pool their resources and thereby tackle cross-border problems in a more effective manner. Environmental degradation, cyber-terrorism and global pandemics have no respect for national borders. The nature of these problems is such that sovereign states must work together and coordinate their efforts. This entails the added benefit of encouraging a sense of cooperation to advance a worthy cause (such as banning chemical weapons via the Chemical Weapons Conventions (1997)).

In addition, economic liberalisation provides greater opportunities for less developed countries to specialise in certain goods and services. This enables those lesser economically developed countries to engage in export-led growth, generate wealth and improve their balance of payments. The subsequent increase in living standards will therefore assist with the process of economic development. This is based upon the old adage that 'a rising tide lifts all boats'. From a similar angle, globalisation makes it easier for people to emigrate in order to gain better prospects in life, which benefits both themselves and the host economy. Immigrants tend to fill job vacancies based upon highly-skilled occupations such as premiership footballers and so-called 'McJobs' such as cleaning (Bloor 2019).

Finally, globalisation may result in more openness over financial transactions which should help combat the twin problems of tax evasion and tax avoidance. There are growing calls for tax justice in order to ensure that the wealthy 1% contribute more. Schemes advocated by progressives (such as the Tobin tax on currency conversions) would also raise tax revenue in order to improve public services. This is a particularly acute problem within less developed countries.

Given the nature of political debate, there are clearly a number of drawbacks with globalisation. The main argument of the anti-globalisation (or alter-globalisation) movement is that developing countries are locked in a desperate 'race to the bottom' in order to entice powerful multi-national organisations. MNCs are able to relocate and outsource employment to those less economically developed countries with the least regulation and the lowest level of corporation tax. This is the inherently exploitative situation presented to the world's most disadvantaged people. For example, Apple has been accused of using sweatshops in the Chinese city of Shenzhen. Images of suicide nets, shared on social media, designed to prevent employees from escaping their working situation is emblematic of the dark effects of globalisation. Workers in much of the developing world are also prevented from joining a trade union by oppressive regimes.

Secondly, the rampant consumerism and unregulated capitalism facilitated by globalisation does lasting damage to the environment. Although globalisation raises awareness of our connection to nature, this does not always translate into effective action. This is particularly noticeable within developing countries reluctant to accept restrictions on economic growth. For instance, gaining agreement to tackle the global environmental emergency has been curtailed by the reluctance of the world's largest emitter of CO_2 emissions (China) to accept the international consensus in this particular area. Globalisation thereby contributes to negative consequences for us all due to the heightened depletion of natural resources.

From a geostrategic perspective, globalisation may also result in an increasingly unstable international system, due to the proliferation of nuclear weapons. Nuclear proliferation can be characterised as either horizontal (with more states gaining a nuclear capacity) or vertical (with more weapons accumulated by existing nuclear powers). For example, India and Pakistan are both nuclear powers with a historic rivalry over the disputed state of Jammu and Kashmir. Despite pressure from the international community, neither state is a signatory to the Nuclear Non-proliferation Treaty (1968). Globalisation also enables terrorist groups and violent non-state actors to proliferate in the cracks between states in the global space that it creates. This argument also applies to extremist groups capable of threatening innocent lives throughout the world.

In an economic sense, cross-border agreements designed to facilitate the process of globalisation present a number of disadvantages for workers in wealthier economies. For instance, outsourcing has resulted in lower wages and an erosion in job security. In the US, the phrase 'being Bangalored' is commonly used when people in sunset industries lose their jobs (such as the so-called 'Rust Belt' in the US). Companies can also threaten to take their operation overseas and thereby ensure that workers comply with a deterioration in pay and working conditions.

There are a number of figures on the left of the political spectrum who claim that globalisation tends to benefit the wealthy. The world-wide Occupy movement points out that the wealthy 1% have captured the political process to the detriment of the remaining 99%. Rather than wealth trickling down to benefit everyone, economic liberalisation enables the rich to hoard their wealth in offshore accounts. Globalisation also enables the transnational elite to evade / avoid paying tax and thereby escape their obligations as citizens of communities. In addition, the removal of trading barriers tends to benefit those with existing economic resources. The result is a system tilted heavily towards those with money and influence. Ultimately, globalisation has led to greater levels of inequality within society.

Another inherent problem with globalisation is that it makes it easier for the spread of fatal diseases to cross territorial borders. During the Ebola virus outbreak in 2013, 11,000 people died from a disease originating from near the Ebola River in the Democratic Republic of Congo. The source of the Ebola virus was thought to be bats that then transmitted the virus to humans (Centers for Disease Control and Prevention 2021). The freedom of movement associated with globalisation undoubtedly poses a greater risk of an outbreak turning into a global pandemic. We are closer to one another than ever before, but contained within that is a heightened risk to our health and wellbeing. The Covid-19 pandemic is the perfect illustration of this and the manner in which globalisation has sped up the possibility of the spread of disease-based crises.

Finally, globalisation can be said to have eroded our sense of national and cultural identity. That which once made us distinct has been replaced by a monocultural world dominated by Western-based multinational companies such as Starbucks and Facebook. Cultural globalisation is actually a misnomer for a bland and homogenised form of Westernisation that, ultimately, erodes cultural pluralism. The magnitude of the issue was brought home when it was found that more people recognise the golden arches of McDonalds than the Christian Cross (Lubin and Badkar 2010).

Having considered both sides of the argument, it is worth noting that the future course and direction of globalisation is an uncertain one. At the present time, even its most enthusiastic supporters would have to concede that globalisation is a deeply uneven process. According to the sociologist Manuel Castells, the term 'variable geometry' describes the asymmetrical nature of globalisation (1996). It is however conceivable that the future course of globalisation could serve all members of society and even the ecosphere. It should also be said that the process is not irreversible and may in time subside due to the forces of nationalism and populism.

The Implications of Globalisation for the Nation-State and Sovereignty

Globalisation entails a compression of the world and a transformation in our conception of self and identity. The world appears to be getting smaller due to technological developments, the affordability of travel and the impact of market forces. Globalisation also influences the integrity of national borders and their economic development. For better or worse, we are now all connected in a multi-layered system of mutual dependence. It is therefore undeniable that globalisation has had a deep and lasting influence upon the nation-state and national sovereignty.

According to the Japanese academic Kenicki Ohmae, globalisation has weakened the nation-state. The apparatus of the state no longer adequately protects a nation from the forces of globalisation (1995). From a similar angle, the noted sociologist Michael Mann (1997) identifies four threats to the nation-state: identity politics, post-nuclear geopolitics, global warming and global capitalism. Whilst the extent of each threat differs, they all offer a direct challenge to the sovereignty of the nation-state. If their arguments are accurate, then globalisation spells the death knell of the nation-state. Given the overwhelming impact of globalisation, territorial borders no longer offer a meaningful demarcation by which to comprehend the complex interactions of the modern era. The Westphalian conception of national sovereignty faces a slow but steady slide into permanent irrelevance.

In order to substantiate this argument, globalisation can be said to have had a profound impact upon the nation-state in three key areas: political, economic and cultural. In the political realm, globalisation undermines the ability of the nation-state to chart its own path. Given the interconnected character of the international system, it is simply impossible for states to retain absolute sovereignty in the economic realm (an argument made manifest by the great recession of the late noughties). However, the most symbolic argument to consider here is that of deeper European integration. Since the 1950s, the nation-states of Europe have formed an 'ever closer union' that renders the traditional conception of national sovereignty increasingly obsolete, as the characteristics that constitute a nation (singular common language, culture, history and social norms) become weakened or less concrete as individuals of different nations mix. Whilst member states still retain a degree of political legitimacy within their own borders, they are tied together in a complex web of mutual dependence. Member states work together to advance their national interests and are subject to sanctions for failing to impose EU-wide rules and directives.

In the economic realm, the world is interconnected like never before. Symbolically housed in Washington D.C., the International Monetary Fund (IMF) and the World Bank regulate the macroeconomic policies of those countries in debt to the global banking system. Structurally assisted programmes impose crippling repayment schemes upon many of the poorest countries in the world. Moreover, the sovereignty of the nation-state is undermined by multinational companies (MNCs). When the combined GDP of leading MNCs is greater than certain developed countries, it is hard to deny that the nation-state has lost some of its relative status.

The global financial and currency system can also determine the economic policies and objectives of even the most developed economies. States therefore have no choice but to pool resources and work alongside transnational organisations. This loss of direct control can only be interpreted as a loss of national sovereignty.

In the cultural realm, globalisation is often called Westernisation due to the spread of western norms. From the perspective of the non-Western world, this represents a modern-day version of cultural imperialism. For instance, the dominance of English-language programmes and American films undermine the national identity that lies at the very heart of the nation-state. The cultural element of globalisation has grown in significance, paralleling the rise of soft power in the global system. The threat is considered so significant that some countries have implemented protectionist measures to prevent their cultural way of life from being undermined, and this of course comes with political and social consequences, as is the case with all 'nationalist' protectionism.

Having said all this, there are those who claim that the nation-state is a robust concept that retains its relevance. In order to support this view, it could be argued that nation-states throughout the world have not been greatly affected by globalisation. Indeed, even the smallest countries retain their *raison d'etre*. For instance, the nation-state is defined by territorial boundaries. It also preserves a monopoly on the legitimate use of political violence in accordance with Max Weber's conceptualisation. Indeed, this definition has become more salient in the modern era as a means of distinguishing the legitimacy of the nation-state from that of terrorist groups. It should also be noted that the nation-state remains the most salient actor on the world stage when compared to international institutions, NGOs and sub-state actors. Based on such arguments, Paul Hirst and Grahame Thompson (1996) claim that the nation-state remains a powerful entity in an era of globalisation, overlapping with a number of the arguments presented by globalisation sceptics or even some transformationalists.

It could also be argued that globalisation has contributed towards an expansion in the power of the nation-state and national sovereignty. Far from being washed up with the tide of globalisation, states have adapted and prospered accordingly. National sovereignty can be viewed thus as a bargaining tool which can be bartered in order to advance the national interest. This could explain why nation-states have willingly joined regional forums designed to foster trade and cooperation. It's worth noting here that power is exercised in a somewhat different manner than ever before due to globalisation. One illustration of this argument is the transformation of the UK from having the largest empire in history to one of the leading proponents of soft power. Globalisation thereby encourages states to achieve their foreign policy objectives via the use of such power.

Whilst globalisation undoubtedly presents challenges for the nation-state, the concept remains a powerful force for three reasons. Firstly, the rules that govern globalisation are largely determined by nation-states – something that can be seen by the machinations of statist obligation construction UN resolutions. Secondly, sovereignty is retained when a member of an international organisation that requires the cessation of a certain degree of individual decision-making capability of its member-states chooses to leave that particular organisation (as in the case of the UK's 'Brexit' from the EU). More importantly, the process of globalisation has actually contributed to a revival of nationalist sentiment. There are few better illustrations of this point than in the United States. In 2016, the Republican candidate Donald Trump was elected on a mandate to 'Make America Great Again', implying that America's 'greatness' had been lost in the contemporary global era, and thus a reversal of such global processes was necessary. During his presidency, he took decisions contrary to the ethos of globalisation: such as a travel ban imposed on majority-Muslim countries or withdrawing the US form the 2015 Paris Climate Accords. Although it is fashionable to claim that globalisation renders the Westphalian system irrelevant, this is far from given. In reality, globalisation has done nothing to prevent states from putting their own interests first, or indeed utilising globalisation for their own ends – a realist argument.

In this vein, economic globalisation also brings undoubted benefits to nation-states. For instance, multinational companies provide governments with added tax revenue. In other words, as multinationals grow larger, they spread globally and largely accumulate wealth (which the state collects in corporation tax). The location of such companies also creates jobs within the host economy. An increase in international trade also requires the existence of global regulatory bodies. The enhanced flow of goods, services and people can only occur via an institutional framework provided and managed by national governments. Such factors ultimately strengthen the ability of nation-states to implement policies that meet their specific national interests.

Finally, the nation-state has in some areas reasserted its ability to control events and implement actions as a response to globalisation. We are bound together in security matters like never before as a result of the threat posed by organisations with a distinctly global reach. Whilst few would contend that globalisation entails a heightened sense of risk, the response to such threats underlines the continued relevance of national sovereignty. The global response to the COVID-19 pandemic is a particularly salient example to consider. Far from being passive victims of globalisation, it is entirely possible for sovereign states to impose differing and unprecedented restrictions upon people's movements and thereby reasserting themselves as an ultimate decision-making power within a given territory.

The Extent to Which Globalisation Addresses Contemporary Issues

In an increasingly interconnected world characterised by a complex web of mutual dependence, the process of globalisation can be utilised to address contemporary issues. Equally, it also presents a series of intricate barriers towards conflict resolution and the threat of global warming. In each dimension, there are both positives and negatives to consider. There are also several dependent factors to highlight when seeking to evaluate the manner and extent to which globalisation addresses these pressing issues.

The very character of globalisation offers opportunities for state and non-state actors to address issues of a transnational character, such as a reduction in global poverty and environmental protection. In these cases, the role of international organisations has proved an increasingly important one. This observation also applies to human rights alongside conflict prevention and resolution. Globalisation similarly enables like-minded individuals to work together and promote worthy goals, such as the protection of human rights. Equally, the process of globalisation accentuates threats of a cross-border character. For instance, technological developments make it easier for terrorist groups and violent non-state actors to promote their cause.

Poverty

Attempts to address the problem of poverty incorporate states, non-state actors and sub-state actors. In a particularly clear illustration, the G8 Summit held at Gleneagles in 2005 agreed to write off the entire debt owed by 18 'Highly Indebted Poor Countries'. It was a decision influenced by campaigns from prominent pressure groups such as Make Poverty History, and it was implemented by a number of progressive political leaders. It remains symbolic of the manner in which globalisation frames our approach to issues that affect billions. In 2021, an estimated 9% of the world's population lived on less than $1.90 a day.

In terms of eradicating poverty, the main focus of the United Nations has centred upon targets agreed by the member states. In the year 2000, the Millennium Declaration was signed, committing countries to combat poverty (along with other related goals such as fighting hunger and disease). The eight Millennium Development Goals (MDGs) entail specific targets and indicators that member states agreed to achieve by the year 2015.

The Millennium Development Goals sought to eradicate extreme poverty and hunger, implement universal primary education, promote gender equality and empower women, reduce child mortality, improve maternal health, ensure environmental sustainability, to develop a global partnership for development and to combat HIV/AIDS alongside other diseases. In 2015, the Sustainable Development Goals (SDGs) replaced the MDGs. There are 17 global goals in total designed to be the 'blueprint to achieve a better and more sustainable future for all' (United Nations 2021). Revealingly, the first goal is that of eradicating poverty and malnutrition. It is also worth noting that the language used is more purposeful than that adopted for the MDGs. In an attempt to ensure these goals are met by the year 2030, data is available in an easy-to-understand manner. The emphasis upon sustainability also reflects the growing salience of environmental issues and sustainable development.

Another aspect of tackling poverty is to open up national economies towards free trade. The so-called Washington Consensus consists of a set of policies based upon deregulation, privatisation and marketisation. The basis of the Washington Consensus is therefore centred firmly upon a free-market philosophy. There are powerful arguments to support the Washington Consensus. Supporters claim that the free market is the best system available for lifting people out of poverty. Liberal theorists are highly supportive of global capitalism as they claim that free trade enhances the level of cooperation between states. According to the World Bank (2021a), more than a billion people have escaped extreme poverty since the early

1990s and poverty rates in 2019 were lower than they had ever been, although rising slightly in 2020.

From the opposing angle, the alter-globalisation movement is heavily critical of the Washington Consensus. They claim that policies imposed upon national governments serve the interests of the wealthy and exploit those marginalised within the global economy. The invisible hand of Adam Smith (1999; 2009) actually prevents those at the bottom from escaping a structure systematically biased against them. The recent coronavirus pandemic also has a disproportionately negative impact upon the world's poorest people.

As with much else within the field of International Relations, a great deal depends upon the perspective taken. From the predominant Western viewpoint, globalisation is often viewed as a welcome economic development. There is undoubtedly much merit in this argument. However, for those who exist at the periphery of the world economy globalisation is clearly an uneven process with several adverse effects over which they have little control. Whilst there has been some progress in lifting people out of poverty, globalisation also tends to exacerbate inequality between wealthy states and those in the Global South. In theoretical terms, this is often heard from dependency theorists (Prebisch 1950) and the world systems approach (Wallerstein 1979).

Another issue to consider is the provision of foreign aid from wealthy governments. Those in favour claim that financial assistance can be targeted towards poverty reduction schemes. Opponents however argue that foreign aid is routinely misappropriated by powerful elites, particularly within authoritarian and dictatorial regimes. In addition, the level of corruption within a recipient state prevents aid from reaching those most in need. The provision of foreign aid also results in a dependency culture that undermines self-reliance and initiative. It could also be argued that foreign aid actually contributes further towards global inequality.

It must be acknowledged that there is little evidence to suggest that aid has a positive impact upon poverty levels. Given the realities of international relations, states tend to pursue their own interests via foreign aid. For instance, the UK government has been accused of providing aid to Malaysia to fund a project linked to arms sales. Political considerations are also central towards the provision of aid from the Chinese government. Furthermore, wealthy governments have failed to meet the guidelines laid down in the 1987 Brundtland Report – which introduced the concept of sustainable development and how it could be achieved.

Conflict

There is a glaring contradiction that lies at the very heart of globalisation. In one sense, globalisation contributes towards a more peaceful world order. The spread of democratic norms underpinned by economic interdependence reduces the number of conflicts between states. Equally, globalisation can exacerbate conflict and contribute towards heightened levels of political instability. This can entail several related problems such as an influx of refugees, armed insurgencies against the ruling government and inter-ethnic conflict.

One of the most interesting case studies to consider here is that of global terrorism. In an age of globalisation, terrorism has shifted from an essentially state-bound or regional problem to a global phenomenon. Its method of funding, communication and expansionist objectives have all become globalised over time. For example, Islamic State (also known as ISIL/ISIS/IS/ Daesh) broadcasts its message to a potential audience of billions via social media. Indeed, despite its historical connections, the goal of an Islamic state under the leadership of a caliph (a political-religious ruler and considered a successor to the Prophet Muhammad) has been symptomatic of the globalised era.

Regarding terrorism, globalisation enhances the threat posed throughout the world. Due to the erosion in conventional state boundaries, terrorist groups find it easier to target states and other actors. However, this is not a one-sided process. Globalisation also allows states to co-ordinate efforts to combat terrorism. Sovereign states continually exchange information on known terrorists and their associated activities, a great illustration of this being the 'Five Eyes' intelligence alliance between Australia, Canada, New Zealand, the US and the UK. The international fight against terrorism can at times lead to an unlikely alliance between countries with apparently little in common. Just as terrorist groups have become globalised, so too has the response from states to the threat of global terrorism.

The impact of globalisation is particularly evident in regards to the spread of information. At one time, states had a near monopoly on the use of propaganda whilst terrorist groups had restricted means by which to spread their message. More importantly, the agents of the state often had effective means of censorship. However, due to technological developments, governments throughout the world find it almost impossible to control the flow of information and the 'spin' placed upon it. New social media provides the oxygen of publicity for violent and extremist groups to disseminate their worldview and gain support. This provides the added benefit of gaining funding, recruitment, and the platform to offer a spectacle for all the world to see.

Terrorist groups have also become more problematic for states to deal with because of changes in their structure. Terrorist cells now operate locally which means that states can only tackle the spread of terrorism one cell at a time. This tactical change has made it more problematic for governments to defeat extremist groups. This is particularly notable within ISIS strongholds in Syria and Iraq. Such groups endorse the unofficial maxim of globalisation in theory and practice: 'think locally, act globally'.

Human Rights

The international human rights agenda can be dated back to the UN Declaration of Human Rights (UDHR), signed on 10 December 1948. For the very first time, a common standard for universal human rights was agreed upon by the signatory nations. It marked a unique moment in world history and was indicative of a new world order determined to avoid another period of turmoil, persecution and genocide.

The UDHR demonstrates that sovereign states are both willing and able to specify fundamental human rights. This has since been extended towards protecting the most vulnerable, such as refugees, prisoners, and children. With the benefit of hindsight, the UDHR helped lay the foundation for further treaties that broadened the concept of human rights. There is even a sufficient body of international human rights law to justify the use of the phrase International Bill of Rights. Once hailed as 'a Magna Carta for all humanity' (Klug 2015), the International Bill of Human Rights seeks to bring together a number of rights into one codified document (United Nations General Assembly 1948). It consists of the five core human rights treaties of the UN that function to advance the fundamental freedoms and to protect fundamental human rights.

Perhaps the clearest illustration of globalisation in the context of human rights is the UN Human Rights Council (UNHRC). Created in 2006, the UNHRC investigates allegations of human rights violations within member states. The UNHRC replaced the UN Commission on Human Rights, which had been previously criticised for allowing countries with a poor record on human rights to join the organisation. However, the UNHRC has not been without criticism. For instance, the US has accused the organisation of holding an anti-Israeli bias. To support this claim, the Council has passed more resolutions condemning Israel than the rest of the world combined. Washington objects to the focus upon Israel, although this ignores the point that the use of veto powers in the UN Security Council shields Israel from their actions in Gaza and the West Bank. The Trump administration withdrew the United States from the UNHRC – the first country ever to do so. Having said this, the UNHRC has taken steps to defend rights in despotic regimes such as Myanmar, Burundi, and the Democratic Republic of the Congo. The UNHRC could therefore be seen as an illustration of globalisation and its impact upon the protection of human rights from both a positive and more critical angle.

The effectiveness of human rights within the contemporary era is subject to heated debate. Despite globalisation helping to raise and promote awareness of human rights, ensuring compliance remains highly problematic due to various reasons. First and foremost, the international organisations responsible for implementing global governance lack sufficient resources to enforce compliance upon rogue states. For instance, the international community has been unable to exert any lasting influence upon North Korea. The Kim dynasty has violated human rights for several decades. Having chosen isolation and rejected globalisation, the regime in Pyongyang remains largely impervious to pressure from any form of global governance.

Another illustration of this argument concerns the International Criminal Court (ICC). Established with the Rome Statute of 1998, the ICC deals with the violation of human rights with a remit to cover areas such as genocide, land grabs and war crimes. However, the effectiveness of this legally independent (albeit UN-associated) institution is constrained due to relatively powerful countries refusing to join. This includes China, Israel, Iraq and of course the United States. Even the Philippines left the organisation under President Duterte in protest at the ICC launching an investigation in their country.

Secondly, the effectiveness of the human rights agenda is undermined by its Eurocentric (or Western-centric) bias. In some parts of the world, the concept of individual rights lacks legitimacy. It is revealing to note that the continent of Asia lacks a regional human rights organisation comparable to the European Court of Human Rights (ECtHR). In addition, the Arab League has long taken the view that national sovereignty should apply on a literal basis. It could even be said that the documents that specify universal human rights are largely 'paper rights' in certain parts of the world.

In contrast to the flowery rhetoric of global governance, there is no international court to administer human rights law. In reality, only a handful of quasi-judicial bodies exist within the umbrella of the United Nations. Although the aforementioned ICC has expanded its jurisdiction, it still leaves a wide remit of human rights abuses free from investigation. It is also problematic to circumvent the principle of national sovereignty. This is a particular problem when faced with populist leaders, especially in the current age where illiberal democratic norms appear to be becoming increasingly popular (Mudde 2019, Müller 2016). Furthermore, globalisation has increased public demand for social protection whilst decreasing the capacity of the state to provide it. Some states genuinely find it difficult to protect human rights due to the immense power of multinational companies, global markets, and the IMF/ World Bank. Globalisation could therefore be said to undermine the ability of a hollowed-out state to ensure adherence to human rights.

From a more positive angle, international institutions are able to nudge recalcitrant states towards better behaviour. International human rights law provides a framework by which to govern the actions of states. As with people, most states follow the law because it is the law. This tautology is made more effective when reinforced with a veneer of legitimacy and a set of effective sanctions (e.g. trade and diplomatic restrictions). Globalisation has also increased the salience of human rights within the international community.

As a process, globalisation undoubtedly sheds greater light upon human rights abuses. The ability of authoritarian regimes to cover up a violation of human rights has been greatly curtailed by the spread of technology. Protestors and dissidents can upload and share images throughout the world in a manner unimaginable in the past. Technological developments also enable like-minded groups to work together to enforce social change. That said, the problems of monitoring and implementing international human rights law remain largely unresolved.

The Environment

International cooperation in this area emerged during the growing awareness of environmental issues in the 1970s. The UN Environmental Programme (UNEP) was established in 1972 to co-ordinate the environmental activity of member states. However, the UNEP is institutionally weak and provides ineffective protection. As with much else provided by the United Nations, its effectiveness is hampered by a constrained mandate and a lack of funding.

In an era of globalisation, there have been a series of multilateral agreements that seek to address environmental issues. In 1992, the UN Conference on Environment and Development (also known as the Rio Summit) provided a forum in which member states could collaborate on issues such as sustainability. It established a global environmental agenda that has since been developed during subsequent conferences. The UN Conference on Sustainable Development created the Climate Change Convention. It was also agreed that signatory states would not carry out any activity on the lands of indigenous peoples that might cause environmental damage. Finally, the Rio Summit instigated a process that led towards a firmer commitment towards the Convention on Biological Diversity.

In the specific area of environmental protection, the international community has often been prepared to reach agreements and demonstrate a common show of unity. According to the WTO, there are over 250 multilateral environmental agreements (MEAs) currently in force dealing with a multiplicity of environmental issues. Some of those agreements have been truly historic. For instance, due to the 2015 Paris Agreement, signatories pledged to reduce their carbon emissions. However, it has proven difficult to persuade the most powerful countries to take the required action. Most notably, the United States failed to ratify the Kyoto Protocol. Partly because of this, global emissions were on the rise in 2005 (the year the Kyoto Protocol became international law). China has also been reluctant to deal effectively with carbon emissions, whilst the Trump administration withdrew from the Paris Agreement – although later re-joined under the Biden administration in 2021.

Given the pressing nature of climate change, there have been proposals to implement a truly effective governing body or centralised institution. Even the strongest defenders of national sovereignty recognise that international agreements are neither legally binding nor effective enough to tackle the climate crisis. There have, for instance, been proposals for a World Environment Organisation (WEO). However, the US prefers voluntary initiatives to ensure that economic interests are protected. This also matches the national interests of several emerging economies, such as the BRICS.

It has also been proposed that environmental issues should be directly incorporated into the WTO. The WTO can apply legal pressure and resolve trade disputes. However, critics claim that this would fail to address underlying market failures or improve rulemaking in terms of environmental protection. Providing greater power for the WTO is also problematic for those critical of the Washington Consensus and its adverse impact upon the Global South.

Perhaps the main problem posed by environmental degradation is that states are often reluctant to cast aside the advantages provided by retaining the status quo. Whilst creating a more effective system of global governance is laudable, there is insufficient political will to surrender national sovereignty. Environmental degradation is a problem for all countries and demands a complete rethink of the Westphalian system to be resolved in an adequate manner. There is also to some extent a trade-off between economic development and environmental protection.

When it comes to the international community and the environment, the narrative has typically been 'too little too late'. Given its gathering pace and irreversible character, the society of states has a clear interest in resolving the problem. However, this has proved immensely difficult to implement. More than any other issue, environmental degradation demands effective collective cooperation from the international community on an unprecedented global scale. Globalisation has not yet managed to circumvent the barriers presented by sovereignty and national interests.

Conclusion

This chapter sought to provide an overview of the role and significance of the state and globalisation. It provided an outline of concepts such as the nation-state, national sovereignty and mutual dependence. The impact of globalisation was weighed up in terms of both positives and negatives. Whilst it is arguably too soon to provide a definitive conclusion, globalisation may well hold significant implications for the future of the nation-state. According to some, the nation-state needs a radical rethink in an era characterised by globalisation.

It must however be acknowledged that globalisation provides the means by which transnational issues can be addressed. It is surely important to note that there is nothing deterministic about globalisation and the future of the state. Change is a constant within global politics. Hence, given the evidence outlined, there seems little to suggest that the notion of 'the state' will be any different. The following chapter will provide a consideration of global governance. Taking forward some of the themes explored in this chapter, the implications of globalisation will be examined in regards to its political and economic dimensions. This will lead towards a consideration of human rights and the environment.

BOX 2.1 – KEY TERMS FROM CHAPTER TWO

Sovereignty

Sovereignty can be defined as the ability of a state to set rules and regulations within its territorial boundaries. National sovereignty is a fundamental element of global politics and most countries seek to establish sovereignty within the framework of a nation-state. The concept of national sovereignty lies at the very heart of understanding International Relations. However, there is a debate over the relevance of the term within the contemporary realm. According to hyper-globalists, national sovereignty has lost its traditional meaning in an era characterised by the process of globalisation. The realist perspective however asserts that nation-states remain the most significant actors within global politics. Theoretical perspectives should be supported by evidence, and the response to the coronavirus crisis gives credence to both sides of the debate.

Nation-state

A nation-state is a theoretical construct based on the belief that a nation should be able to define its own borders and exercise control over them. Throughout history, the contours of the globe have been drawn by independence movements seeking to properly delineate their own nation-state. As well as being a theoretical construct, the nation-state is a legal concept dating back to the Treaty of Westphalia in 1648. Westphalian sovereignty is the decree that every nation-state is considered sovereign over its defined territory. The Westphalian system is built upon the principles of non-interference and equality of nations under international law. The ability of a nation to determine its own path is a fundamental right. Intervention in another country can only be justified on humanitarian grounds.

Non-state actors

The realist perspective within International Relations views the state as the legitimate source of power and authority over any given territory. In order to substantiate this argument, there is no part of the world in which the nation-state does not have some territorial claim. This observation even applies to disputes between competing states. Having said this, the liberal perspective tends to emphasise the importance of non-state actors. International relations can only be understood with reference to the role of non-state actors. For instance, the economic might of multinational companies dwarfs those of even the largest states.

Given the economic might of such organisations, national governments often negotiate directly with MNCs. The influence of multinationals is such that nation-states may have little choice but to acquiesce to the demands of these monolithic companies.

Globalisation

Globalisation can be thought of as the increasing interdependence of nation-states within the contemporary era. Globalisation can be applied in a number of different ways towards our understanding of international relations. These primarily relate to the economic realm, the political sphere and the cultural dimension. Global actors are mutually dependent because events in one part of the world impact upon others at remarkable speed. Globalisation increasingly dominates the conversation over our understanding of global politics. There are several themes to consider here including the consequences for national sovereignty and the extent to which globalisation helps to resolve contemporary issues. To realists, globalisation does not change the fundamental basis of international relations. The global system should be viewed via the prism of survival, self-help and statism. Liberals however tend to view globalisation as a transformative process upon global politics with major implications as to how we should comprehend national sovereignty.

Economic Globalisation

Economic globalisation reflects intensified and enhanced levels of mutual dependence via the movement of goods, services, capital and labour. As a consequence of economic globalisation, an economy could never completely protect itself from a slowdown in international trade (as shown dramatically during the credit crunch). The process of economic globalisation is based upon the assumption that each state has a clear benefit from engaging in trade. The liberal perspective has long argued that economic globalisation contains within it the bonds of eternal (or perpetual) peace. It is an argument that can be traced back to the philosopher Immanuel Kant (1991) and was modified via the 'golden arches' theory of Thomas Friedman (1996).

Political Globalisation

Political globalisation depicts the binding relationships that have fostered amongst different countries from a habit of cooperation. This is underpinned by mutual dependence amongst a multitude of actors on the world stage. As a result of political globalisation, decisions taken by a powerful state may impact in a significant and multi-faceted manner upon others. The international system is characterised by a complex political system with a diverse range of state, non-state and even sub-state actors. In regards to the latter, transnational groups can at times shape the dynamics of the political process. A number of academics even claim that political globalisation holds major implications for the nation-state. This is the argument put forward by a school of thought known as the hyper-globalists. However, sceptics such as Ha-Joon Chang take a more pessimistic view of the process. For instance, Chang (2002) describes the World Bank, the IMF and the WTO as the 'unholy alliance' which forces less developed countries to adopt a free trade approach.

Cultural Globalisation

Cultural globalisation refers to the exchange of ideas, meanings and values throughout the world. Cultural globalisation both extends and intensifies social relations throughout the globe. It is a process underpinned by the consumption of cultures distributed via new media sources. The liberal perspective claims that cultural globalisation is a positive development. For instance, it has created shared norms and values across borders. Cultural flattening of differences amongst nations and regions also contributes towards a shared mindset. In the contemporary era, the Internet and social media provide a powerful means of mobilisation for political reform. Cultural globalisation is often criticised for eroding cultural differences. For instance, Jeremy Seabrook (2005) argues that globalisation relegates all local cultures to an inferior status. Globalisation also implies a civilised mode of living with an implicit promise of prosperity and security. Anything that deviates from the cultural norm is therefore seen as second-rate. It has also been argued that cultural globalisation contributes towards a sense of homogenisation. In a world increasingly characterised by soft power, the ability to impose a cultural mindset on less powerful countries is a modern-day form of imperialism.

Homogenisation and Monoculture

In a cultural sense, homogenisation refers to a reduction in cultural diversity via the popularisation and circulation of a wide array of cultural symbols. The homogenisation of culture refers to intangible factors alongside physical objects. According to figures and pressure groups within the alter-globalisation movement, homogenisation is a form of neoimperialism exercised by Western countries and companies (Veltmeyer 2016). Cultural homogenisation is seen as problematic because it leads to an erosion of national identity. Monoculturalism is the practice of preserving and advocating a single culture via the exclusion of external influences. A monocultural society comes to exist through racial homogeneity, nationalistic tendencies and geographical/political isolation. The practice of monoculturalism marks an attempt to shut out external influences and is commonly associated with a totalitarian regime. In terms of a binary understanding, monoculturalism is the opposite of multiculturalism (the latter term can be defined as the broadening diversity and identity that has come to characterise the era in which we live). On a final note, a global monoculture entails the dominance of a single culture. Unlike traditional imperialism, it does not require military force. A global monoculture could therefore be seen as a prominent illustration of soft power (Nye 1990).

Interconnectedness

Interconnectedness refers to the mutual reliance of two or more actors within international relations. Interconnectedness is fostered via international forums that provoke dialogue and cooperation. Interconnectedness underlines the extent and significance of globalisation. As with other aspects of globalisation, there are both positive and negative elements to consider. For better or worse, the world appears to be shrinking due to rapid developments within communication and technology.

World Government

World government refers to the idea of a common political authority within the realm of international relations. A world government would thereby entail a law-making body, an executive capable of implementing decisions and a judicial system. Each branch of government would be based upon a supranational approach and thereby exist above the nation-state. For instance, a judicial body would be able to impose sanctions upon those countries that break international law. Whilst it is clear that a world government does not exist, there is a system of governance in place that exhibits some of these features. Although the nearest equivalent to a global law-making assembly is the United Nations, it is not a law-making body in the sense of a domestic legislature. The closest thing the global commons has to an executive branch is the UN Security Council. And, the closest thing the international community has to a judicial branch is the International Criminal Court (ICC) that sits in The Hague. There are also a number of judicial bodies that oversee international conventions (such as the European Court of Human Rights).

Global Governance

First and foremost, global governance is distinct from the concept of world government. The latter consists of a unified system with the three recognised branches of government unified under a common system. Global governance however merely refers to those institutions and organisations that specify the rules and framework of the global system. Global governance is an all-encompassing term that seeks to create an institutionalised structure capable of regulating the behaviour of both state and non-state actors. There are a number of international organisations that hold a specific remit over certain areas. For instance, the World Bank seeks to eradicate poverty by the provision of financial assistance to poorer countries. In addition, the International Monetary Fund (IMF) is tasked with ensuring global monetary cooperation, financial stability and the smooth flow of world trade.

BOX 2.2 – KEY POINTS FOR CHAPTER TWO

1. The process of globalisation is driven by several factors.

2. There are various dimensions of globalisation.

3. The impact of globalisation entails both positives and negatives.

4. There are various perspectives that seek to highlight the implications of globalisation.

5. Most commentators accept that globalisation has fundamentally altered the concept of national sovereignty, but this is contested.

6. The nation-state remains a fundamental element within international relations.

7. Globalisation seeks to address and resolve issues such as alleviating poverty, preventing conflict, upholding human rights and protecting the environment.

3

Global Governance: Political and Economic Governance

Taking the themes and concepts explored in the opening two chapters, this chapter concerns itself with the development of global governance. It begins by sketching an outline of the very epicentre of global governance - the United Nations (UN). The role, significance and changing role of the North Atlantic Treaty Organisation (NATO) will then be assessed, before an evaluation of the institutions that lie at the very heart of 'the Washington Consensus'. From here, how the institutions of global governance seek to address issues within contemporary international relations such as the WTO, the G7 (formerly the G8) and the G20 will become the focus of inquiry. This chapter seeks to go beyond the realism-liberalism dichotomy so as to consider alternative theoretical interpretations of the subject matter.

Political Global Governance

The United Nations

As with the League of Nations before it, the United Nations emerged out of a desire to create a world centred upon peace and the rule of law in the aftermath of total war. US President Franklin D. Roosevelt first used the term to describe the Allied countries fighting the Axis powers during the Second World War, and as such the history of the UN is intrinsically tied to the end of the conflict in much the same way, as stated above, that the League of Nations was tied to the outcome of the First World War. In 1942, a short document was signed which later became known as 'The Declaration by The United Nations'. Representatives of twenty-two nations added their signatures to those of the 'four policemen' (the US, the Soviet Union, China and the UK). In 1945, the UN Conference on International Organisation was held in San Francisco to finalise the details of the organisation.

The United Nations was born out of an understandable willingness to avoid the problems that had plagued the League of Nations. The horrors of the Second World War exposed the inherent flaws within an idealistic organisation devoid of any effective sanctions against rogue states. The absence of the United States also meant that the organisation would prove powerless against the rise of fascism. In order to make progress towards a more peaceful and stable world order, the United Nations Charter was signed in 1945. The UN Charter consists of a preamble and a series of articles grouped together into Chapters. The preamble to the Charter (United Nations 1945) refers to 'we the peoples of the UN' and underlines the importance of human rights, justice and social progress, whilst declaring the aim to prevent succeeding generations from the scourge of war. The preamble also provides a commitment to tolerance, peace and security. The core of the document is contained in Chapters three to fifteen, which outline the role and powers of the various institutions that constitute the organisation. In relation to international law, Chapter seven authorises the Security Council to use military force to resolve disputes. The UN Charter commits the organisation to uphold peace and security, develop cooperation between nations and promote progress in terms of living standards and human rights.

Right from the very beginning, the UN adopted a decision-making structure that matched the power balance of the immediate post-war settlement. Within the Security Council, the UN body responsible for the establishment of peacekeeping operations and the authorisation of military action, five permanent members (P5) represented the victorious powers emerging from the war against European fascism and Japanese imperialism: The US, France, The UK, The USSR and the Republic of China. In 1971, the People's Republic of China replaced the Taiwan-based Republic of China on the UN Security Council, and in 1991 the Russian Federation upheld the permanent membership once held by the USSR prior to its collapse. Despite calls to expand its membership, the permanent five have remained a feature of the Security Council since the mid-1940s.

Having outlined the origin and development of the organisation, we will now consider each branch of global governance. Given the importance of the Security Council, it seems fitting to begin with this quasi-executive branch. The legislative and judicial functions will also be considered.

UN Security Council (UNSC)

Under Chapter Six of the UN Charter, the UN Security Council (UNSC) may investigate any dispute if there is a threat to international peace and security. The UNSC is also authorised to recommend appropriate procedures and measures to resolve the dispute. The real power within the UN lies with the UNSC, consisting of fifteen members. There are five permanent members (all of whom are nuclear powers) and ten non-permanent members elected for two-year terms by the General Assembly. Decisions taken within the Security Council are binding upon all member states.

Since the turn of the century, a number of resolutions passed by the Security Council have contained major political implications. For instance, the UNSC condemned the Iraqi invasion of Kuwait on the same day as the attack and later authorised the US-led coalition. Chapter 7 allows the UNSC to decide what measures should be adopted by the organisation. This includes the use of armed force in order to maintain or restore international peace and security. Action adopted on this basis is binding upon all members of the General Assembly. Such measures include economic sanctions, ending diplomatic ties and sending peacekeeping troops to conflict zones. However, given the difficulty in reaching a consensus amongst the P5, UN resolutions tend towards strongly-worded condemnations rather than effective actions. This is a particular problem when a member of the P5 acts in a manner that undermines human rights, or when a rogue state has the backing of one of the P5. In addition, these recommendations lack an enforcement mechanism and must therefore be considered a weakness of the organisation.

The UNSC also adopts a number of less important roles. For instance, it endorses new states for admission as members of the UN. During the Cold War, the Soviet Union frequently used its veto powers to prevent new states from joining the organisation. The UNSC also recommends the new Secretary General to the Assembly. In addition, the UNSC has the authority to refer cases to the International Criminal Court (as in 2011 in order to investigate action taken by the Libyan government in response to the outbreak of civil war).

In 2005, the UN member states endorsed the concept of responsibility to protect (R2P) in order to ensure that sovereign states meet their responsibilities. The R2P provides a framework for employing already existing measures to prevent genocide, war crimes, ethnic cleansing and crimes against humanity. The UNSC has the authority to employ the use of force upon this basis. However, taking action as such is a measure of last resort only after all other channels have been exhausted (such as mediation). The UN Secretary-General has published numerous reports on the R2P that expand upon measures available to governments, intergovernmental organisations and civil society.

In terms of an assessment of the UN Security Council, its main weakness relates to the use of veto powers by the permanent five. This means that the

United States, Russia, China, France and the United Kingdom can choose to place their own national interests above those of the international community. Whilst the veto is in fact a technicality, in that nowhere in the UN Charter does it specifically state that the permanent members have that power, resolutions are adopted only if there are at least nine affirmative votes on the 15 member UNSC (and the P5 lack any voice of dissent). The very existence of a veto can, at times, impede the ability of the international community to resolve disputes. It can also lead to glaring double-standards in which major powers can effectively ignore the needs of others. The permanent five also distorts the distribution of power within the organisation. The Global South is marginalised due to the entrenched position of the permanent five. There is also considerable debate over a potential expansion of countries within the Security Council. There is undoubtedly a persuasive case for granting membership to Germany and Japan given their economic weight. Nuclear powers such as India and Pakistan are also excluded from the existing permanent members, which again seems hard to justify, especially given India's economic and regional influence.

In terms of the positives, there have been occasions in which the UN Security Council has worked together to adopt a common and effective strategy. For instance, the international community condemned the Iraqi invasion of Kuwait and provided legitimacy for a US-led intervention during the Gulf War (1990–91). It also provides a forum by which the major powers can discuss shared interests and co-operate on a diplomatic basis.

UN General Assembly (UNGA)

The UN General Assembly (UNGA) is the representative law-making body within the organisation that includes representatives of each member or observer state's mission to the International Organisation. The UNGA is primarily responsible for consideration and approval of the UN budget, the appointment of non-permanent members to the Security Council and the appointment of the UN Secretary General. The UNGA also establishes subsidiary agencies to advance its overall mandate. In accordance with its deliberative role, the General Assembly receives reports from various agencies and offers recommendations.

Voting in the UNGA on important issues (such as the possible expulsion of a member state) is on the basis of a super-majority of those members within the chamber. The majority of non-controversial or contentious issues are resolved via a simple majority with each member state entitled to one vote each. The UNGA can make recommendations on matters within the scope of the organisation, even those that fall under the remit of the Security Council on the basis of Resolution 377. The UNGA can consider matters that appear to present a breach of the peace, or an act of aggression. Apart from approval of budgetary matters, resolutions adopted by the UNGA are not binding. The resolutions brought forward by sponsoring states are largely symbolic, and most of the debate lacks any effectiveness. This has led to an assessment of the UNGA as an ineffective 'talking-shop' that lacks the legitimacy of a genuine law-making institution. For instance, attempts made by the UNGA to tackle global poverty have proved negligible when compared to the magnitude of the problem.

Condemnation by the member states of human rights violations have rarely resulted in decisive action. For instance, delegations from countries accused of such violations such as North Korea and Turkey have actually stormed out of the Assembly. There is also the phenomenon of grandstanding, whereby a representative provokes a symbolic response from those accused. For instance, in 2011 several Western countries walked out of the UNGA after the Iranian President Mahmoud Ahmadinejad denounced the US response to 9/11, stopping short of claiming the terrorist attack a decade earlier was staged. The General Assembly has also witnessed farcical scenes, ranging from lengthy speeches delivered by Fidel Castro (just under 5 hours) and Muammar Gaddafi, to laughter at US President Donald Trump.

As a result of decolonisation, the number of member states within the Global South has increased significantly. The source of diplomatic influence for many of these Less-Economically Developed Countries (LEDCs) is via the floor of the General Assembly. Their common stance is coordinated via the Group of 77 (G77) which was set up during the mid-1960s. However, there is little doubt that political power within the organisation is concentrated in the hands of the permanent five.

Economic and Social Council (ECOSOC)

The UN Economic and Social Council (ECOSOC) is responsible for coordinating the economic and social aspects of the organisation. It seeks to advance a number of worthy objectives such as promoting higher living standards, facilitating international cooperation and protecting universal human rights. The Council is the central forum for discussing global cooperation via a number of specialised agencies and commissions. In doing so, the ECOSOC formulates policy recommendations addressed by the UN member states.

The ECOSOC seeks to co-ordinate its work with a range of non-state actors. For instance, NGOs participate within the Council on the basis of their consultative status. The Council also holds an annual meeting of finance ministers which includes representatives from the IMF and the World Bank. Seats within the ECOSOC are allocated on the basis of geographical representation. This is a contentious process within any international organisation, and there are understandable calls to adopt a more accurate reflection of recent developments within international relations.

Apart from a lack of sufficient resources, the main criticism of the ECOSOC has been the fragmented nature of the multilateral system. The cumbersome character of the decision-making process constrains the capacity of the Council to influence international policies. This has led to demands for reform in order to improve the relevance of the Council. There have also been proposals to establish a forum within the Council in order to counter the influence of the G20. However, this was not approved by the UNGA. The stated aim of the Council is to establish itself as a platform for high-level engagement among member states, financial institutions and other stakeholders. The main focus in recent years has centred upon internationally agreed development goals such as the Sustainable Development Goals (SDGs).

The International Court of Justice (ICJ)

The International Court of Justice (or World Court) aims to settle disputes between states. All members of the United Nations are part of the Statute of the International Court of Justice. Non-UN members may also become parties to the statute and thereby participate in cases heard before the court's attention. The ICJ also offers advice on issues of international law on referral from the United Nations.

The workload of the court covers a wide remit of judicial activity in relation to contentious issues. However, it lacks the legitimacy and resources required to be a truly effective institution. For instance, the United States withdrew from compulsory jurisdiction after the ICJ ruled that it had violated international law during their covert war against the Sandinista-regime in Nicaragua. Only the Security Council has the authority to enforce the rulings of the Court, which means that a member of the permanent five can use their veto. In addition, being a party to the statute does not enable the court to exert jurisdiction over disputes involving those parties. The ability of a powerful country such as the US to prevent a ruling from taking effect is a clear limitation upon the effectiveness of the ICJ.

The ICJ has also been criticised on the basis of its procedures, independence and authority. For instance, the judicial body does not benefit entirely from judicial independence because there is no separation of powers. This means that members of the permanent five can avoid their legal obligations regardless of the judgement reached. Secondly, jurisdiction is constrained to those cases in which both parties have agreed to submit to its final decision. The absence of a binding force means that member states do not have to accept its ruling. For instance, the United States rejected a 2018 ruling which mandated exemptions on humanitarian and civil aviation supplied to Iran. Enforcement therefore rests upon the consent of each state to accept the court's jurisdiction, and that a violation has actually taken place.

It should also be recognised that organisations, individuals and UN agencies cannot bring a case to the attention of the court except in an advisory capacity. This means that potential victims of crimes against humanity may be unable to exercise appropriate legal representation. Crucially, only states can bring cases and become defendants. It is also the case that other judicial courts (notably the International Criminal Court) are independent from the United Nations. Inevitably, this makes it harder for the judicial process to be truly effective.

Despite all of these criticisms, the various organisations of the United Nations deserve praise for advancing a number of worthwhile causes such as the longstanding commitment to eradicating poverty. There have also been occasions when the engagement of the United Nations has helped resolve a dispute. In addition, the condemnation and potential threat of action from the international community may well have been enough to ensure a level of compliance with international laws and conventions. When reaching an assessment of the UN and its various agencies, it must be acknowledged that its effectiveness ultimately rests upon the willingness of the member states to secede authority. In a system based essentially on a Westphalian conception of sovereignty, this will always be an overriding factor.

According to the realist perspective, members have joined the UN in order to advance their security. Membership is also an important marker in terms of national self-determination, a point which reflects the realist focus on sovereignty and the state. However, liberals adopt a rather different perspective. Members have joined and promoted universal values (notably human rights) consistent with an agenda of global governance. The United Nations is a particularly good illustrative manifestation of the institutional peace theory within liberal thought.

The North Atlantic Treaty Organisation (NATO)

The North Atlantic Treaty Organization is an intergovernmental military alliance, separate from the United Nations and its organs, tasked with implementing the 1949 North Atlantic Treaty. The main purpose of the organisation is to maintain collective security against an act of aggression (chiefly against the Soviet Union when the organisation was formed). The principle behind the organisation is an 'open door' policy, which enables countries within the North Atlantic region to join if the applicant can meet the obligations of membership. Since its creation, seventeen countries have formally joined the organisation and twenty others are engaged in the 'Partnership for Peace program', as quasi-members. Membership is open to those who accept liberal democratic values, have US support, and can commit to the security obligations of NATO.

After the collapse of the Soviet Union, the organisation adopted an increasingly humanitarian role. In 1994, NATO undertook its first military action against Bosnian-Serb forces, and in 2001 maintained a united stance supporting the United States. In 2014, member states agreed to establish a Very High Readiness Joint Task Force (VJTF) that could be deployed at short notice against threats to the sovereignty of member states. The VJTF has been dispatched to monitor elections in Afghanistan and provide humanitarian relief in New Orleans and Pakistan.

Over time, the organisation has shown itself to be flexible in the face of changing threats. For instance, as a response to the 2014 Russian annexation of Crimea, NATO deployed multinational battalion battle groups. It was a stark reminder that the institution still retains its purpose in the post-Cold War era. Since 2016, the Enhanced Forward Presence (EFP) has sought to provide a deterrent against potential Russian intervention within Poland and the Baltic states, especially given the events of 2014 in Eastern Ukraine and the annexation of Crimea. Another arena in which the organisation has shown itself adaptable concerns the threat of cyberwarfare. As the activities of hackers (and hostile governments) have become more sophisticated, NATO provides the expertise needed to assist any country exposed to an attack. NATO also co-operates with partner countries in order to deal with cyber threats to the sovereignty of the state.

The context of contemporary debate surrounding the organisation relates to American hegemony and NATO enlargement. The former raises issues concerning the willingness of Washington to perform the unofficial role of the world's policeman. Donald Trump caused anxiety amongst member states when he declared the organisation 'obsolete' during his presidency. In terms of the latter, the enlargement of the organisation has led to an expansion in the influence of NATO. During the late-1990s relationships between NATO and other countries were strengthened by the Partnership for Peace, the Mediterranean Dialogue, and a forum for relations with Russia. The focus of

NATO activities has also expanded to incorporate humanitarian intervention. This may suggest that the organisation retains its relevance, a point that Trump himself later conceded.

During the Cold War, the principle of collective security provided a mutually beneficial link between the United States and other countries in the 'West.' Since the formal dissolution of the Warsaw Pact – the collective security agreement between the Soviet allied states during the Cold War – the purpose and future of the organisation has become uncertain. Whilst in office, the Trump administration sent mixed signals about America's engagement with the organisation. The US has also expressed concern about the inability of member states to meet the official target of allocating at least 2% of their GDP to military provision by the year 2024.

In terms of assessing NATO, there are a number of strengths that warrant highlighting. First and foremost, the organisation has helped spread liberal-democratic values throughout the world. It has also ensured cooperation amongst those members who might have balanced the international system in the favour of another alliance or power-centre (such as Turkey during the Cold War). Equally, NATO has also ensured stability which benefits all its members as a direct result of the collective security it provides, through Article Five of the North Atlantic Treaty: 'The Parties agree that an armed attack against one or more of them in Europe or North America shall be considered an attack against them all' (North Atlantic Treaty Organisation 2019). For instance, the United States has a vested interest in a relatively peaceful and stable Europe; NATO ensures this.

NATO has also contributed to the process of nuclear disarmament. The provision of a security umbrella from the United States (and to a lesser extent the UK and France) has arguably prevented NATO allies from developing their own nuclear capacity. NATO has also provided a diplomatic forum in order to reduce security threats to its members. The organisation therefore prevents situations escalating into full-blown conflict. Most notably, the collective defence benefit provided by Article Five of the NATO Charter (North Atlantic Treaty Organization 2019) remains applicable in the face of aggressive tactics employed by the Russian President Vladimir Putin in both Georgia and Ukraine (two countries that are aspiring to become members of NATO).

In terms of other positives, the structure of its military organisation enables allies to share best practice in areas such as counter-terrorism and rapid response. Its command structure also enables NATO members to mobilise resources and personnel more effectively than any other comparable international organisation. NATO also provides a cost-effective means by which member states ensure their mutual defence. Members gain the benefits of collective security for allocating around 2% of the GDP on defence. Members of the alliance are therefore able to share the costs (and risks) of dealing with any given situation.

In addition, NATO helps to maintain peace and stability outside of its borders. Since the end of the Cold War NATO forces have been sent to Bosnia, Afghanistan and Kosovo. NATO has also worked to combat the spread of Islamic terrorism by training local forces in Afghanistan and Iraq. For instance, it provides surveillance aircraft to help locate ISIS strongholds and shares military intelligence to anticipate emerging threats. The organisation has also sought to counter the spread of piracy within the Gulf of Aden and off the Horn of Africa, protecting international shipping lanes. Moreover, NATO has addressed the refugee crisis in Europe by providing assistance with home placement and visa applications.

In historical terms, NATO is arguably the most successful intergovernmental defence organisation. The military alliance between the US and other NATO countries contributed to the defeat and downfall of the Soviet Union. Indeed, in some ways NATO is a victim of its own success. Given its clearly defined purpose during the Cold War, NATO may well have exhausted its usefulness. There were certainly figures within the Trump administration who took the view that Washington should place its own narrow interests above those of the organisation (Wolff 2018).

From the opposing angle, there are certain issues that need to be resolved regarding the continued existence of NATO. Firstly, membership of the organisation could be viewed as a disadvantage from the perspective of the country in question. For instance, American troops have been sent into conflict zones with no direct interests at stake. The United States (and other members) have also been dragged into military engagement regardless of their own specific interests. Indeed, the United States actually came close to launching a nuclear attack during the Cuban Missile Crisis in 1962, due to Soviet objections regarding Turkey's presence within NATO. Even though the Crisis was de-escalated, the role of NATO in forging the closest incident humanity has come to nuclear war is undeniable.

Secondly, the NATO budget has historically been overly reliant upon the United States. In the name of fairness, it may be time for others to 'pick up the tab.' Having said this, an over-reliance upon American dollars places some members into a very difficult position. The United States could engage in action that NATO allies oppose and yet feel obligated to support. The development of a full-scale European army would help to counter the conundrum raised here. Germany and France are supportive of this approach (The Economist 2019), but the UK has long endorsed the 'special relationship' with Washington.

The expansion of NATO also creates greater levels of risk for existing member states. As the organisation continues to enlarge, there is a degree of risk posed by potential conflict. At the present time, the role of NATO within the Syrian Civil War holds the potential capacity to escalate into a lengthy quagmire. That said, membership of the organisation has fostered a habit of diplomacy amongst potential rivals. For instance, membership of NATO may well have prevented an escalation of conflict between Greece and Turkey over the status of Cyprus.

Another weakness inherent within the organisation is the inability to ensure that members maintain their democratic status. Populist leaders and movements have imposed illiberal policies in Turkey, Hungary and Poland. The same argument could also apply to the Trump administration. Yet having said this, it may be more realistic to maintain such links and seek to influence those countries within the structure of the organisation.

In terms of an overall assessment, the role and significance of the organisation continues to develop and evolve. During the Cold War, NATO provided a necessary and ultimately successful alliance against a common enemy. Since then, the organisation has adopted a more humanitarian perspective. The terrorist action of 9/11 provided a reminder that the principle of collective security remains relevant in a dangerous world. Equally, it must be acknowledged that 9/11 was not technically an attack from another country. Diplomatic support for Washington might have simply been a reflection of the power imbalance within the organisation.

Now that we've considered NATO, the next area to reflect on is the economic realm of global governance. The clear starting-point here is the free-market approach characterised as the Washington Consensus. The main focus will therefore centre on the IMF and World Bank.

Economic Global Governance

The International Monetary Fund (IMF) and the World Bank

The International Monetary Fund is responsible for the stability of the world's monetary system, whilst the objective of the World Bank is to offer financial assistance to countries that need it. The IMF and World Bank promote a set of market-based economic policies prescribed by institutions based in the District of Columbia (DC). This is more commonly known as the Washington Consensus.

A loan from the IMF is conditional upon implementing certain policies and meeting a series of requirements (namely adjusting its economic policies). If these conditions are not met or the necessary adjustments are not made, the IMF can withhold its funding. Policies consistent with structural adjustment take the form of austerity, trade liberalisation and depreciation of the exchange rate. Governments must also balance their books via privatisation of state-owned assets and the removal of state subsidies. It is also a condition that governance is improved via tackling corruption and avoiding profligate spending.

The World Bank provides loans and grants to LEDCs in order to combat poverty. The World Bank identifies the priorities of the recipient economy (such as developing human capital) and targets financial assistance accordingly. The World Bank also distributes grants to social enterprises that provide services to lower-income groups. Finally, the World Bank communicates with other international organisations in regards to protecting the environment and the provision of health services.

It is of course mutually beneficial that countries in receipt of a loan are able to repay the debt. As such, the IMF and World Bank provide loans at a market-rate of interest. The main condition of gaining a loan is to adjust the domestic economy and thereby ensure it can service the repayment. The stability of the entire global financial system depends upon the capacity of recipients to finance their loan. Those in receipt of financial assistance have a decent track record in terms of repaying the money with full interest over the duration of the loan.

An assessment of the strengths and weaknesses of both institutions should be placed in the context of the Washington Consensus. In terms of arguments in favour, the IMF and World Bank have helped to transform the economic situation facing countries plagued by bad governance (such as military juntas in Latin American countries). As one of the largest economies in the world, Brazil is a particularly good illustration of this argument. For a country that once suffered from hyper-inflation, the GDP of the Brazilian economy overtook the UK in 2011.

Secondly, market-based reforms championed by the IMF and World Bank have lowered the cost of consumer goods and services. Countries in serious debt have no other option but to implement fiscally prudent policies which benefit their economy in the long-run. Allowing prices to reach their equilibrium based upon demand and supply is often preferable to profligate policies from unaccountable elites. In addition, financial assistance provided by the IMF and World Bank may have helped lift millions out of poverty (World Bank 2018). For instance, economic growth in Central and Latin America has been considerable, whilst debt levels have been significantly lowered. This has undoubtedly helped to transform the economic prospects facing many of the poorest within the global economy.

In addition, the approach favoured by the IMF and the World Bank has generally worked better than the import-substitution industrialisation favoured during the 1960s. Market-based economies have usually performed much better than those based upon a statist alternative. The contrast between the two Koreas is a particularly illuminating one to consider. The Republic of Korea received assistance from the IMF / World Bank and implemented market-based policies. In contrast, North Korea is not a member of either institution.

As for counter arguments, policies implemented on the basis of structurally adjusting the debtor state's economies have contributed towards the economic crisis in Argentina and Mexico. The Argentinian monetary crisis of 2001/2 was particularly revealing as it was the initial 'poster-boy' of the Washington Consensus. Riots broke out after the government restricted people's ability to withdraw cash from banks, following the conditions set in line with the IMF. Moreover, reforms do not always lead to intended consequences. For instance, many former state-owned assets in Russia have links to oligarchs and organised crime.

Both dependency and World Systems theorists point out that Structural Adjustment Programmes (SAPs) have failed to break the debilitating economic dependence upon the West. After independence, the institutions that uphold the ideology of unregulated capitalism have maintained the dependency of the Global South upon the developed North. The IMF and the World Bank ensure that countries rich in natural resources remain locked in a system of economic dependence. For instance, the removal of protectionist measures within the Global South has undoubtedly benefited multinational companies (such as Primark) and the vested interests of the wealthy. The Washington Consensus also ensures that profit comes before people.

It is striking to consider that several economies within sub-Saharan Africa have failed to develop in spite of implementing the conditions imposed by the Washington Consensus. The structural causes of economic underdevelopment are sometimes resistant to a magic formula, implemented from external sources. Most notably, the level of economic growth recorded within African countries during the 1980s and 90s fell below the figures recorded in previous decades. The former Chief Economist of the World Bank Joseph Stiglitz has been particularly critical of the 'one size fits all' treatment of individual economies (2015).

Finally, the policies implemented by these institutions have undermined national sovereignty within the recipient countries. Those who receive loans and grants are unable to implement economic policies suitable for their own growth and development. It is difficult to deny that the lender effectively determines the fiscal and monetary policies adopted by the recipient. Austerity can have severe consequences for state spending on health, education and agriculture even in a relatively wealthy economy, potentially even adapting wider political norms surrounding equality, elitism and government efficacy. However, it could also be argued that the financial discipline associated with SAPs is ultimately in the best interests of the nation concerned.

The World Trade Organisation (WTO)

Based in Geneva, the World Trade Organisation (WTO) is an intergovernmental organisation responsible for the regulation of international trade in goods, services and intellectual property. One of the largest global economic organisations in the world, the WTO replaced the General Agreement on Tariffs and Trade (GATT) in 1995. The WTO seeks to ensure that trade flows as smoothly, predictably and freely as possible.

The main objective of the WTO is to resolve disputes and thereby prevent a debilitating trade war between two or more nations. Acting as a neutral arbiter prevents the implementation of 'beggar-thy-neighbour' protectionist policies. The WTO also provides a framework for negotiating trade agreements and ensuring that signatories adhere to them. However, the organisation is perhaps best-known for its multilateral agreements reached after lengthy negotiations. The main barrier towards progress in the most recent round of talks has been a lack of consensus between the developed North and the Global South. During the Doha round of talks, attempts to make globalisation more inclusive have proved particularly difficult over the issue of agricultural subsidies. The Doha round represents a series of negotiations which commenced in November 2001 in order to lower trade barriers and facilitate increased global trade.

Under the rules of the WTO, a country cannot discriminate between their trading partners. Granting a country 'most favoured nation' status is prohibited except under circumstances relating to national security and environmental protection. The WTO therefore provides a more welcoming domain for the conduct of global trade. In doing so, the organisation has helped reduce transaction costs and thereby stimulate economic development.

In terms of assessment, there has been a significant increase in the level of international trade since the 1990s. World trade as a percentage of GDP has risen from around 40% in 1990 to just under 60% in 2018 (World Bank 2021b). This has been facilitated by the WTO in either preventing or limiting protectionist policies, such as tariffs. It could also be argued that the WTO provides a blueprint for free trade agreements as virtually all preferential trade agreements make explicit reference to the organisation.

There are however several valid criticisms raised by pressure groups, indigenous peoples and academics. Perhaps the most significant is that the institution serves the interests of multinational companies at the expense of those disadvantaged in the Global South. In doing so, the WTO exacerbates inequality within the global economy. Most notably, the rules and regulations maintained by the WTO have resulted in economic hardship for those forced to make a living in the poorest parts of the global economy. For instance, agreements reached in the field of agriculture and health have restricted access to food and medicine. The inflexible character of the most favoured nation clause has also contributed to lost export revenue amongst the least developed countries (LEDCs).

Economists such as Martin Khor (2000) argue that the WTO exhibits a systemic bias towards wealthy countries and multinational companies. For instance, rich economies are able to maintain import duties and quotas that restrict access to potentially lucrative markets. In contrast, the rules of the organisation prevent LEDCs from protecting their own infant industries. Negotiations are also biased towards the developed North because LEDCs lack the ability to participate on an effective basis. It was somewhat telling that the 2003 Cancún meetings of the Doha Round broke down when developed countries objected to calls from LEDCs to gain greater access to agricultural markets in wealthier countries.

The unrepresentative and non-inclusive character of negotiations has resulted in further criticism of the organisation. The advocacy group 'Third World Network' (1999) has described the WTO as: 'the most non-transparent of international organisations [as a result of] the vast majority of developing countries have very little real say.' In addition, the WTO often seems unwilling to ensure that developed countries meet their obligations or address issues surrounding the environment. Powerful states have also been able to ignore commitments made concerning the protection of cultural traditions amongst indigenous peoples. On a final note, it has also been argued that the WTO has imposed policies that have dismantled state provision within less developed countries. This has led to criticism that such action has contributed to economic damage and food insecurity.

The G8 and G20

For several years, the 'Group of 8' (G8) was one of the most important groupings within international relations. The organisation consisted of the most developed industrialised economies (United States, United Kingdom, France, Germany, Japan, Canada, Italy and Russia). However, the organisation became known as the 'Group of 7' (G7) after the Russian Federation annexed Crimea in 2014 and was consequently suspended from the group. In 2017, Russia formally announced their permanent withdrawal from the organisation.

Since the end of the 1990s, the 'Group of 20' (G20) has provided a forum for the wealthiest economies on the global stage. The shift from the G7 to the G20 is indicative of broader trends within the global economy. Many of those states who are members of the G7 are heavily in debt to the world banking system. Membership of the G20 is also a more accurate reflection, taking into account emerging economies such as the so-called BRICS (Brazil, Russia, India, China and South Africa), alongside other regional economic powers like Argentina, Saudi Arabia and Indonesia.

It must be acknowledged that action taken on a coordinated basis by the G7 (or G20) states can have a positive and lasting impact upon the global economy. For instance, the G20 agreed to a package of debt relief for low-income nations in 2020. Given that the organisation accounts for approximately 90% of global GDP, any action taken is important. As a forum for diplomatic relations amongst the most powerful economies, the role of both organisations is also a substantial one. The very existence of the G7 (and G20) underlines the extent to which the world economy operates on the basis of mutual dependence and global governance.

Having said this, there are a series of cogent criticisms levied at the G7 and G20. Of these, the most significant is the arbitrary and self-appointed character of membership. For instance, the G20 excludes states that may qualify for a position as one of the top-20 'largest' economies, such as Switzerland or Taiwan. Another issue presented by the G20 is the lack of representation for Spain, Sweden and the Netherlands, although this is partially offset by the presence of the European Union. There is also further criticism over the exclusion of rapidly emerging economies such as Nigeria or Thailand.

Another common criticism of the G7/G20 is the manner in which members can have a detrimental impact upon the Global South. The organisations institutionalise the major imbalance and inequities within the global economic system. The G7 and G20 have therefore been placed alongside a broader critique of globalisation and its uneven character. Alongside the IMF and World Bank, the G7/G20 are part of an institutional structure that exploits less developed economies.

The Significance of How Global Economic Governance Addresses Poverty

The distribution of wealth within the global economy is highly uneven. According to Oxfam, the twenty-six wealthiest people on the planet have the same net worth as the poorest half (Elliott 2019). In terms of states, the distribution of wealth is also deeply uneven. The wealthier economies are heavily concentrated within the developed North whilst the underdeveloped elements can be found within the Global South. The combined economy of the developed North accounts for around four-fifths of global income despite housing just one-quarter of the world's population. Countries within the developed North also tend to be more democratic, record a higher life expectancy and are more equal than those in the Global South. This broad phenomenon is often referred to as: 'the Global North-South divide'.

The causes and consequences of the uneven character of the North-South divide is the subject of much debate. In terms of theoretical perspectives, the world systems approach claims that the global economy is based upon an unjust division of labour, whereby the majority of the world's wealth is concentrated in the core economies following the exploitation of the periphery. Theorists who favour the free-market approach maintain that an uneven distribution of wealth is merely a reflection of how the global market operates. They claim that economies that adopt the Washington Consensus have often generated rapid economic growth and development.

In order to properly address the issue of world poverty, it is important to place the issue within the context of globalisation. According to the World Bank (World Bank 2018), the number of those living in extreme poverty has decreased by over one billion since 1990. This would seem to suggest that globalisation has led to increased wealth and enhanced opportunities globally. Having said this, those who are more critical of globalisation highlight the uneven nature of the global economy. The institutions of global governance (notably the IMF and the World Bank) enforce a system that benefits the wealthy at the expense of those working in sweatshops (Klein 2000). This also reflects the realist critique of liberalism and globalisation. Realists claim that the liberal international order is ultimately compliant on upholding a self-help and egotistical anarchy.

As the term implies, world systems theory considers international relations as a global system with an economic division of labour between the core, semi-periphery and periphery. Each of these sections tends to specialise within a particular aspect of economic activity. For instance, core countries focus upon capital-intensive production whilst those in the periphery focus upon labour-intensive industries. The crucial argument is that the world system operates to the benefit of core countries and constrains the economic and political development of those at the margins.

Arguably the most well-known theorist within the world systems perspective is Immanuel Wallerstein (1974). He identified the core of the system as one located within the developed North, whilst the periphery consists of the underdeveloped world. Although states can change from peripheral to semi-peripheral and core states, this division of labour remains a constant feature within the economic system. Irrespective of who sits atop the structure of the international system, those at the periphery will always be subject to economic manipulation from governments (and firms) located within the core on the basis of resource extraction and the existence of cheap labour.

From a broadly similar perspective, dependency theory stipulates that poorer countries are deliberately impoverished in order to meet the demands of the global bourgeoisie. The economic system therefore operates to the advantage of a transnational class. The perspective emerged in the 1960s as a response to the lack of economic development within Latin American countries. Theorists such as Raul Prebisch (1950) challenged the conventional wisdom that underdeveloped economies were simply at an earlier stage of development than wealthier countries. According to the dominant perspective of the time, underdeveloped economies would eventually make progress by adopting similar policies and strategies to those of the 'West.' Instead, dependency theorists argued that poorer countries face overwhelming barriers within a class-based system that operates against their interests.

Economic dependency is facilitated via the capitalist system and the provision of foreign aid. In terms of the former, wealthy and powerful Europeans created an economic system that purposely exploited economic resources within their colonies. The slave trade remains an obvious example of how workers were subjugated in order to maximise profit for slave owners. Slavery also reflects the racist mindset operating within the mechanics and machinations of imperialism and colonialism. Furthermore, foreign aid is often provided on the basis of geostrategic aims rather than economic need (as in the case of the United States with Israel). According to this perspective, the wealthy are always in a position to exert power over those in a relatively weaker political position. For instance, Teresa Hayter (1971) claims that the true purpose of foreign aid is to maintain a global capitalist system that works in favour of the ruling class. The provision of foreign aid is beneficial to the wealthier countries because it buys the political support of recipient countries. Hayter also notes that financial assistance rarely goes to the poor themselves, but to the political elite and other strategically important actors.

In terms of an explanation of poverty and the North-South divide, the explanatory capacity of these theories has come under challenge. In one sense, decolonisation undermines their overall argument. The overt exploitation of the past no longer offers an accurate portrayal of how the global system operates. Even the argument that sweatshops are exploitative can be challenged. Workers in factories run by multinational companies often receive relatively higher wages and better working conditions than within domestically owned workplaces (Aisbett et. al. 2021). Although pressure groups campaign vigorously against sweatshops, it could be argued that economies are simply utilising their comparative advantage in cheap labour that is provided for by their politico-legal milieu, and stance on human and workers' rights. Historically, this was the path adopted by the United Kingdom during the Industrial Revolution.

Having said this, companies located within the core economies make huge profits and, on the whole, do not pay workers a wage that reflects their overall contribution. In addition, wealthy economies remain in a highly advantageous position. For instance, the level of economic influence wielded by the Chinese government provides Beijing with considerable leverage over countries within Africa. Less developed countries have also accumulated huge debts due to unfavourable loans and currency manipulation from former colonial powers.

There is clearly no consensus over the cause of poverty and those measures needed to reduce poverty. The predominant view from Western governments is that the solution lies firmly in terms of economic development. The adaptation of market economies, good governance and other related measures provides a pathway out of poverty. It is a view based upon the assumption that market forces should be the stimulus for economic growth. The alternative angle claims that global poverty is linked to structural disparities. This is most commonly expressed within the core-periphery model of economic development. However, it has also been argued that poverty is caused by a number of factors that reflect a shared responsibility between 'North' and 'South'. This nuanced approach stipulates that corruption, the absence of proper financial institutions and territorial disputes have their roots in the actions of the wealthy alongside governments within poorer regions.

In defining poverty, the terms 'absolute' and 'relative' are added in common usage to distinguish different phenomena that can broadly be understood as 'poverty'. 'Absolute poverty' is defined by the United Nations as: 'a condition characterised by severe deprivation of basic human needs ... It depends not only on income but also on access to services' (United Nations 1995). Absolute poverty is sometimes referred to as extreme (or abject) poverty. The World Bank estimates that the international poverty line is approximately US$1 a day (based on 1996 prices). Measuring poverty on this basis has always been the orthodox method available. For instance, absolute poverty has been a central concept in relation to the Millennium / Sustainable Development Goals agreed upon by the United Nations in 2016.

'Relative poverty', however, is used on the basis of individual countries as an arbitrary measure predicated upon average incomes within that particular society. This is the most common alternative measure to 'absolute poverty' although there are others at hand, such as 'subjective poverty' (which offers an assessment of how people feel about their situation) or the Multidimensional Poverty Index (MPI). Published by the Oxford Poverty and Human Development Initiative (OPHI), the MPI measures deprivation of basic needs (OPHI 2021). The MPI helps to determine the most likely cause of poverty, but not all countries employ it as a measure.

The absolute measure adopted by the United Nations has been criticised for failing to take into account the depth of global poverty. The orthodox approach is also criticised for ignoring the relative measure of poverty and its subjective element. As with all quantitative measurements used within the social sciences, it suffers from a lack of accuracy concerning consumer prices and the calculation of purchasing power parity (PPP).

Classical Economic Development Theory, Structural Theory and Neoclassical Development Theory

There are various theoretical perspectives offering insight into global governance and the North-South divide. Of these, classical economic development theory adopts an unmistakably free-market outlook. The classical approach claims that governments should not intervene within the marketplace. Instead, the allocation of economic resources is best achieved via the multifaceted interaction of firms and consumers. In doing so, prices will reach a market-clearing rate based upon fluctuations in supply and demand. Economic development rests upon a free-market approach that places faith in what the former US President Ronald Reagan once called 'the magic of the marketplace'.

The assumption that lies behind classical economic theory is that poverty is the responsibility of the individual concerned. Unlike other theoretical perspectives, it does not identify the structure of the global economy as a problem. Ultimately, it is down to the individual to make progress towards economic development. This demands the same characteristics that others have adhered to, regardless of their social background. It could be argued that this perspective intends to empower the individual as opposed to the state, reinforcing the importance and potential of individual agency.

Structural theorists such as Hans W. Singer (1998) adopt a very different approach. Structural theory prescribes an interventionist role for the state, particularly in the early stages of industrialisation, in order to foster economic development. Governments must alter the entire structure of their domestic economy in order to encourage economic growth. This may take a number of forms such as import-substitution industrialisation and export-oriented industrialisation. The overall aim is to transform and modernise the economy towards a more industrialised approach. The role of the government in terms of economic development is of absolute central importance. The government, rather than the marketplace, is the key source of economic progress. In economic terminology, the structural approach advocates a mixed economy based upon a strategy of Keynesianism, following the thought of the twentieth century economist John Maynard Keynes (2015).

As the term suggests, neoclassical development theory is an updated version of the classical school of economic thought. During the eighteenth and nineteenth centuries, classical economists such as David Ricardo (1817) and Adam Smith (1999) argued forcefully in favour of market forces. Concepts such as 'the invisible hand of the market' and 'comparative advantage' would benefit all members of society. The World Bank and the IMF moved closer towards a neoclassical approach in response to the global debt crisis of the 1980s. The current market-based package of austerity, privatisation and trade liberalisation is a clear illustration of an ideology based upon neoclassical economics, one that has become increasingly observable since the global economic crisis of 2008. The structural adjustment programmes, discussed above, are emblematic of the neoclassical approach to economic development.

The Extent to Which These Institutions Address Contemporary Global Issues

The Membership and Structure of the UN

The UN Security Council is the main decision-making body within the United Nations. The UNSC determines the existence of a possible threat to peace, or if a state has undertaken an act of aggression. It has the authority to call upon the parties involved to settle the dispute via peaceful means and offer recommendations for a settlement. The UNSC seeks to avoid conflict and thereby maintain international peace and security.

In terms of taking effective action, the UNSC can impose sanctions and authorise the use of coercion. Article 42 of the UN Charter enables the Council to utilise force if non-military measures have been proved inadequate. It can also pass resolutions in order to approve any form of humanitarian intervention it deems upholds the purpose of the UN and the Charter. In all cases, action taken by the international community must navigate the barriers presented by geostrategic interests and the contested application of humanitarian intervention. The Security Council is often charged with adopting a selective definition of the term and for exhibiting glaring double standards. However, the main issue to consider is the ability of the permanent five (P5) to use their technical veto powers.

The Use of the Technical Veto

The UN Security Council consists of five permanent members and ten non-permanent members. In order for a Security Council resolution to pass, the threshold is nine votes including total unanimity amongst the P5. As such, if any one of the P5 votes against the other four, the resolution is terminated. This means that although the UN Charter does not explicitly state that each of the P5 hold the power to veto a resolution, the necessity of unanimity between the P5 creates veto power on a technicality. Since the end of the Cold War, the UN Security Council has authorised the use of force in situations that would have once been viewed as an internal conflict. There have also been attempts to gain international involvement in order to avoid unilateral action from the United States.

In terms of employing their technical veto power, the main culprit has been the Russian Federation, utilising this technicality on over one-hundred occasions. Since 2011, the principal justification for the Russian veto has been international action relating to the Syrian Civil War. Vladimir Putin has long been supportive of the Assad regime and offered protection against coordinated action from the United Nations. The US is second, with a total of over 80 uses of the veto as of 2021. In contrast, neither France nor the UK have used their veto since 1989, in which they, alongside the US, blocked draft resolution S/21048 demanding the immediate withdrawal of foreign troops from Panama following military intervention by the US. Given their growing salience within international relations, the majority of Chinese vetoes have occurred since the mid-1990s. As with Russia, the main reason has been their support for the Syrian government.

The barriers presented by the use of the veto by the P5 makes it difficult to garner official authorisation for humanitarian intervention. It also leads towards a selective form of intervention which necessitates the use of unauthorised action. For instance, NATO's intervention in order to address human rights violations within Kosovo occurred without UN support. The same situation occurred with intervention led by the United States to protect the Kurds in Northern Iraq. In terms of the latter, humanitarian intervention led by the US sought to protect Kurdish refugees fleeing their homes in northern Iraq in the aftermath of the Gulf War of 1990–91. As with many other examples of humanitarian intervention, a no-fly zone was enforced in order to facilitate the mass movement of refugees. The Kurdish minority had long faced oppression from the Saddam Hussein regime in Iraq. The US-led intervention continued until the mid-1990s in order to prevent further aggression against the Kurdish people.

In such cases, the UN Security Council could be described as an ineffective institution when faced with clear human rights violations. The Security Council has also failed to investigate the use of chemical weapons by the Assad regime in Syria. The civil war in Syria is a complex situation with several stakeholders involved. In terms of authorisation, the main issue has been the reluctance of the Russian government to support action against a key (albeit unreliable) ally in the Middle East. Although widely respected, the UN Security Council has also proved unable to reverse the proliferation of nuclear weapons and thereby ensure wider disarmament. This, hence, has perhaps limited the key function of the UN – to ensure international security.

On a more positive note, the UN Security Council can also authorise major projects driven by the organisation. In 2015 the Sustainable Development Goals were adopted by the United Nations in order to end poverty and protect our planetary ecology. Without initial support from members of the Security Council, the sustainable development goals would not have made much progress. Members of the UN are pledged to end extreme poverty in all forms by the year 2030. These admirable goals partly reflect a growing recognition that international security requires a comprehensive consideration of the various causes of terrorism (such as poverty). Equally, there is also an acceptance that environmental damage holds major economic consequences. In theoretical terms, there is a tacit acknowledgment that such issues are interrelated and interdependent.

Pressure for Reform and Critique

The IMF and World Bank are both committed towards seeking an end to global poverty. Although the IMF and World Bank can claim some credit for economic improvements amongst countries in receipt of SAPs, they are also criticised for failing to resolve the problem posed by global poverty.

Structural adjustment programmes have been criticised from several angles. Figures from the alter-globalisation movement have claimed that such programmes have done little to alleviate the problem of extreme poverty (Stiglitz 2002). This is particularly noticeable within sub-Saharan Africa. The stark economic failure of this underdeveloped region of the world underlines the multi-causal nature of poverty. The eradication of poverty is, to some extent, resistant to policies imposed via external international organisations.

Another common criticism of the IMF and World Bank concerns the neocolonialist nature of its policies. Leslie Sklair (2002) observes that those who own and control the institutions that drive globalisation wield a great deal of power in the global system. In this manner, according to Sklair, globalisation serves the interests of a transnational capitalist class. Both the IMF and World Bank legitimise and implement Western-centric assumptions concerning economic growth. The world systems (and dependency theory) perspective claims that such institutions are part of an international economic order designed to dominate those on the periphery. It could also be argued that such policies undermine national sovereignty as they shape the economic policy of recipient countries. Furthermore, the implementation of such policies have exacerbated the problem of poverty. SAPs have led to hunger, inadequate health care and a lack of educational opportunities for some of the very poorest within the global economy. The combination of such policies has worsened the already deep-seated problem of poverty.

Many of those who are critical of the IMF and World Bank claim that market-oriented policies suit the vested interests of the powerful at the expense of those living at the margins. Loans are provided on the proviso that recipients restructure their economies towards the demands of global capitalism rather than those of their own citizens. This line of criticism is particularly vocal amongst pressure groups that aim to raise awareness of world poverty. Marxists also claim that SAPs stuff the pockets of the wealthy global bourgeoisie at the expense of workers. The Washington Consensus thereby upholds and exacerbates the conflict between the privileged and the powerless. The inequity of the global economic system was graphically exposed during the credit crunch. The Covid-19 pandemic also underlines the tendency of the developed North to place their own interests above those of the Global South. Any balanced assessment of the IMF and World Bank must surely recognise that these institutions are very much part of the problem of global inequality (as well as a potential solution to the issue).

In order to address these criticisms, the IMF and World Bank have recently introduced Poverty Reduction Strategy Papers (PRSPs). These are documents published before a country may be considered for debt relief, and before low-income countries can receive aid from most major donors. The IMF stipulates that the papers are formulated according to five principles (country-driven, result-oriented, comprehensive, working towards partnerships and offering a long-term perspective). The overall objective is to ensure that recipients are focused upon the reduction of poverty within their own population. They are also intended to assist recipients towards meeting the UN's developmental goals.

Whilst reforms have been welcomed, a number of countries have found it difficult to match the intentions of such policies. For instance, budgetary funds intended to reduce poverty have been misallocated. The papers have also been criticised for increasing aid conditionality even though they were designed to empower the recipient. The IMF and World Bank have also been criticised for failing to define exactly what 'civil participation' entails. Inevitably, this may mean that PRSPs are approved regardless of fulfilment.

The Role and Significance of Global Civil Society and Non-State Actors

The traditional focus of International Relations has centred upon the interaction between states. The state-centric approach of the subject matter owes much to the predominance of realist figures such as Hans Morgenthau and Kenneth Waltz. Liberalism however seeks to emphasise the role and significance of non-state actors. It should therefore be evident that an appreciation of non-state actors requires us to view the world through a liberal lens. The same observation applies to the interconnected character of global civil society (Keohane and Nye 1977). This is particularly evident in the realm of human rights, protection of the environment and measures to alleviate poverty.

When seeking to properly identify the role of non-state actors, the obvious starting-point would be NGOs and International Non-Governmental

Organisations (INGOs). The significance of NGOs is dependent upon the size of their membership, the ability to mobilise public support and the attitude adopted by national governments. This is particularly noticeable when such groups hold insider status within a particular government (or international organisation). Equally, such groups can also be outsiders in the policymaking process with little real say in matters. It is said that those who make the most noise have the least impact, and there is certainly some veracity to that observation.

NGOs (and INGOs) are often most needed in those states in which the ruling regime is greatly reluctant to award them any real influence. In an autocratic or dictatorial system, there is very little civil society to speak of. The ruling regime will seek to restrict the public space available for such groups to operate and thrive. In these situations, NGOs (and INGOs) aim to put pressure on Western governments and international institutions to take effective action against those regimes that commit acts of genocide and ethnic cleansing. A revealing case study to consider here is the persecution of the Rohingya people in Myanmar under the leadership of Aung San Suu Kyi. A former winner of the Nobel Peace prize, Aung San Suu Kyi was once lauded by NGOs for her endorsement of democratic values. However, since coming to power she has defended the actions of the military within the International Court of Justice in regards to their persecution of Rohingya Muslims. Ironically, she was ousted from power, and later jailed, in 2021 during a military coup in Myanmar.

As with any promotional pressure groups, NGOs seek to aggregate the interests and will of individual citizens. There is a strong normative element to the action (and interaction) of such organisations. The Western-centric bias of human rights does present something of an image problem for such organisations within those regions of the world that lack a rights-based culture. The impact of NGOs that seek to uphold human rights is also made more difficult due to the importance of national sovereignty within international relations.

In the context of sustainable development, civil society is widely assumed to have a positive impact. Given the growing salience of environmental issues, opportunities have been created for the engagement and involvement of NGOs. Given the global character of the problem, environmental groups such as Greenpeace can at times shame governments into action. The significance of NGOs (and INGOs) is underlined by the influence such groups have upon intergovernmental deliberations. The pluralist character of global governance enables such groups to contribute effectively towards negotiations.

Those of a cosmopolitan perspective tend to praise the impact of such organisations. In an increasingly interdependent world, they could be viewed as constructive players that influence the political process. For instance, the 1997 Ottawa Treaty owes much to the International Campaign to Ban Landmines. The establishment of the International Criminal Court also entailed a major role for INGOs in terms of offering information and advice.

From a more sceptical angle, it must be acknowledged that states remain far more important on the global stage than pressure groups. NGOs and civil society groups do not have anything comparable to the power of national governments. The international system remains state-centric, and governments can shape the political agenda in a way that pressure groups simply cannot. Indeed, it is states that ultimately decide to engage with such groups and act upon the advice offered. Politicians have real power and capability to adapt policy, whilst civil society and groups that seek to represent worthy causes only have influence. Given the sheer number of NGOs (and civil society groups), politicians almost certainly ignore them more often than they pay attention to them. A similar observation could also be applied towards multinational companies exposed for employing poor labour practices (Klein 2000).

On a final note, NGOs (and INGOs) have themselves been criticised for their lack of democratic accountability. The leadership of the organisation may not be elected and therefore lack a legitimate democratic mandate to make binding decisions. The legitimacy of such organisations has also been questioned due to the dominance of northern-based groups who claim to speak on behalf of the Global South. Such groups are also challenged for cementing – rather than dismantling – international power structures (Sending and Neumann 2006).

Conclusion

This chapter primarily sought to consider the political and economic dimension of global governance. The principal focus has been on the UN, due to its centrality within the framework of global governance. However, other institutions such as NATO have also been considered. The role of the IMF and World Bank is a particularly salient section when seeking to understand the impact and significance of global governance. The focus of this section has also included other relevant institutions – such as the WTO, the G7/8 and the G20 – opening a pathway to a greater discussion in the next chapter of global governance in relation to human rights and environmental governance.

BOX 3.1 – KEY TERMS FROM CHAPTER THREE

NGOs

Non-governmental organisations (NGOs) are non-profit organisations in-dependent of any government. NGOs operate at practically every level of governance, from the local to the international. Indeed, there are millions of NGOs in the world exerting pressure upon the political process on be-half of a specific cause. Pressure groups such as Amnesty International raise awareness of humanitarian issues to gain the attention of deci-sion-makers (e.g. the treatment of refugees). As with all pressure groups, NGOs foster a heightened level of
political participation and spread political information. They also act as a mediator between the people and those within the decision-making process.

In those countries with relatively weak levels of governance, NGOs can often bridge the gap between the agents of the state and the local community. They can also mobilise resources and activists in an effective manner. For instance, the Bangladeshi-based group 'Building Resources Across Communities' (BRAC) makes an important contribution to social development amongst the very poorest countries. In addition, NGOs act as representatives for many of the most marginalised and overlooked causes within global politics. On the other hand, they can also act as lobbyists for corporations. The main issues facing NGOs are a lack of adequate resources to translate good intentions into decisive action. Giv-en the dynamics of state sovereignty, NGOs do at times require the tacit support of national governments.

Structural Adjustment Programmes (SAPs)

Structural adjustment programmes (SAPs) are loans provided by the International Monetary Fund and the World Bank. In order to receive financial assistance, states experiencing economic difficulties must imple-ment a set of policies known as 'the Washington Consensus'; consisting of privatisation,
marketisation and deregulation. Debtor countries are also required to address their borrowing deficit and open up their domestic markets to international competition. SAPs impose a form of fiscal discipline based upon austerity and currency depreciation so as to reduce the balance of payment deficit. In the short-term, such policies have led to high levels of unemployment and an increase in the number of people living in poverty.

However, debt restructuring can result in long-term benefits for the country involved.

The United Nations (UN)

The UN is an intergovernmental organisation resting at the very heart of global governance. The organisation is guided by the principles contained within its founding Charter signed in 1945. All members of the General Assembly are bound by the articles of the Charter. As the name clearly suggests, virtually all countries in the world are members of the United Nations. In becoming a member of the organisation, the sovereignty of a member state is recognised by all other member states. However, there are certain countries that lack universal recognition within the international community; Palestine, for instance, as a disputed 'Non-member observer state'.

The UN Security Council (UNSC)

The UN Security Council is responsible for the establishment of peace-keeping operations and the authorisation of military action. The fifteen members of the UN Security Council can also recommend the admission of new members to the General Assembly, approve any amendments made to the UN Charter and investigate disputes. More importantly, the Security Council is the only body within the UN able to issue binding resolutions. The ability of the UN Security Council to maintain peace and security is hamstring by vetoes exercised by the P5. Since 1992, Russia has exercised the greatest number of vetoes, closely followed by the US. The deployment of peacekeepers is also constrained by a lack of legitimacy amongst warring parties. This has often proved problematic in various trouble-spots throughout the world.

NATO

The North Atlantic Treaty Organisation (NATO) is an intergovernmental military alliance with a membership of thirty states. The organisation is based upon a system of collective defence in which an attack on one is an attack upon all, following the fifth article of the North Atlantic Treaty. To date, the only time Article Five has ever been implemented was in response to the 9/11 terrorist attacks on American soil. In addition, any of the member states can invoke Article Four which states that: 'parties will consult together whenever, in the opinion of any of them, the territorial integrity, political independence or security of any of the parties is threat-ened' (North Atlantic Treaty 2019). Article Four has been invoked over the civil war in Syria and the annexation of Crimea in 2014. The latter was strongly condemned and led to the creation of a new spearhead force in NATO countries close to the Russian border.

International Monetary Fund (IMF)

The International Monetary Fund is a financial institution with a member-ship encompassing virtually every country in the world. The aims of the IMF are to secure financial stability, facilitate international trade, foster monetary cooperation, promote sustainable economic growth and reduce poverty. Along with the World Bank, the IMF plays an absolutely central role in the maintenance of the Washington Consensus. Funding for the IMF mainly derives from quotas based upon the economic significance of member states. Voting power is also based upon the quota system, with each member entitled to a basic vote plus one additional vote for each special drawing right (the unit of account used in the organisation). The basic voting system is biased towards the smaller economies, whilst additional votes favour the wealthier economies.

As with other institutions enmeshed within the system of global govern-ance, there have been calls to provide a louder voice for developing countries. Given the shift in the balance of power within the global econ-omy, the IMF is arguably in need of a major overhaul. Another issue of contention is the relationship between debtors and creditors. The voting system creates a system based upon the dominance of creditor states whilst marginalising poorer countries who contribute less to the organisa-tion's resources.

World Bank

The World Bank provides loans and grants to lesser developed econo-mies. In common with the IMF, the allocation of voting amongst mem-ber states is based upon their relative economic importance and their contribution to the organisation. In 2010, the voting system was amended in order to provide a stronger voice for emerging economies such as Brazil, India and Turkey. The voting power of several developed countries was reduced but the allocation awarded to the United States remained unchanged. Every President of the World Bank has been an American citizen. The structurally assisted programmes issued by the World Bank (and the IMF) are a result of negotiations between the government concerned and the Washington-based institutions. Such programmes are based upon the long-term objective of poverty reduction. Despite a rapid level of economic development, the largest borrower from the World Bank is currently China.

World Trade Organisation (WTO)

The World Trade Organisation is the largest international economic organisation in the world. The WTO deals with the regulation of trade in goods, services and intellectual property between participating countries. It achieves this via providing a framework for negotiating trade agreements and a process for dispute resolution via independent judges. The WTO prohibits discrimination between trading partners although exceptions are allowed for national security and environmental protection. The WTO is an intergovernmental organisation which replaced the General Agreement on Tariffs and Trade (GATT) during the mid-1990s. In terms of its impact and significance, the WTO facilitates the process of global trade by providing a regulatory framework. In a practical sense, it seeks to limit the implementation of protectionist policies and prevent the damaging effects of a trade war. For instance, a decoupling of the mutually dependent trading relationship between Beijing and Washington would have serious economic consequences for the global economy.

G8/G7

The Group of Eight (G8) was an intergovernmental forum formed in 1997 by representatives from the most significant economies in the developed world (France, the US, Germany, the UK, Japan, Italy, Canada and Russia). After the annexation of Crimea in 2014, the Russian Federation was suspended from the group and the term G7 is now used. The Group of 7 is used as a reference to the member states involved and the annual summit of the various heads of government. Since 2009, the focus has shifted more towards the G20 as the main economic council of wealthy economies. Whilst the G7 can make a credible claim to be the steering group for the 'West', there is little doubt that the credit crunch exposed the stark reality of the international financial system. Many of the G7 economies owe vast sums of money to other countries – most notably Japan, with a debt-to-GDP ratio that exceeds 200% (O'Neill 2021). The shift towards the G20 is symbolic of a broader development within the global economy from the 'West' towards emerging economies.

G20

The G20 is an international forum for the governments (and central bank governors) of the world's 19 largest economies alongside the European Union. Taken together, the G20 accounts for around 90% of global income and 80% of global trade. The economic clout of the organisation is such that statements and decisions adopted by the G20 have major repercussions for the global economy. In 2020, the G20 pledged to do 'whatever it takes' to combat the coronavirus pandemic and announced that members had launched a stimulus package worth US$5 trillion (Wintour and Rankin 2020).

North-South divide

The global economy can be divided into the developed North and the underdeveloped South. However, this is not an exact distinction and requires a degree of flexibility in terms of application. The developed North is often characterised as the West and there is some veracity to this. However, the developed world also includes East Asian economies such as Japan and South Korea. The Global South is slightly clearer to identify as it incorporates the vast majority of countries within sub-Saharan Africa, Latin America and the Caribbean. The Middle Eastern states are usually categorised as part of the South with the exception of Israel and the oil-rich Gulf states. It should also be noted that the phrase has to some degree been challenged by the rise of the BRIC economies. There has for instance been genuine progress in terms of reducing poverty levels within the underdeveloped South (with the exception of sub-Saharan Africa). Countries in the North also tend to be liberal democracies with a more even distribution of income than those in the South. Countries in the underdeveloped world often suffer from a number of interlinked problems, ranging from corruption to overdependence upon agricultural products.

Dependency theory

Dependency theory offers a rather different perspective on International Relations than the conventional realist-liberal debate. Dependency theory stipulates that the international economic system is built upon class conflict and the exploitation of the poor. Dependency theory emerged during the 1960s and 70s in order to address the lack of economic development within the 'third world'. As a theoretical body of thought, it aims to look beyond the traditional Western-centric explanations for underdevelopment (such as a failure to implement the 'right' set of economic policies).

Dependency theory stipulates that the international political economy is biased in favour of the wealthy nations and thereby prevents the development of newly independent countries. One of the main figures within dependency theory defines economic dependence as 'a situation in which the economy of certain countries is conditioned by the development and expansion of another economy to which the former is subjected' (Dos Santos 1970, 231). As a perspective from the left of the political spectrum, it claims that a clear division exists between the core and the periphery. Those countries at the centre of the global economic system have created a set of rules that suit their own interests at the expense of those at the periphery (such as former colonies). There is also an international division of labour in place whereby multinational companies manipulate those working at the margins. Economies within the periphery provide both cheap labour and natural resources. The structure of the global economy thereby serves the wealthy bourgeoisie at the expense of the oppressed. The Washington Consensus imposed by the IMF and World Bank is merely the latest instalment of colonialism and neoimperialism.

BOX 3.2 – KEY POINTS FOR CHAPTER THREE

1. The United Nations lies at the very epicentre of global governance.

2. The Security Council acts as a quasi-executive branch of global governance, whilst the legislative role is performed by the General Assembly.

3. Several institutions are responsible for the judicial branch of global governance.

4. NATO has evolved considerably since the end of the Cold War.

5. The Washington Consensus serves to promote policies such as privatisation and marketisation.

6. There are a number of theoretical perspectives critical of the Washington Consensus.

7. The distribution of power is shifting towards the G20 and emerging economies rather than the G7.

4

Global Governance: Human Rights and Environmental Governance

Chapter four applies the aforementioned concept of global governance to the protection of human rights and our shared environment. This chapter begins with an examination of attempts by the international community to uphold the universality of human rights. Humanitarian intervention will be contextualised via the prism of international law, judicial institutions and the impact on national sovereignty. This invites a discussion of selective intervention, the responsibility to protect and Western hypocrisy on the topic of human rights. Equally, this section moves towards a discussion of the role, significance and impact of measures to address climate change. The chapter ends with an examination of the ways and extent to which institutions of global governance address and resolve pressing global issues.

Human Rights

Origins and Development of International Human Rights Law and Institutions

Whilst human rights are a relative concept, the international community often justifies humanitarian intervention on the assumption that the concept is a universal one. Human rights are upheld via domestic legislation alongside a number of international agreements and judicial bodies. There is an inherent moral (and often legal) character to the concept of human rights. Since the turn of the century, there has been an increase in the number of institutions and agreements that seek to uphold human rights.

Before we consider the various sources of authority in regards to defining human rights, there is a useful distinction to be made between positive and negative rights. The former consists of those rights that place a positive duty upon others (usually the state). An example would be the right to healthcare and social welfare provided by the government. A negative right consists of the right to non-interference (such as freedom of speech and religious worship). These are sometimes called 'civil rights' and entail those rights consistent with being a citizen of that particular state. The exercise of rights is also beholden on the recognition of an obligation to others, and that rights cannot be taken away unless due process has been followed. In addition, positive and negative rights are grounded upon the principle of equal opportunities regardless of social background. The United Nations Universal Declaration of Human Rights (UDHR) lists both positive and negative rights.

The doctrine of human rights has been influential within international law and various institutions of global governance. This process of influence has occurred alongside an expansion in the scope and scale of human rights within the context of global politics. The main sources of international law derive from treaties, conventions and general principles recognised by state and non-state actors. The obvious reference point remains the UDHR. Signed in 1948, the UDHR entails thirty articles affirming the rights of the individual. Although the declaration is not legally binding, it does provide a framework for the debate surrounding the protection of human rights and a template for humanitarian intervention. The UDHR has also provided the background for subsequent treaties and agreements within international law. Most notably, it marked the first step towards the formation of the International Bill of Human Rights. The three opening Articles set the tone of the document that reflect liberal discourse, emphasising: (a) that all are entitled to free and equal rights and dignity, (b) that no distinction shall be made on access to such rights based upon sovereign legal jurisdiction, and (c) that 'Everyone has the right to life, liberty and the security of person' (United Nations 1948). Other key elements include Article Seven (which deals with discrimination) and Article 20 (freedom of assembly and association).

Treaties consist of a formal written agreement between sovereign states (and in some cases international organisations) which are considered binding within international law. Treaties form a contract between the signatories involved and can take a number of forms, such as protocols, covenants and pacts. Treaties therefore impose a set of obligations recognised and upheld by the signatories. A breach of contract can result in sanctions imposed by quasi-judicial bodies. Treaties often have a regional basis and can at times play a central role within the process of regional integration. For instance, the European Court of Human Rights maintains human rights amongst every member-state of the Council of Europe, under the 1950 European Convention of Human Rights (ECHR), and thus this includes not just all continental European states, Belarus aside, but also Russia, Turkey, Azerbaijan, Georgia and Armenia to name but a few.

A convention is an agreement between different countries that is also binding upon the signatory states. International conventions cover a wide remit of areas such as trade, disarmament and human rights. Conventions play a surprisingly influential role within the anarchic system of states. In contrast, general principles consist of normative values such as justice and equitable treatment. In the context of international law, general principles act as 'gap fillers' when codified and uncodified elements do not provide a satisfactory course of action. For instance, the principles surrounding warfare consist of five inter-related areas: military necessity, unnecessary suffering, proportionality, discrimination and chivalry. As a core element of international human rights law, the Geneva Conventions have been ratified by 196 states, including all 193 United Nations member-states.

A small number of institutions are responsible for the implementation of international human rights law. First and foremost, institutions such as the ICJ and the ICC have undoubtedly helped to advance the human rights agenda. Once considered the preserve of the domestic realm, such institutions provide a framework of global governance to uphold the universality of human rights. International institutions have imposed sanctions against those who might at one time have escaped censure due to their broader significance within the Cold War. It should also be acknowledged that some of these institutions are relatively new, which should be considered when reaching an assessment of the ICC.

The effectiveness of said institutions is dependent upon a number of factors. Of these, arguably the most significant factor is the role played by national governments. The role of international institutions cannot be viewed separately from the support (or lack of support) provided by national institutions in terms of protecting human rights. The successful protection of human rights requires action at the national and international level (Cassel 2001), and thus, in a realist frame, befall subject to the demands of national interest, as all else. There are also other applicable factors to consider, such as public awareness of human rights, the impact of NGOs and the political culture of those countries in question. There was, for instance, sufficient scope within the United States for the Biden administration to present the ICC as an unwelcome intrusion upon national sovereignty, following the policy of past administrations.

The UDHR remains the most important element of international human rights law. All signatories are obligated to protect and promote human rights for their citizens in accordance with the declaration. It also provides a global standard for all others to accept. This however needs to be balanced alongside the reluctance of certain states to uphold the declaration. The abuse of human rights can at times be the direct consequence of states pursuing their own national interests (such as Israeli military strikes against residents in Gaza). In all cases, the Westphalian conception of state sovereignty trumps international law. Indeed, Articles two through seven of the UN Charter protect such claims and thereby limit external intervention (even on humanitarian grounds). Thus, international law in relation to human rights can be considered somewhat contradictory. The Human Rights Committee of the UN has also been subject to criticism for its lack of effectiveness. As with any assessment of the UN, the reluctance of the international community to transfer power and authority is a key factor.

Key Issues in Dealing with Human Rights

The Impact of Human Rights on State Sovereignty

There is an inescapable conflict between the sanctity of state sovereignty and humanitarian intervention in order to protect human rights. The institutions of global governance clearly have the capacity to implement decisions that undermine the sovereignty of the state. However, in regards to a failed (or failing) state, action taken by the international community may actually restore the sovereignty of the ruling regime. For instance, the UN mission in Sierra Leone from 1999 to 2006 helped bring stability and re-establish normality after a lengthy civil war. It should also be noted that some governments actively seek the involvement of external forces in order to restore the territorial integrity of the state.

Violation of human rights inevitably leads towards a consideration of humanitarian intervention from the international community. Given the universal character of human rights, a rogue state places its sovereignty under threat when acting in a manner contrary to international human rights law. The very existence of legal precedent in this area underlines the porous nature of state boundaries (Guillaume 2011). Authoritarian regimes in particular are more likely to ignore the rules, norms and conventions surrounding the universal character of human rights. In contrast, those countries with a political culture that respects human rights and associated liberal-democratic values are least likely to experience outside interference from the international community. Having said this, the charge of Western hypocrisy is often valid in the case of human rights abuses in countries based in North America and Europe. The United States and their allies have been reluctant to address human rights abuses in several Western countries, placing political reality above abstract normative rhetoric concerning human rights.

States that continually violate human rights are more likely to face sanctions from international institutions. For instance, in the context of the ECHR, both Russia and Turkey have been frequent visitors to the courts in Strasbourg. Nonetheless, exhibiting a tradition of liberal democracy does not necessarily mean that the government in question will fully adhere to human rights legislation. As a result of its draconian measures against terrorist organisations, the UK government has at times found itself in contravention of the ECHR.

In terms of international courts, the inability to impose effective sanctions upon rogue states such as North Korea and Venezuela underlines the undoubted significance of national sovereignty. Although there has been a great deal of progress in terms of global governance since the establishment of the UDHR, there's only so much that international institutions can do without impeding upon the sovereignty of states. This observation is central towards an understanding of the selective character of humanitarian intervention and its relative success. Academic research suggests that international human rights legislation has the least effect on those states that need it the most (Hafner-Burton and Tsutsui, 2005).

The Rise of Humanitarian Intervention in the 1990s

Humanitarian intervention has proved an increasingly marked feature of global politics since the end of the Cold War. The landscape of international relations changed dramatically after the collapse of the Soviet Union. The international community gained greater scope to intervene without provoking a Soviet reprisal. A unipolar world characterised by American hegemony presented an opportunity to establish a new world order based upon liberal values of democracy and the rule of law.

Humanitarian intervention may consist of: (a) military coercion against another state with the aim of bringing any violation of human rights to an end in a given territory, or (b) the use of non-military intervention such as economic sanctions or forceful aid provision. The target of humanitarian intervention via the international community has typically been rogue states and/or failed states, although this is not always the case. Non-state organisations with global ambitions may also be targeted by the international community.

There are several factors that determine the effectiveness or otherwise of humanitarian intervention. In an era characterised by an increasing reliance upon soft power, official authorisation from the United Nations undoubtedly confers a degree of legitimacy upon the intervention. However, this alone is insufficient for the intervention to secure legitimacy from the stakeholders affected. In many cases, the warring parties have chosen not to recognise the legitimacy of external interference from the UN. Other factors include the relative capacity of the actors concerned, the political will to act and the existence of an exit strategy.

In terms of a successful intervention, one illustration to consider would be the 1994–95 intervention in Haiti. In the mid-1990s, Operation Uphold Democracy was designed to remove the military regime that seized power after the election of President Jean-Bertrand Aristide in 1991. The US-led intervention had the necessary political will, capacity and legitimacy to secure a clear objective (namely the restoration of democracy). The UN Mission in Haiti sent peacekeeping troops in order to maintain law and order until their eventual withdrawal in the year 2000. A similar observation applies to the actions of the international community in East Timor. The UN Transitional Administration in East Timor (UNTAET) provided an interim civil administration and a peacekeeping presence for three years until national independence was secured in 2002.

In stark contrast, the UN Assistance Mission for Rwanda (UNAMIR) is widely regarded as an abject failure. The international community was highly reluctant to intervene in the ethnic cleansing that ensued between Hutus and Tutsis. Right from the very beginning, there was a lack of clarity concerning UNAMIR's rules of engagement and overall mandate. After the initial intervention by Belgium, and the collapse of any international will to intervene; realists claimed that Rwanda was yet another illustration of power politics. Despite the liberal rhetoric of the UN, national interest triumphed over any moral considerations. The total death count in the Rwandan Civil War ranges from half a million to just over a million (about 70% of the Tutsi population). Estimates of sexual violence against women vary from around a quarter to half a million incidents (Human Rights Watch 1996).

It is too early to reach an accurate judgement about some of the on-going illustrations of humanitarian intervention. For instance, the UN is currently engaged in combat with what remains of ISIS. The international community has become involved due to human rights violations within territory controlled by Islamic extremists. There are also justifiable concerns as to the spillover implications within Syria. Fourteen countries led by the United States have executed airstrikes on Islamic State forces. With the support of the Syrian government, Russian forces have also launched bombing raids against Islamic State fighters located in Syrian territory. Whilst Islamic State has been driven back from areas in Iraq and Syria, the organisation remains a threat to international security and it would be too early to declare victory over them. If this does eventually occur, it will be one of the most successful interventions in recent years, albeit staggered and lacking in widespread mutual conduction.

Reasons for Selective Interventionism, Development of Responsibility to Protect and Conflict with State Sovereignty

There are many reasons for the reluctance of the international community to intervene when faced with a humanitarian crisis. Of these, perhaps the most important is the centrality of national interests. For instance, the cause of a humanitarian crisis may be a strategic ally of the United States. This is often couched within the charge of Western hypocrisy. Similarly, the perpetrating regime may be an important ally of China or the Russian Federation. This can often lead to criticism of double standards from the permanent five of the UN Security Council, potentially blocking a resolution that would allow for intervention in the name of their own interests, and as such, wilfully undermining international security.

Secondly, humanitarian intervention may prove difficult to achieve due to the power balance between various states. During the Cold War, there were clearly defined spheres of influence within the liberal democratic and communist world. Humanitarian intervention within that defined sphere of influence could have instigated all-out war between the US and the Soviet Union. As a consequence, intervention was always on a selective basis. Dictatorial regimes committed several atrocities with the support of either Washington or Moscow.

Another plausible explanation for selective intervention is the inability of the international community to reach a common position. Any member of the P5 can impose a technical veto upon possible UN intervention stemming from Article Seven. Selective intervention is also the result of the international community's reluctance to address violations of human rights by powerful states. For instance, human rights violations by the Chinese government against dissidents have been met with a muted response from the international community. It seems highly improbable that territory controlled by The People's Republic of China would be subject to any form of humanitarian intervention. This observation also applies to other great powers on the world stage, and those states supported by a powerful ally (such as Israel with the US).

Martin Binder (2015, 2017) argues that the response from the UN is based upon four factors. The first of these is the extent of human suffering and the pressure generated by such violations. UN intervention also depends upon the threat to neighbouring countries and regions. This may derive from the spread of terrorism, civil strife and an influx of refugees (as in the case of Bosnia during the 1990s). The UN must also consider the ability of a target state to resist such intervention. This was certainly a consideration in the case of the Gaddafi regime in Libya, prior to the 2011 intervention. Finally, humanitarian intervention can be further understood by the level of material and reputational resources available to the UN (as in the case of the Ivory Coast in 2004). The combination of such factors offers a valid explanation of selective intervention.

The actual consequences of selective intervention are debatable. On the downside, it could be argued that it undermines the entire legitimacy of the United Nations. Successful intervention on humanitarian grounds requires this crucial element of soft power (Nye, 1990), and legitimacy is undermined when intervention is designed to serve the economic interests of the powerful. However, it could also be argued that selectivity is desirable because it prevents the UN becoming embroiled in poorly thought-out commitments (Roberts and Zaum, 2008). For instance, the UN has been reluctant to intervene in the Syrian Civil War due to its sheer complexity. It must also be acknowledged that the Assad regime has support in the Security Council from both Russia and China.

The relationship between state sovereignty and the responsibility to protect (R2P) is a fascinating issue to consider. It is based upon the principle that sovereignty comes with certain duties and obligations that broadly match with the most basic predicates or norms of liberal democracy. These are based upon the norms and values inherent within international law (most notably over human rights). The principle has formed debate over planned intervention in countries such as Libya, Kenya and Sudan.

It is often claimed that the doctrine of R2P is an infringement upon the sovereignty of the state. This seems a relatively uncontroversial judgement given that it enables the UN and the wider international community to intervene as an act of last resort. However, the former Secretary General of the UN, Ban Ki-moon, argues that R2P actually reinforces sovereignty. This is because the international community intervenes without consent only when that state concerned is allowing (or committing) mass atrocities. In these situations, the state no longer upholds the duties and in certain cases may be unable to do so. Intervention thereby supports – rather than undermines – the sovereignty of the state.

In order to properly assess the relationship between state sovereignty and the R2P doctrine, it is useful to consider real-life examples. Although authorisation was secured in the case of Libya in 2011, there was criticism of the selective character of humanitarian intervention and as a means to achieve regime change. The notion of R2P was therefore undermined due to the phenomenon of 'mission creep' within a failed state. This term is used to describe an unplanned long-term commitment arising during the course of a military campaign. In the same year, both China and Russia vetoed an attempt by the United States to gain a resolution invoking R2P within the Syrian Civil War. The Russian Federation and the Chinese government claimed that Washington had abused the doctrine within Libya and therefore acted contrary to the notion of upholding state sovereignty.

The most controversial aspect of the R2P is the third pillar and the use of military intervention. The use of military instruments as a necessary adjunct to successful intervention on humanitarian grounds has its detractors and supporters. The deployment of troops and other military hardware undoubtedly raises the stakes in the debate concerning R2P and the sovereignty of the state. Given the complexity of cost-benefit analysis, the international community will always have to balance a number of variables when considering military intervention on humanitarian grounds.

Western Double Standards / Hypocrisy

As far as humanitarian intervention is concerned, the charge of Western hypocrisy is based upon two factors. Firstly, the 'West' adopts a selective approach towards humanitarian intervention. Some of the most powerful countries within global affairs have opposed humanitarian intervention against an important ally. For instance, Israel is a long-term ally of the United States and repeated human rights violations against the Palestinians have been largely ignored by the UNSC, of which the US is a permanent member. In contrast, the actions of rogue states, as classified by Washington, have been dealt with on an effective and co-ordinated basis. The 'West' has also been complicit in turning a blind eye to the actions of human rights abuses in supportive states. For example, violations against journalists and members of minority groups within Saudi Arabia have been largely ignored. To take just one example, in 2018 the journalist Jamal Khashoggi was murdered in the Saudi consulate in Istanbul, Turkey after his criticism of the Saudi government.

As a consequence of Western hypocrisy, the international community has often refused to intervene, regardless of the humanitarian tragedy unfolding. This usually occurs either because: (a) an ally of the West has been involved in some manner (such as Saudi Arabian forces in Yemen), or (b) there were no vital national interests involved. The latter is the more common of the two and can be applied to humanitarian crises in Darfur (2003–2009) and Sri

Lanka (1983–2009). In the case of the former, attempts by the Sudanese government to defeat separatists have contributed to thousands of casualties. Rather, in the case of the latter, the Sri Lankan government had a hand in the murder of thousands in their conflict against the Tamil Tigers. The 'West' have also been accused of hypocrisy in their failure to deal effectively with the quagmire of the Syrian Civil War, which began during the Arab Spring.

Accusations of hypocrisy were particularly noticeable during the Cold War. In order to defeat the threat and spread of Soviet Communism, the United States and its Western allies supported a number of right-wing dictatorial regimes. Human rights violations were a feature of several Western allies, including the Shah of Iran and General Pinochet in Chile. However, the West was prepared to ignore such violations in order to keep on friendly terms with important strategic allies – gaining both political and financial capital in the process. After the end of the Cold War, former allies did on occasion become enemies. In such cases, they were able to use military hardware previously purchased from Western powers.

A particularly clear illustration of this argument concerned Iraq under Saddam Hussein. During the Iran-Iraq War (1980–88), the US and the UK provided arms to Iraq. However, during both the Gulf War (1990–91) and the Iraq War (2003), US-led invasions of Iraq saw these exact same arms used against the US. Despite claims of humanitarian intervention in the 2003 instance, the US Bush administration and the Blair-led British government were accused of seeking international authorisation and legitimacy for the invasion of Iraq in order to impose regime change. The appearance of ulterior motives in the 2003 American-led intervention in Iraq remains one of the most controversial military conflicts of the twenty-first century.

Environmental Governance

The Role and Significance of the United Nations Framework Convention on Climate Change

The United Nations Framework Convention on Climate Change (UNFCCC) is an international environmental Treaty dating back to the 1992 Rio de Janeiro Summit. Officially, the role of the United Nations Framework Convention on Climate Change (2021) is to 'stabilise greenhouse gas concentrations in the atmosphere at a level that would prevent dangerous anthropogenic interference with the climate system'. The UNFCCC is also the name of the UN Secretariat department thus responsible for the implementation of the convention.

The UNFCCC specifies limits upon greenhouse gas emissions and provides a framework for a series of international environmental agreements. The signatories to the convention have met on an annual basis since the mid-1990s. Signatory nations establish national measurements of greenhouse gas emissions. Having said this, the significance of the convention is greatly limited by the absence of an effective enforcement mechanism. It is also constrained by the barriers posed by national sovereignty and disagreement amongst states over how to approach the issue of climate change, let alone a common measure of emissions.

The first major agreement under the UNFCCC was the Kyoto Protocol, signed in 1997. The first stage of the Kyoto Protocol established legally binding obligations for developed countries to reduce greenhouse gas emissions by an average 5% reduction in comparison to 1990 levels over the five-year period (2008-2012). The second stage was negotiated via the Doha amendment. However, this being said, implementation of the second stage was limited and the Kyoto process eventually lost momentum. Attention then shifted towards the Paris Agreement which was outlined and agreed upon at the end of 2015.

In terms of its positive impact, the convention enjoys a broad sense of legitimacy due to the urgent need to tackle climate change. It is telling to note that membership is near unanimous, with almost all states becoming members of the convention. It has also provided a stable basis in order to make progress towards emission targets. For instance, the Kyoto Protocol represented the first-ever legally binding agreement to address climate change. It is also worth noting that the original Kyoto Protocol reduced CO_2 emissions beyond the targets set (Shishlov et al.. 2016). However, there are several limitations that need highlighting when reaching an assessment of the UNFCCC.

The most important constraint upon the UN convention is the lack of an effective enforcement mechanism. This has undoubtedly contributed to the failure of the UNFCCC to meet the goals of carbon dioxide emissions. Although the Kyoto Protocol did have a legal mechanism in place, its effectiveness was limited by the refusal of several major emitters to sign up to uphold the accord, chiefly the US. The multilateral character of the institution also makes it problematic to secure an effective and lasting agreement. Most notably, there is a sharp division between the developed world and the less developed economies. The North-South divide has been graphically exposed within a number of international environmental agreements. The withdrawal of major economies (such as Canada, the US and Japan) from the second stage of Kyoto greatly undermined its overall impact. In the absence of a supranational set of institutions, it seems improbable that divisions between the wealthy economies and LEDCs can ever be fully resolved.

There is also the tendency towards building consensus on the basis of the lowest common denominator. Given the need for unanimity, it is often possible for countries to raise objections in relation to their own national or economic interests and thereby stall the overall process. This, inevitably, results in the failure to achieve a meaningful and lasting response to climate change. This has also contributed towards certain countries switching towards alternative agreements. For instance, the Climate and Clean Air coalition sought to reduce short-lived climate pollutants. It is a voluntary partnership led by governments throughout the world. In addition, the use of benchmarks is widely seen as inequitable given the vast difference in economic costs towards meeting overall targets.

Given the existence of Article Three in the convention, climate measures have sought to avoid restricting international trade. Some would argue there is an unavoidable tension here between economic development and protection of the environment. Given the existence of state sovereignty based upon the Westphalian conception, there is always the opportunity to prioritise growth and development over limiting the negative externalities caused by economic activity. Perhaps the clearest illustration of this argument is China – the country with the largest carbon emissions footprint (Climate Action Tracker 2021).

Any assessment of the UNFCCC requires a comparison with other environmental agreements. In the case of ozone depletion, the Montreal Protocol (1987) can claim a greater level of success than the agreements undertaken as part of the UN convention. The regulatory framework agreed upon at Montreal has been shown to be more effective than attempts to address climate change in the Kyoto agreement. Environmental agreements reached on a regional or even bilateral basis can also be considered as part of a broader assessment of the UNFCCC.

The Intergovernmental Panel on Climate Change

The Intergovernmental Panel on Climate Change (IPCC) is dedicated to providing the world with scientific information relevant towards an understanding of climate change. The IPCC is an intergovernmental body of the United Nations that provides reports that contribute towards the work of the aforementioned UNFCCC. Established in 1988, membership of the IPCC is open to the World Meteorological Organisation and the UN Environment Programme (UNEP).

The IPCC does not carry out original research or monitor climate change. Instead, it offers an assessment of published literature on an objective and measured basis. In terms of its positives, the IPCC can be said to stimulate research into climate science. For instance, reports entail an assessment on research gaps in order to generate further investigation. The fifth assessment report, published in 2013 by the IPCC, provided valuable scientific input into the Paris Agreement. According to its official website, the planned sixth assessment report is the most ambitious in the history of the organisation, due to be released fully in 2022 and with the first Working Group Report published in 2021 (Intergovernmental Panel on Climate Change 2021).

Scientists and associated experts contribute to the process on a voluntary basis. The eventual report is then reviewed by representatives of national governments. This level of oversight derives from the concern expressed by the Reagan administration (1980–88) about the unrestrained influence of independent scientists and UN bodies. Reports produced by the IPCC therefore require some input from official representatives of participating governments. The summary for the policymakers section is subject to line-by-line approval from delegates in order to reflect the views of various governments.

The significance of the IPCC is based upon the reputation formed within the scientific community. It represents the leading authority on climate change and, in recognition of this, the institution was awarded the Nobel Peace Prize in 2007. It would be impossible to imagine the UNFCCC operating effectively without some input from the IPCC. However, this being said, the panel has been subject to a degree of justifiable criticism. Of these, perhaps the most important critique is that some of the data published has been incorrect (IPCC, 2010). For instance, the projected date for the melting of the Himalayan glaciers overstates the impact of climate change. The publication of incorrect data is a serious matter as it enables climate change deniers to claim that the issue as a whole is a hoax. In the United States, right-wing politicians have often seized upon these mistakes. For instance, the Republican Senator James Inhofe once claimed that 'man-made global warming is the greatest hoax ever perpetrated on the American people' (Cosgrove-Mather 2005). It also creates the political environment in which figures within the Trump administration (including the President himself) could downplay the significance of the threat, contributing to the rejection of the 2015 Paris Agreement prior to the Biden administration reversing this position in 2021.

From the opposing angle, the IPCC has faced criticism for its conservative character. In doing so, it has been accused of minimising the pace and impact of sea temperature rises. Publication of reports based upon the lowest common denominator does little to address the seriousness of a problem facing all of humanity. Scientific research has shown that estimates offered by the IPCC understate the risk of a projected rise in sea levels. This, for instance, is a critique often taken up by radical pressure groups, such as Extinction Rebellion (2019), who cite the conservatism of the IPCC as part of the 'climate emergency' issue.

As with other provisions of information, there is always the problem that data soon becomes out-of-date. Since the IPCC works on a schedule, any significant findings that do not meet the submissions deadline will not be included in the published report. This is a major shortcoming given that reports are widely regarded as the ultimate scientific authority into the matter, and that our knowledge of the changing climate constantly adapts. It has also been claimed that political lobbying from the United States has impacted the leadership of the Panel (Pearce 2002). Under the influence of ExxonMobil, the Bush administration sought to remove a climate scientist from the chairmanship of the IPCC. This clearly undermines the autonomy of the international panel. Whilst the IPCC enables a more informed decision, it does not necessarily mean that decisions taken are in any way free from political influence. On a final note, it has also been claimed that the voluntary basis of providing information deters scientific experts in the field.

The 2021 COP-26 Meeting in Glasgow

In 2021, the UN's Conference of the Parties (COP) held its 26th summit in Glasgow, UK. The high-profile conference brought together the majority of the world's countries in an attempt to tackle climate change. The high-profile conference is a very clear illustration of global governance in action. However, the failure of the world's largest polluter, China, to send its premier, Xi Jinping, dealt a major blow to the overall credibility of the conference (Ortega 2021). The effectiveness of any final agreement reached at the conference was also hampered by the non-attendance of the Russian president, Vladimir Putin.

In common with other forums of global governance, the UN's COP26 is constrained by the concept of national sovereignty. Governments always have the capacity to announce policies that match their own perceived national interests. For instance, Prime Minister Narendra Modi announced that India would cut its emissions to net zero by 2070. The goal is in clear contrast to the summit's overall commitment for states to reach net-zero by 2050. In terms of meeting environmental goals, there is no institution within the UN effective enough to ensure that countries meet their commitments. This problem is particularly acute in the context of major polluters. As an emerging economy and one of the BRICS, India is the third largest polluter in the world. The same critique applies to China, who announced a commitment to achieve carbon neutrality by 2060. However, the United States (and the EU) aim to achieve net zero ten years earlier. Essentially, it seems unlikely that such targets can be coordinated. The Glasgow Climate Pact also failed to gain unanimous agreement to limit temperature rises to 1.5 degrees Celsius. Equally, its central pledge to 'phase out' the use of coal was replaced with the pledge to 'phase down' the use of coal.

It must of course be noted that the conference did achieve certain goals. For instance, it should not be neglected that this is the first ever climate agreement to 'phase down' the use of coal. The deal also provides more financial assistance to developing countries to help adapt to the impact of climate change. There was also a bilateral agreement reached between the United States and China on emissions. However, the conference faced the same problems that all such agreements tend to run into, such as placing the short-term national interest above long-term considerations for future generations.

The Extent to Which These Institutions Address and Resolve Contemporary Global Issues

The concept of state sovereignty lies at the fulcrum of understanding global politics. It has direct and indirect implications in regards to human rights, the environment and efforts made by the international community to prevent conflict. Within its defined territory, the state is able to implement policies that reflect its own perceived interests. The effectiveness of international law is thereby heavily constrained by the concept of state sovereignty.

In principle, relations between states are based upon equality. As such, one state cannot force another to adopt a particular course of action and no state has the right to intervene within another. This means that states must rely upon international agreements, treaties and protocols in order to address issues of a transnational or truly global character. In seeking to prevent conflict, there are numerous agreements that states should adhere to. In regards to environmental protection and upholding human rights, it should be noted that the overwhelming majority of international organisations and regional bodies are intergovernmental. Only supranational institutions have the authority to compel states to adopt a certain course of action, and these are conspicuously absent in relation to human rights and the environment. The inherent problem with intergovernmental institutions is the tendency to reach a compromise absent of any decisive action.

Another related issue to consider is that international law generally suffers from a lack of adequate enforcement. International institutions are often under-funded. There is also a marked propensity towards vague and generalised wording alongside very little actual substance behind the self-congratulatory rhetoric of international agreements. There is, for instance, no effective enforcement mechanism available to impose sanctions upon the United States as to its treatment of detainees at the Guantanamo Bay Detention Facility, in Cuba. Washington D.C. is not a signatory to the Rome Statute of the International Criminal Court, and none of its allies exercise much influence over the world's only military superpower. Imposing sanctions against a member of the permanent five is also deeply problematic. Based upon Article 94 of the UN Charter, any judicial criticism made against one of the P5 (or its allies) would almost certainly be vetoed within the Security Council, undermining the power of international law in the face of the sovereign national interests of the P5 states. Moreover, if the UNSC refuses to enforce a judgement against another state there is no method of forcing the state to comply.

Having said this, the process of globalisation has to some degree changed how sovereignty operates. The international community is now more willing to accept that intervention is justifiable on humanitarian grounds than in previous years. The very existence of international human rights law also provides an institutional framework by which to protect and uphold the universality of such rights. Furthermore, the interconnectedness of globalisation enables some states to escape the debilitating dichotomy between economic growth and environmental protection. Equally, there is a growing emphasis amongst sovereign states upon sustainable development that is consistent with the overall themes of globalisation.

In regards to dealing with conflict, international law is widely seen as ineffective in addressing and resolving issues arising. The conditions for just war (*jus ad bellum*) and the conduct of just war (*jus in bello*) are binding upon all states. For instance, there is an obligation to make every effort to avoid killing non-combatants during a military conflict. However, this does allow states to target combatants who intentionally make use of human shields (as used by Hamas during the 2014 Gaza War). Laws also apply to individuals and members of the armed forces. Parties are bound by the laws of warfare to the extent that compliance does not in any way interfere with legitimate military goals. This is a relatively open-ended phrase that provides national armies with a wide degree of interpretation.

Secondly, the laws of war are based upon consensus. As a consequence, the content and interpretation of such laws are at times contested, which dilutes their meaning and value. For instance, there is no consensus on the contested issue of private security combatants or mercenaries. The international quasi-judicial system lacks the resources to fully implement the Geneva Conventions on the humanitarian treatment of both combatants and non-combatants in war. The ability to bring rogue states and powerful states to justice is always highly problematic for institutions. As with human rights and the protection of the environment, the key stumbling block is that of state sovereignty.

The Performance of the International Courts, Including Controversies

The performance of the international judicial system is subject to a number of valid criticisms. Of these, the most common is that of systemic bias. For example, the ICC has been accused of displaying a certain bias against Israel. The Israeli Prime Minister Benjamin Netanyahu once called a report into alleged war crimes by the Israeli state against Palestinians as 'pure anti-Semitism' (Heller 2019). It should be noted that Israel is not a signatory of the International Criminal Court.

The Court has also been criticised for demonstrating a bias against African countries. Each of the forty-four individuals indicted by the prosecutor's office come from the African continent. It is a figure which seems incongruous, especially given that alleged human rights abuses are identifiable in every region of the world. In 2017, three African states threatened to leave the court due to accusations of bias. However, the ICC has pointed out that its record reflects requests made by governments within Africa. It is also claimed that the African Court of Human and Peoples' Rights has been unwilling (or unable) to pursue human rights violations in the continent alone.

Another controversial area is that trials can only be brought against individuals rather than countries and organisations. From a similar angle the remit of the court could be expanded as its present range only covers genocide, crimes against humanity and war crimes. A further problem undermining the effectiveness of the ICC is that almost a third of states (most notably the United States) have refused to grant the court jurisdiction in their territories. As a result, the ICC has been unable to properly address human rights abuses amongst powerful entities like China and the United States. According to Amnesty International (2021), torture and repression is implemented by the Chinese government against political opponents to the government alongside ethnic minorities, such as the Uyghur Muslims in Xinjiang. Moreover, the treatment of dissidents and minority groups is characterised by arbitrary detention and forced indoctrination, labelled as 're-education' (Newlines Institute 2021).

Shallow Ecology Versus Deep Ecology

The term ecologism is often interpreted as the study of our 'natural household'. Ecologism is based upon an assumption that all living organisms (both human and non-human) are mutually dependent within a broader ecosystem. The main ideological division amongst ecologists is between so-called 'shallow-greens' and 'deep-greens'.

In terms of their view on human nature, shallow-green ecologists are anthropocentric, where humanity is at the centre of their outlook and ultimate concerns. Shallow-greens therefore advocate an enlightened lifestyle choice and adopt a moderate stance within the political process. The shallow-green approach also views capitalism as consistent with the broader objectives of the environmentalist movement. Individuals can adopt their consumerist habits in order to protect the environment. In accordance with shallow-green thinking, the path towards lasting influence lies in a constructive engagement with the political process. It is therefore a strand of thought relatively close to the centre of the political spectrum and places an emphasis on adapting behaviour within our already existent frameworks of economics and politics.

In complete contrast, deep-green ecology adopts a radically different approach. Whereas shallow-greens are anthropocentric, deep-greens are ecocentric. Deep-green ecologists argue that our purpose in life should be to live in harmony with nature, as opposed to privileging ourselves over it. The most significant contribution from deep-green ecology derives from the 'Gaia hypothesis' where James Lovelock (1979) argued that Gaia (the Ancient Greek Goddess of the Earth) will destroy anything that presents a threat to it. For Lovelock, the view that 'we' need to save the planet is an anthropocentric fallacy.

According to shallow-greens, those who adopt ecocentric assumptions are more interested in philosophical thought rather than achievable objectives. From the opposing angle, shallow ecologism is used in a prerogative sense for compromising the entire ethos of the green movement. Deep-greens contend that the conventional political process will never provide an opportunity for securing the goals of ecologism. Most notably, powerful vested interests like the military-industrial complex will always block the green cause. There is also the question of gaining public support. Nonetheless, it may be the case that human behaviour within a democratic system is never going to change in an adequate manner.

Sustainable Development and the Tragedy of the Commons

Sustainable development can be defined as that level of development that meets the needs of the present without compromising the ability of future generations to meet their needs. It usually entails an environmental dimension and provides the basis for targets agreed upon by the United Nations. Sustainable development can also be viewed as a form of generational justice between the living and those yet to be born. This latter point reflects the Burkean concept of a social contract between those who are dead, those who are living and those still yet to be.

The actual meaning of sustainable development is unclear because there is no agreed consensus as to what should be sustained. The term has also expanded from the original Brundtland Report towards something of a public relations-exercise. On a deeper level, there is arguably no such thing as a sustainable use of a non-renewable resource. As many of the planet's resources are non-renewable, sustainable usage of such resources may well prove impossible. If we adopt a pessimistic outlook, economic development may eventually lead towards the depletion of non-renewable resources. Simply put, it is undoubtedly very difficult to reconcile economic development with the protection of the environment.

The tragedy of the commons bears an obvious relationship to the issue of sustainable development. Individuals in pursuit of their own narrow interests act in a manner contrary to that of the common good. The global commons are therefore under threat from the rational actions of consumers and companies. Given the dynamics of globalisation, governments can do relatively little to mitigate consumer choice and decisions taken by major companies. Whilst they can impose policies and nudge economic agents towards the correct behaviour, this alone is not enough.

The tragedy of the commons casts considerable insight into economic growth and development. According to the basic economic problem, we need to allocate limited resources towards the satisfaction of unlimited wants. A capitalist economic system facilitates consumer choice and could therefore be viewed as consistent with protection of the environment. Shallow-greens contend that consumers are able to adopt their behaviour in order to preserve the global commons. Deep-greens however do not believe that capitalism is consistent with ecologism. It is an economic system based upon instant gratification rather than long-term considerations of the environment.

The tragedy of the commons illustrates the true complexity of ensuring sustainable development. In the absence of a world government, it seems improbable that states will sacrifice their own interests for some common greater good. It also requires democratic governments to place the interests of future generations over that of securing re-election. This has often proved a recurring problem when seeking to reach an effective international agreement in order to address environmental concerns. Powerful states in particular have often declared that their domestic way of life will not be threatened by international institutions.

Strengths and Weaknesses of International Agreements - Including Key Highlights from Rio, Kyoto, Copenhagen and Paris

During the 1992 Earth Summit, held in Rio de Janeiro, the member states of the United Nations came together and settled upon a number of common themes. The Rio Declaration outlined 27 principles intended to guide countries towards sustainable development. The Earth Summit resulted in the Rio Declaration on Environment and Development. The Earth Summit at Rio also instigated a series of international agreements that signify a co-ordinated attempt to combat global warming. It ultimately laid the foundation for later agreements reached at Kyoto (1997), Copenhagen (2009) and Paris (2015).

The impact and significance of the Rio Summit is somewhat mixed. On the plus side, agreement was reached so that signatories should not carry out any activities on the lands of indigenous peoples that would cause environmental degradation. The Rio Summit also instigated the UNFCCC. However, the convention lacks an enforcement mechanism. It should also be noted that the world's largest economy (the US) refused to sign the proposed convention on biological diversity.

The Kyoto Protocol implemented the objective of the UNFCCC. It commits signatories to reduce their greenhouse gas emissions. It is based on the scientific consensus that global warming is a man-made phenomenon. Adopted in 1997, the Kyoto Protocol finally entered into force in 2005. Perhaps the main success of Kyoto is the notion of differentiated responsibilities. In order to secure agreement amongst a range of countries at very different stages of economic development, it was acknowledged that each country holds different capabilities in relation to addressing climate change. The obligation was stronger upon developed economies based on their historical role in damaging the atmosphere.

The first commitment period secured compliance from signatory states, but several states refused to participate in the second stage. Although the second commitment period was finalised in 2012, a number of major economies failed to accept the new targets such as Canada, Russia and Japan. Most notably, the United States Senate refused to ratify the Kyoto Protocol.

The Copenhagen Summit marked the fifteenth conference of the parties to the UNFCCC. According to timelines agreed upon before the summit, the Copenhagen summit of 2009 pledged to outline the framework for climate change mitigation beyond 2012. The resultant accord agreed that measures should be taken to keep temperature increases below 2 degrees centigrade.

Developed countries also pledged $100 billion a year to help developing countries. However, it was not legally binding and did not specify any binding commitment to reduce CO2 emissions. Given disagreements amongst the sovereign states, the document did not receive unanimous approval. Within the media, the summit was widely described as 'Broken-hagen'.

Under the aforementioned UNFCCC, the Paris Agreement on greenhouse gases and global warming was adopted on 12 December 2015. The long-term temperature goal is to limit the increase to 1.5 degrees Celsius. There is also an obligation that signatories report on their contribution towards tackling global warming. Although virtually all countries are signatories the Trump administration pledged to withdraw from the Agreement and did so, prior to the successor Biden administration formally re-joining in February 2021. The impact of the Paris Agreement is also weakened over a lack of clarity as to which clauses are voluntary and legally obligatory.

Obstacles to International Cooperation and Agreement

The refusal of the Trump administration to accept and implement the Paris Agreement is indicative of a deeper malaise within international relations. In a number of cases, member states place their own perceived national interests above a threat to the global commons. Westphalian sovereignty is one of the most significant barriers towards international cooperation and agreement.

In order for a sovereign state to sign up to and adhere to international agreements, it must view that agreement as a match with their own interests. In order for states to view international agreements in such a manner, a number of associated variables may prove relevant. Most notably, a democratic society must have the space for a civil society to exist that favours action to address climate change. States must also feel they have little choice but to accept the international consensus. Naturally, a global superpower, such as the US, has greater leeway to ignore such agreements when compared to less powerful states. Having said this, even a minor power such as New Zealand refused to accept the second stage of the Kyoto Protocol, a state often thought of as adhering to international norms and collective interest.

A similar situation applies to the protection of human rights. The language of those documents that uphold the universal character of human rights derives from an individualistic and Liberal mindset. This is built upon assumptions that do not necessarily translate well to certain parts of the world. For instance, it was only in 2004 that the Arab League adopted the principles contained in the UDHR. Even then, the UN High Commissioner for Human Rights said that the Arab Charter was incompatible with universal human rights (particularly regarding women's rights and capital punishment for children). The Charter has also been criticised for setting human rights standards below the internationally recognised norm.

Autocratic and totalitarian regimes have routinely ignored such documents in the knowledge that the international community adopts an inconsistent approach to human rights violations. It is a fact that powerful states such as China (or regional powers like Israel) have routinely ignored international human rights law with no effective sanctions from the UN. Similarly, the US has violated human rights in their treatment of terrorist suspects without facing any major consequences (Amnesty International 2020).

There is also a major division between the developed and developing worlds with regards to climate change. Once again, this can cause considerable difficulties when seeking to secure an agreement to reconcile different interests and perspectives. From the viewpoint of the developed world, the level of pollution generated by the developing world is of major concern. It also provides a potentially unfair advantage for LEDCs over developed economies. Similarly, the Global South can rightly point out that the worst culprits in terms of carbon emissions are the developed economies in the Global North. This has made it very difficult to gain agreement over emission targets, with the North favouring current measures whereas the South prefers historic levels.

Concerning tackling global poverty, the gap between the developed and developing world also poses certain problems. To the developing world, the global marketplace is protected by developed countries in the case of agriculture. Despite their free-market rhetoric, the farming sector of prominent Western economies is heavily protected. There is also a degree of hypocrisy shown by the developed North in regards to market-based policies. The Washington Consensus preaches that those states in economic difficulties should implement policies of marketisation and privatisation, whilst developed countries are free to impose trade restrictions. Given that access to lucrative markets in North America and Europe would greatly assist economic growth in the emerging economies, the issue will always prove significant during negotiations in the WTO.

Finally, there is a clear division over responsibility in regards to environmental damage and global poverty. Given their economic development, it may seem obvious that the developed world is more responsible for pollution than the emerging economies. However, the reality is more complex as China is now the biggest polluter on the planet (Ortega 2021; Union of Concerned Scientists 2020). Given its considerable economic power and influence; other countries are understandably reluctant to take action against Beijing.

In regards to global poverty, economic development within Africa has been hampered by the legacy of colonialism. The accumulated wealth of former colonialists is based to some extent upon the exploitation of labour and natural resources within their former colonies. This however is problematic to address within international forums (such as potential repatriations). Gaining an accurate measurement is also a difficult one to resolve in the context of emissions. Given the lack of supranational bodies, it is always problematic to identify precise data out of those states that manipulate their own figures.

The Role and Significance of the Global Civil Society and Non-state Actors

Global civil society can be thought of as activists and pressure groups that operate across national borders. Often defined in a narrow sense as new social movements, global civil society seeks to influence policymakers in governments and international institutions. The main focus of global civil society tends to be upon liberal values such as the protection of human rights. A number of organisations fit neatly into our understanding of global civil society, such as trade unions, indigenous groups, charities, faith-based organisations and NGOs.

The term global civil society has grown in popularity since the end of the Cold War and the resultant emergence of globalisation. Sometimes dubbed the 'third sector' (after states and commerce), global civil society has the capacity to mobilise people and shape the decision-making process. In order to underline the significance of the third sector, one estimate suggests that NGOs across forty countries employ approximately 54 million full time workers with a volunteer workforce of over 350 million (Jezard 2018).

The impact of NGOs upon the political process is debatable. From a positive angle, they provide expertise and improve the quality of legislation. They also perform a democratic function as they hold institutions and decision-makers to account. NGOs and global civil society can raise awareness of crimes against humanity and genocide. They may even force governments who might be reluctant to intervene on humanitarian grounds to assist victims of human rights abuses. In a more practical sense, such organisations routinely provide public services to many of the most vulnerable. They also foster engagement amongst citizens and seek to empower communities (particularly those who speak on behalf of indigenous groups). This may even entail providing disaster preparedness and management.

On the flipside, the impact of such groups is often relatively low within autocratic regimes. Governments that operate on this basis tend to marginalise (or just ignore) the third sector. Whilst NGOs and other associated groups can, and indeed do, raise international awareness, they may have very little direct influence upon certain regimes. This observation also applies to those countries which lack a political culture that encourages debate, transparency and engagement. As with other pressure groups, overall influence depends upon several inter-related factors.

It should also be acknowledged that technological developments tend to assist their operations. Activities that would at one time have been censored or suppressed can often be shared throughout the world at the click of a button. The wave of democratic reforms that characterised the Arab Spring is a particularly striking illustration of this argument. It has also proved easier to mobilise civil society groups via the use of technology (such as during the 2007 Saffron Revolution in Myanmar). In addition, drone technology has been harnessed by environmental groups in order to expose illegal poaching of endangered species.

Conclusion

Chapter four sought to consider the attempts made on behalf of the international community to uphold universal human rights and global environmentalism. Intervention on a humanitarian basis provides considerable insight into notions of international law, judicial bodies and the sovereignty of the state. An examination of humanitarian intervention inevitably leads us towards the charge of hypocrisy. Equally, the international community also faces a number of salient issues and barriers that are integral towards the fight against climate change, running up against questions of power and influence over the international system as a whole.

BOX 4.1 - KEY TERMS FROM CHAPTER FOUR

Human Rights

Within the context of international relations, human rights can be defined as a set of freedoms and liberties applicable to citizens of a particular state. The purpose of international human rights law is to respect, protect and fulfil universal human rights. As parties to international organisations and treaties, signatory states are obligated to protect and uphold these fundamental rights. As a grounding for international law, human rights legislation primarily exists amongst agreements between sovereign states. There is also a significant number of multilateral treaties applicable towards the conduct of warfare, the rights of children and refugees. Although not binding in a strictly legal sense, there are certain instruments that contribute to associated political duties (such as the responsibility to protect). The concept of human rights holds implications towards the conduct of humanitarian intervention and the application of international law. Whilst the significance of human rights has greatly expanded, upholding human rights remains limited by the Westphalian concept of national sovereignty. There is no international court to administer international human rights legislation. However, there are international tribunals and quasi-judicial bodies under the auspices of the United Nations. There are also regional institutions that administer human rights legislation such as the Inter-American Court of Human Rights. It should also be noted that there is no shared consensus upon the actual meaning of rights and duties.

International Law

The concept of universal jurisdiction of international law is based upon *jus cogens* and *erga omnes*. The former is a principle in which no derogation is permitted amongst sovereign states. Whilst there is no universal agreement regarding which norms are classified as *jus cogens*, it is widely accepted that the concept prevents both genocide and enslavement. Wars of aggression, torture and territorial expansion may also be considered. The concept of *erga omnes* is a phrase which means 'towards all or everyone'. In a legal sense, rights or obligations are therefore applicable regardless of social background. In well over a hundred countries, national human rights institutions have been created in order to monitor and protect human rights within jurisdiction in a given country. The basis for such legislation is the Paris Principles which were later adopted by the UN.

International Court of Justice (ICJ)

The ICJ has jurisdiction over disputes between states, and provides advisory opinions on points of international law. Established via the UN Charter, the World Court must adhere to the statute of the International Court of Justice. In terms of its structure, the ICJ consists of fifteen judges elected by the General Assembly and the Security Council. Article Six stipulates that all judges should be elected based upon their competence in order to ensure judicial independence. There is also an informal convention in place whereby seats are allocated on a geographical basis. For most of the Court's history, a judge from at least one of the permanent five from the UN Security Council has resided upon the judicial benches. Whilst the UN Security Council is authorised to enforce the rulings of the Court, enforcement is subject to veto powers exercised by the P5. Inevitably, this is a major drawback in terms of the effectiveness of the International Court of Justice. The exclusion of NGOs and groups seeking national self-determination also limits the effectiveness of the ICJ. Only states are allowed to be parties in contentious cases, although they could voice the interests and opinions of nations that seek the right to self-determination. Although the ICJ is based upon judicial independence, this has on occasions been undermined by the influence of the more powerful states.

International Criminal Court (ICC)

The ICC is an intergovernmental organisation with the power to prosecute individuals for genocide, war crimes and crimes against humanity. The ICC only exercises jurisdiction when national courts are unwilling or unable to prosecute. The ICC complements existing national judicial systems and considers a wide number of on-going cases. For instance, the judicial body recently investigated alleged war crimes and crimes against humanity by all parties in the ongoing South Ossetia conflict. The ICC is a relatively recent institution within the system of global governance. Since 2002, the International Criminal Court has investigated and prosecuted crimes committed in situations referred to the Court's attention by the Security Council. The ICC has four principal organs and the President is the most senior judge chosen by their peers in the Judicial Division.

International Tribunals

International tribunals under the authority of organisations such as the
United Nations can either be permanent or temporary. Unlike other UN
agencies, both institutions are housed in the Netherlands. On
occasions, the United Nations has created specific tribunals on a
temporary basis to investigate and prosecute war criminals. For
instance, the International Criminal Tribunal for the former Yugoslavia
(ICTY) was established to prosecute serious crimes committed during
the Yugoslav Wars. Created on the basis of a UN resolution, over 160
individuals were indicted over the course of its existence. The ICTY
considered four clusters of crimes such as breaches of the Geneva
Convention, genocide and violations of the laws of warfare. There are
also international tribunals within a specific region. For instance,
interpretation of African Union treaties is the sole responsibility of the
African Court of Justice. Over the historical development of the
international tribunal system, the courts have been primarily concerned
with crimes against humanity committed within the African continent. As
with other aspects of international law, there are also issues
surrounding its Western-centric understanding of universal human
rights. Indeed, Muslim theorists suggest that human well-being is
divinely ordained whilst Asian states champion community values above
those of the individual.

Human Rights / Universal Human Rights

On 10 December 1948, the UN General Assembly adopted a famous
document for all peoples and all nations throughout the world. The
Universal Declaration of Human Rights (UDHR) makes a firm
commitment to uphold the basic dignity of the individual. There are thirty
articles in total, covering a wide remit of human rights from freedom of
opinion to laws against discrimination. In historical terms, the UDHR
has offered a blueprint for the implementation of human rights. Many of
the newly independent countries adopted those rights within their own
codified constitutions during decolonisation. On the basis of the UDHR,
the international community has since expanded the scope of treaties
and conventions concerning human rights. Many of the international
institutions that implement a system of global governance are primarily
concerned with upholding the universal and indivisible character of
human rights. There has undoubtedly been progress made towards the
protection of universal human rights. Most notably, it provides a
legitimate basis for the concept of humanitarian intervention. Equally, it

must also be acknowledged that the international community is far from maintaining these values for all members of humanity. Whilst the UDHR remains a powerful instrument with a lengthy pedigree, the implementation of human rights legislation is constrained by an inability to protect and uphold human rights.

Humanitarian Intervention

Humanitarian intervention is defined as the use of military coercion with the aim of ending human rights violations within the host state (or region). The primary agent of alleviating human suffering is the UN – although great powers and regional powers can adopt a leading role without prior approval from the UN. The use of non-military forms of intervention such as economic sanctions and humanitarian aid may also be considered as part of a broader strategy. Humanitarian intervention entails three related characteristics. First and foremost, it consists of either the threat or use of military force. Secondly, humanitarian intervention involves sending military forces into the territory or airspace of another sovereign state. Finally, it is a coordinated response to situations that do not necessarily pose a direct threat to another's national interests. There have been a number of successful peacekeeping operations from the UN in countries ranging from El Salvador to Cambodia. However, in some cases peacekeeping has proved to be more complex including Somalia and Rwanda. The effectiveness of humanitarian intervention depends upon several factors such as the legitimacy of the international community's efforts, the existence of consent from the host state and the political will of participant states. Under international law, the use of force is authorised on the basis of either Chapter Seven of the UN Charter or as self-defence against armed attack. There is however a clear tension between national sovereignty and the exercise of humanitarian intervention. The debate over humanitarian intervention will always be an interplay of normative ethical issues and national interests.

United Nations Framework Convention on Climate Change (UNFCCC)

As the principal global covenant on climate change, the United Nations Framework Convention on Climate Change (UNFCCC) dates back to the Rio Summit in 1992. The aim of the UNFCCC is to stabilise greenhouse gas emissions into the atmosphere via non-binding limits upon countries. There is no enforcement mechanism but the framework outlines how international treaties may be negotiated to specify further action. The UNFCCC eventually entered into force two years later once a sufficient number of countries had ratified the Treaty. Since 1995, the parties to the convention have met on an annual basis in order to assess progress towards combating climate change. As a consequence of this, the Kyoto Protocol in 1997 established legally binding obligations upon developed countries to reduce their emissions. In 2010, the UN Climate Change Conference also specified a limit on future global warming. In the latest environmental agreement signed in 2016, the Paris Agreement seeks to limit greenhouse gas emissions by implementing the long-term goal of increasing the global average temperature to well below 2 degrees centigrade above pre-industrial levels. It also commits signatories to limit the increase to 1.5 degrees centigrade by the second half of this century. Finally, the Paris Agreement seeks to increase the ability of parties to adapt to the adverse impact of climate change. The UNFCCC applies to virtually all countries in the world.

Intergovernmental Panel on Climate Change (IPCC)

The IPCC is dedicated to providing scientific information relevant towards our understanding of climate change. The IPCC also offers potential responses to the problem of climate change. The IPCC was established in 1988 by the World Meteorological Organisation and the UN Environmental Programme (UNEP). The IPCC produces periodic reports that offer critical scientific input into the aforementioned United Nations Framework Convention on Climate Change (UNFCCC). The IPCC assesses published literature rather than conducting original research, and thereby stimulates scientific debate upon the issue of climate change. Reports published by the IPCC contain proposals for policymakers which go through a line-by-line process of approval by delegates from participating governments. The IPCC is therefore an internationally recognised authority on the existential threat posed by climate change.

Global Commons

The term 'global commons' depicts those international, supranational and resource domains in which common-pool resources are available. The global commons therefore includes shared natural resources such as the Antarctic, cyberspace and the atmosphere. Management of the global commons requires a legal structure that can deal with the dilemma posed by the tragedy of the commons. Systems need to be in place in order to prevent the depletion of non-renewable resources. In order to achieve this, there are several environmental treaties and associated protocols within international relations. Following the Stockholm Intergovernmental Conference in 1972, international environmental agreements have grown in terms of both scope and salience.

Tragedy of the Commons

The tragedy of the commons is a term widely used within the social sciences. It describes the situation in which individuals acting on their own rational self-interest behave in a manner contrary to that of the common good. Over time, such actions will result in a depletion of environmental resources. The term derives from a seminal article from the ecologist Garret Hardin (1968, 1244) and his famous quote that 'freedom in a commons brings ruin to all.' In a political context, the tragedy of the commons is commonly applied to the concept of sustainable development and the debate over global warming. The rational self-interest of individuals (and states) leads inevitably towards the overuse of non-renewable resources. The implications of the tragedy of the commons are therefore stark in terms of how we manage scarce resources based upon our unlimited wants. Attempts to address the tragedy of the commons presents a major problem in terms of global governance.

Sustainability / Sustainable Development

The terms sustainability and sustainable development are used interchangeably and relate to the environmental dimension of international relations. They can be thought of as that level of development that meets the needs of the present without compromising the ability of future generations to meet their own economic needs. Concerted attempts to address the issue of sustainability and sustainable development underline the mutual dependence of the global commons. The main forum for ensuring sustainability and long-term development is the United Nations. There are currently 17 sustainable development goals (SDGs) adopted by member states throughout the world. The SDGs are built upon an assumption that economic growth is compatible with protection of the environment. The issues raised by sustainability and sustainable development have undoubtedly gained greater prominence in recent years. Despite this, making real and lasting progress towards these goals by the year 2030 is difficult due to the lack of a higher supreme authority. As with all institutions and agreements associated with the concept of global governance, there is a reliance upon states to 'do the right thing'. Inevitably, this is highly problematic to achieve in practice. For instance, emerging economies are reluctant to accept any restrictions upon their own economic development from developed countries. Moreover, governments throughout the world place their own economic interests over those of the environment following the logic posed by the tragedy of the commons. The scientific evidence shows time and time again that we are living well beyond our environmental means.

BOX 4.2 – KEY POINTS FOR CHAPTER FOUR

1. International law is interpreted and upheld via a number of institutions.

2. One of the main areas of international law is the protection of human rights.

3. The universal character of human rights impacts the sovereignty of the state.

4. Humanitarian intervention is often criticised on the basis of hypocrisy and double standards.

5. The role and significance of the UNFCCC has grown considerably since 1992.

6. International law seeks to address issues such as preventing conflict and protecting the environment.

7. The significance of global civil society and non-state actors has grown over time.

5

Power and Development

The fifth chapter provides a detailed analysis of power and its broader importance. The typology of power plays a key role within this section alongside the consequences of polarity. The aim of the chapter is to place recent developments within the context of power and polarity. This entails a consideration of concepts such as hegemony, unilateralism and multilateralism. The various systems of government are also considered, ranging from stable democracies to failed states. In order to comprehend power and developments, the Middle East will be offered as a case study of a regional system of power relations.

Types of Power: 'Hard' and 'Soft' Power

The distinction between hard and soft power is a significant feature within the discourse of International Relations. In basic terms, hard power is the use (or threat) of force via military or economic resources. It is also based upon tangible resources such as the size of a state's nuclear arsenal or its armed forces. Soft power however is attractive or persuasive power. Unlike hard power, it is grounded upon intangible factors such as culture and ideology.

The academic most closely associated with 'soft power' is Joseph Nye. Nye defined soft power as the ability to shape the preferences of other countries via non-coercive methods. In contrast, hard power consists of ordering others to get what they want via the use (or threat) of force. Nye (1990) popularised the concept of soft power in his book '*Bound to lead*' which examined the changing nature of American foreign policy. Since then, the concept has been developed further as an integral part of international relations, power dynamics and foreign policy (Nye 2003). For instance, the diplomat Robert Cooper (2004) emphasises the importance of legitimacy towards the effective exercise of soft power.

The concept has shifted from the world of academia to its usage by policymakers such as Robert Gates, Tony Blair or Xi Jinping. For instance, the term has also gained added credence from an index of soft power, whereby every state has its soft power potential ranked, published by Portland Communications (2019). In 2019, for instance, France came top of the list – whilst the United States came in fifth place. In regards to the inclusion of international organisations into this mix, the Elcano Institute (2021) rated the European Union the highest for soft power presence in its 2020 Global Presence Index, higher than the US or China.

Hard power is a more conventional view of power politics. Hard power entails the use of military and economic means to determine the behaviour of other international actors. As the term clearly implies, hard power consists of an aggressive means to pressurise other agents to act in a certain manner. Hard power entails the ability to wield the 'carrot and the stick' in order to make others submit to demands. The former consists of economic inducements whilst the latter represents a credible and effective existential threat. In the case of the US, the high proportion of foreign aid allocated to Israel is an example of the former, whilst the threat of military action against rogue states is an illustration of the latter.

The concepts of hard and soft power are to some extent reflective of the binary debate that tends to govern our understanding of International Relations. The realist perspective is built around assumptions that gravitate towards talk of hard power. According to the realist stance, power stems from tangible resources that enable a country to get others to act in a manner that suits their particular interests. States can only ensure their survival via a military deterrent of some form. They must also forge alliances with others, delineated via the means of coercion. In an anarchic system, states must live by the maxim 'if you want peace … prepare for war.' Given the predominance of the realist perspective, it seems reasonable to assume that most of us hold an understanding of hard power as the status quo of what 'power' entails.

Soft power emerges from a slightly different set of assumptions. To some extent, it derives from a liberal lens due to its focus upon measures that might lead to a better world. The emphasis upon volunteer programmes is more consistent with a liberal worldview rather than a hard-headed realist conception of International Relations. Having said this, soft power is a descriptive rather than normative term. Soft power is entirely consistent with both democratic *and* dictatorial regimes. Tyrannical leaders such as Hitler, Mugabe and Stalin exercised a great deal of soft power due to their cult of personality. As Joseph Nye neatly points out 'it is not necessarily better to twist minds than to twist arms' (Nye 2006). He also reminds us that soft power is neither a form of idealism or even liberalism, it's merely a way of obtaining a desired outcome. Crucially, it does not contradict the realist perspective of International Relations.

The effectiveness of hard and soft power depends on a number of factors. In both cases, the most important is the credibility of the threat itself. Given its overwhelming military resources, it is entirely conceivable that the US could respond in a manner that matches the bombastic rhetoric of Donald Trump. This argument also applies in the economic realm. However, this is not to say that Washington can always utilise these resources in an effective manner. The President of the United States faces a number of constitutional constraints based upon an intricate system of checks and balances. For instance, the US Senate can reject treaties signed by the President. There are also times when the President is unable to gain international support for the use of power and therefore cannot offer a realistic threat.

Another dependent factor to consider is the legitimacy underpinning the use of power. The activities of the organisation concerned need to be perceived as legitimate in order to be effective. For instance, the spread of American cultural values within Eastern Europe during the Cold War proved a useful strategy in changing hearts and minds. Many of those living in the satellite states of the Soviet Union welcomed the materialistic goods offered by the American Dream. In stark contrast, the US has a credibility problem throughout most of the Arab world. In the case of hard power, the possession of a nuclear arsenal is rarely going to be seen as a legitimate strategy to employ. Despite having the capacity to plunge the planet into a nuclear winter, US President Lyndon Johnson once lamented 'the only power I've got is nuclear and I can't even use that!'.

A further factor to consider in terms of the effectiveness of hard and soft power is the accessibility of resources. Only the very wealthiest states have the financial capacity to maintain significant military forces and/or place economic pressure upon others. Smaller states however must rely upon their soft power. There are at present over thirty-six countries that do not have an army to defend their territory (Macias 2018). In addition, the historical legacy and constitution of a state may well determine the strength and effectiveness of its soft power. For instance, since 1945 Japan has relied upon resources provided by its alliance with Washington.

Another factor to consider here is that of time. The mobilisation of hard power is more straightforward because tangible resources can be mobilised relatively quickly. This usually means that hard power is more appropriate in the short-term. The persuasive element of soft power takes far longer to construct because of its intangible character. Whilst hard power entails coercion, the behaviour of those affected is involuntary. On the contrary, soft power changes attitudes gradually and on an entirely voluntary basis. In terms of effectiveness, consent offers a much better long-term basis for the successful exercise of power than coercion and conflict.

It is widely accepted that the changing dynamics of international relations have assisted the effectiveness of soft power (Gallarotti 2011). Soft power is the more effective strategy due to its sustainability over time. The ability to co-opt others in a persuasive manner is a far more salient illustration of how politics operates in an age of globalisation.

The changing nature of power was underlined graphically during the US-led invasion of Iraq. The strategy adopted by the Bush administration can be said to have failed in two ways. Firstly, decisionmakers ignored the need for sufficient military intelligence from their allies. Secondly, the question of how to generate legitimacy for the invasion was never adequately considered. These mistakes served to undermine America's standing in the world. Over time, this has been exacerbated by the treatment of enemy combatants held in the Abu Ghraib and Guantanamo Bay detention centres.

On a final note, the term 'smart power' is increasingly used. Smart power is the capacity to combine elements of hard and soft power in ways that are mutually reinforcing. Armitage and Nye (2007, 5) define the concept as 'an approach that underscores the necessity of a strong military, but also invests heavily in alliances, partnerships, and institutions.' An example of the effective use of smart power is the attempt by the United States to strengthen its presence within Africa. The Emergency Plan for AIDS Relief is the largest-ever commitment made by any country towards a global health initiative. This initiative has been combined with a financial aid programme tied to the practice of good governance. In addition, the US has just under 30 military bases on the continent. Such examples to some degree underline the argument that the borders between the two concepts have become blurred. Indeed, some foreign policy strategies may be perceived as an effective combination of both modalities of power (Smith-Windsor 2000).

The Differing Significance of For Classifications of State Power, Polarity and World Order, and Regime Types

Classifications of State Power: Great Powers

Great powers can be defined as those who are recognised as holding the ability and capacity to project their influence on a global scale. The status of a great power is conventionally characterised on the basis of three criteria: power capabilities, spatial aspects and status dimensions. In terms of its spatial dimension, a great power should hold and exert influence within the inter-state system. This helps us to distinguish a regional power, such as Iraq, from a great power with an actual presence upon the world stage, such as France. Finally, there has to be some formal or informal recognition from others. The status entails both rights and obligations within an institution-alised structure.

Whilst the term is inherently contentious, it is usually clear who the great powers are based upon these three criteria. For instance, great powers meet on a regular basis in a formal setting, such as the economically advanced states of the G7. Great powers also possess a significant element of military, economic and diplomatic power. For instance, the five permanent members sitting on the UN Security Council possess nuclear weapons and the ability to exercise their veto. Great powers are also likely to be invited on an informal basis to help resolve complex disputes, such as the contact group dealing with the political fall-out in the Balkans during the wars of the 1990s (US, UK, France, Germany, Russia, and representatives from NATO and the EU).

There is however no universal agreement as to what exactly constitutes a great power. Milena Sterio (2013, xii) claims that 'the great powers are an exclusive club of the most powerful states economically, militarily, politically and strategically.' From the neorealist position, Kenneth Waltz (1993) identifies five criteria of a great power: population/territory, resource endowment, economic capability, political stability and military strength. During the nineteenth century, the German historian Leopold von Ranke (2011, 43) observed in an 1833 essay that a great power 'must be able to maintain itself against all others.'

Although each contribution is useful, none of them completely clarifies matters due to the absence of a precise measurement. Accordingly, there are several grey areas that are presented here. For instance, both Japan and Germany could be considered great powers in terms of their economic clout (Gunning and Baron 2014). Having said this, neither country has a permanent seat on the UN Security Council. As a result of their historical baggage, neither country projects a far-reaching military presence abroad. In addition, Mohan Malik (2011) has argued that India should be classed as a great power although the country is often classed as an emerging power.

Given the vague character of the term 'great power', it might be more useful to distinguish between superpowers and middle-ranking powers. For instance, it probably makes more sense to categorise four of the five permanent members of the UNSC as middle-ranking powers because their combined military resources are dwarfed by the US. However, this observation is not unanimously accepted by either analysts or policymakers. One thing we can say with certainty is that the status of a great power comes with responsibilities attached. The maintenance of order and stability within the anarchic system requires some degree of intervention from great powers. This could even be applied to an international organisation such as the EU.

Those countries and organisations that may be classed as great powers fluctuate over time. In recent years, China has made impressive strides in both its economic and military standing. This has led some to predict that China will eventually be classed as a superpower, and that the distribution of power within international relations will gravitate towards bipolarity. Since the mid-noughties, there have been a number of proposals for an informal special relationship between the US and China, primarily upon an economic basis. This would be known as the group of 2 (or G2).

Although tensions have always existed between the great powers, direct military conflicts are largely a thing of the past. The academic Joshua Baron (2013) argues that the main reason for this welcome trend centres upon the primacy of American military power. Secondly, there is a degree of consensus among great powers that military force is no longer an effective tool for resolving disputes. Since the Cuban Missile Crisis, influential Western nations have largely resolved disputes amongst themselves in a peaceful manner via diplomacy. The 'West' has also been keen to avoid an escalation of political tensions with either China or Russia. This brings us to the category of 'The Superpower'.

Classifications of State Power: Superpowers

A 'superpower' is more than first among equals, it is first *without* equals. As the hegemonic state, a superpower swaggers around the global stage. The source of their power derives from both hard and soft power, although there is often an overt and unmistakable emphasis upon the former. It is the only country that meets the criteria laid down by scholars such as Paul Dukes (2000, 1), who describes a superpower as one 'able to conduct a global strategy including the possibility of destroying the world: to command vast economic potential and influence; and to present a universal ideology.'

In a system characterised by unipolarity, only one state, by definition, is classed as a superpower. Under a bipolar system, there are two superpowers in existence. During the Cold War, there were two rival superpowers with a defined sphere of influence. International politics was shaped by an ideological battle for the very future of mankind. In proxy wars during that time, the US and USSR supported an assortment of insurgents and governments throughout the world. The division between the two superpowers was embedded within two military alliances facing off against each other. Although there were attempts to create a form of global governance and foster a sense of multilateralism, the period between 1945 and 1991 was overshadowed by relations between the two superpowers.

Since the collapse of the USSR, the US has emerged as the world's only military superpower. As a hegemonic power, even the symbolism of its diplomatic actions can have major repercussions in various hotspots of the world. For instance, Donald Trump's surprise decision to move the American embassy from Tel Aviv to Jerusalem empowered the Israeli state. In addition, his description of Jerusalem as the 'undivided capital of Israel' is of a magnitude that no other state could reasonably command.

In the post-Cold War era, the US experienced what became known as 'the unipolar moment'. The United States no longer had to contain the spread of communism. Given the realities of the new world order, Samuel Huntington (1999, 36) observed that the United States was now the only country 'with pre-eminence in every domain of power...with the reach and capabilities to promote its interests in virtually every part of the world.' To underline his point, in 1999 the French Foreign Minister, Hubert Verdine, memorably described the US as a 'hyper-power', due to its dominance within international relations.

Samuel Huntington (1999, 35–36) similarly argued that the world should be characterised as a hybrid system known as a 'uni-multipolar system' with one superpower alongside several major powers. In a uni-multipolar system, there are a number of emerging powers. This is most noticeable within the economic realm with China likely to overtake the US on the basis of current economic trends. China may also utilise its military capacity in order to secure a geostrategic advantage in the South China Sea. Having said this, China still lacks the necessary level of soft power comparable to a truly global superpower.

The military and political resources held by Russia also presents some counter-balance to American hegemony. The Russian Federation has a military presence within the Middle East that limits the ability of the United States to impose its own particular agenda in the region (notably in its relations with Iran and Syria). Having said this, the Russian Federation is nowhere close to the geopolitical status of the former Soviet Union. In the Global Firepower ranking to determine a nation's Power Index, Russia is ranked a distant second to the United States (Global Fire Power 2021).

In this uni-multipolar system, another emerging superpower to consider is the European Union. When conventional wisdom gravitates towards military capacity, it is problematic to classify the EU in this manner. However, the soft power of the organisation is highly impressive. It is the world's largest single market and has diplomatic representation at the top table of global governance. The civilian power of the EU demands a re-examination of traditional realist conceptions of power within the academic field.

The term 'potential superpower' offers a useful conceptual toolkit to comprehend contemporary international relations. In the economic realm, the emerging powers of the BRICS could be classed in such a manner. This is likely to have implications for the future distribution of power within international relations. For instance, relations between Washington and Beijing are likely to have considerable economic and political consequences. Given the economic might of the two nations, a trade war between Washington and Beijing would have a devastating impact upon the global economy.

The European Union may also be described as a potential superpower, particularly if it continues to enhance its capacity within the realm of hard power. The process of European integration has already created a Common Foreign and Security Policy. In terms of its defence capacity, the EU can also mobilise a multi-national battlegroup. Having said all this, forecasting future superpowers will always prove a hostage to fortune. During the 1980s, it was widely predicted that Japan would overtake the United States as the world's largest economy. However, the country experienced a major economic slowdown known as the 'lost decade'. A similar fate may befall China at some stage, although this would be speculation. It is also entirely probable that emerging powers will decline in influence due to an interplay of domestic and external factors. Indeed, it is worth reminding ourselves that during the mid-80s a third of the world's population lived under a communist system of government. Even the United States might experience a rapid decline comparable to other historical superpowers of the past (Kennedy 1987).

On a final note, it is important to recognise that there are considerable limitations upon the ability of a superpower to either coerce or persuade others. For instance, the US has singularly failed to secure an end to the Syrian Civil War or bring lasting peace to the Arab-Israeli conflict. It is also telling that Washington has repeatedly sought to gain support from various allies and organisations. Despite its overwhelming military capacity, American foreign policy is largely consistent with a strategy of multilateralism.

Classifications of State Power: Emerging Powers

There is a perplexing list of acronyms that seek to bracket emerging countries together. However, there is no objective measure of classifying an emerging power from other ranks of power. The one constant characteristic of an emerging power is the existence of a rapidly growing economy. This is based upon the assumption that economic development is a prerequisite for an expansion in both political and military presence. By definition, an emerging power seeks to gain a more powerful role and enhanced status amongst the hierarchy of states. It therefore needs sufficient resources to enhance their relative position.

Alongside a burgeoning economy, there are other dimensions of state power that determine a country's status as an emerging power. These include geography, population, resources, military capacity, diplomacy and national identity. Only a great power (or a superpower) can be said to hold all seven dimensions of state power. On this basis, it is clear that South Africa can only be an emerging power because of its decision to abandon its nuclear weapons programme. In addition, India is classed as an emerging power due to social underdevelopment amongst its population. Unlike great powers, it still has a relatively high rate of illiteracy and malnutrition (Panda et al. 2020).

Another characteristic of an emerging power is an attempt to enhance their influence in global affairs. This can be achieved via an expansion in their military capacity, or in a greater ability to utilise their economic resources. Emerging powers can also be classified via a willingness to be identified by others in this manner. The G20 for instance consists of emerging economic powers such as Indonesia, Mexico and Turkey. Along with Nigeria, these so-called 'MINTs' are predicted to become the next batch of emerging economies.

As with other relative terms, there is a debate as to which international actors have moved from their previous status of an emerging power. For instance, the EU is widely considered to have passed from an emerging power to a potential superpower (Moravcsik 2009, 2010). There is considerable evidence to support this view. The EU is in possession of significant political and economic power, a spatial presence and status throughout world affairs. The emergence of the European Union has been facilitated by the growing significance of what Joseph Nye dubbed soft power.

There are a number of emerging powers who undoubtedly have the potential to follow the same trajectory as the European Union. According to the political scientist David Robinson (2011), India is now a great power. For instance, India has the second largest army in the world and is the second most populous country in the world. In terms of a qualitative measurement, the State Power Index for 2017 ranked India, underlined by its nuclear capacity and ambitions, above both France and the United Kingdom. However, according to the Global Diplomacy Index (Lowy Institute 2019) India still sits behind countries such as Turkey and Spain, ranking at twelfth globally.

In the case of Brazil, it could be argued that it will eventually emerge as a great power with an important position in terms of its sphere of influence. As the leading regional power of South America, Brazil's strength lies in its military capacity and a rapidly expanding economy. It is perhaps worth noting here that Brazil is also a member of the G4, which campaigns for a permanent seat on the UNSC (alongside India, Japan and Germany). This is clearly indicative of how the country's policymakers perceive Brazil's relative power.

When considering a typology of states, it is important to note that overlaps are commonplace. For instance, China is rightly referred to as an emerging superpower based upon its economic might. Confusingly, it is sometimes classed as a great power or superpower. Equally, the Russian Federation emerged as the successor state to a superpower (the Soviet Union). Whilst Russia is often called a great power, it is also classed as an emerging power as part of the BRICS. It could also be argued that Russia is actually re-emerging as a global force. Given that such vague typologies exist, there will always be some level of overlap to consider.

Polarity and The Implications of Power Structures

Polarity describes the various modes by which power is distributed within the international system of states. Although the term is commonly applied to states, it is also applicable to international organisations. There are three main categories of polarity and the distinction between each holds implications for global peace and stability. These three modalities of polarity dynamics are: unipolar, bipolar and multipolar.

In order to provide a proper assessment, it is important to define the actual meaning of stability within the context of international relations. According to the neorealist Kenneth Waltz (1979), stability refers to the avoidance of warfare or conflict. This is a definition which recognises that a conflict of interests is inevitable, but that armed conflict is not. Developing this point further, Karl Deutsch and J. David Singer (1964, 390) define stability as 'the probability that the system retains all of its essential characteristics; that no single nation becomes dominant; that most of its members continue to survive; and that large-scale war does not occur'. Their definition introduces the notion of equilibrium (or balance) amongst states, avoiding the emergence of a single state that structurally dominates the entire global power system without any potential rival – a 'hegemon'.

Unipolarity

In a unipolar system, there is a single state classed as a superpower. In a system based upon unipolarity, the hegemonic state has the capacity to act as the unofficial world's policeman. In doing so, the hegemon maintains order within the inherently anarchic international system of states.

There are a number of illuminating historical illustrations of a hegemonic power acting as the world's policemen, both atop and in control of the global power structure. Between 1815 and 1914, the British Empire intervened in regional wars to balance out power alliances between rival states. However, it is not the case that a hegemonic power is necessarily willing to intervene in every facet of foreign affairs. A superpower will invariably be limited by its own national interests, its capacity to mobilise resources, domestic politics and a historical tendency to overreach (Kennedy 1987). More importantly, international law is based upon the concept of non-intervention and a tacit acceptance that all nations are equal. This is vested in the Latin phrase: *par in parem non habet imperium* (equals have no sovereignty over one another).

Given its massive levels of military spending, the United States has often expressed a desire to place a limit upon its overseas military commitments. Administrations from both main parties have applied pressure upon their allies to shoulder more of the burden. It is also the case that the world's only military superpower has sought to gain support from key allies. For instance, when it commits ground troops or enforces a no-fly zone it does so with the assistance of others (as in the case of Libya in 2011).

The willingness of a hegemonic power to act as the world's policeman by military intervention can oscillate considerably. Since the War on Terror was launched in 2001, the US has repeatedly engaged in military action. However, it has also chosen not to intervene despite the capacity to take swift and decisive action, as in the earlier case of Rwanda in 1994. This reflects a conflicting tradition within the states between engagement and isolation, and these forces continue to shape contemporary American foreign policy.

According to some theorists, a unipolar system provides the best guarantee of stability. For instance, William Wohlforth (1999) claims that unipolarity is peaceful because the distribution of power removes the problem of hegemonic rivalry. Secondly, it reduces the stakes associated with balance of power considerations amongst major states. Wohlforth's argument is based upon hegemonic stability theory, which stipulates that the larger the concentration of power into the hands of the pre-eminent state, the more peaceful the international order will be. Hegemonic stability theory is associated with a number of theorists, but it dates back to Charles P. Kindleberger (1973).

However, this theory has been subject to criticism. Professor Nuno P. Monteiro (2011) argues that warfare is endemic to a unipolar system. Taking issue with Wohlforth, he argues that unipolarity results in two distinct types of war. These include wars contested by a superpower against relatively weaker states, and those involving two (or more) minor powers. It is an argument supported by the immediate aftermath of the end of the Cold War. The United States has been at war for over half of this period, whilst warfare between relatively smaller powers has occurred repeatedly since the early 1990s.

The dependent factor to consider here are the intentions that drive the global hegemon. A benign hegemon is likely to ensure peace and stability in accordance with its role as the world's global norms forger and enforcer. They can place their own narrow interests to one side in order to uphold the status quo. In stark contrast, a predatory hegemon will use its power purely for its own benefit. In the absence of any effective counterbalance, a predatory hegemon is free to pursue its own interests without any due regard for the broader international system. This can easily lead to instability within the global system and a potential shift in polarity or power dynamics.

Bipolarity

The term bipolarity is applied to a political system in which two powers of roughly equal strength act as a check upon the power of their opponent. The most obvious example of a bipolar system remains the Cold War between the US and the USSR. Under bipolarity, a superpower acts as a security guarantor for weaker states. In a nuclear age, the stability of a bipolar system rests upon the concept of 'Mutually Assured Destruction' (MAD). MAD is built upon the assumption that the potential devastation of nuclear war guarantees that neither side will launch a first strike. During the Cold War, both superpowers claimed to possess nuclear weapons solely to act as a deterrent. As a result of an arms race, both sides accumulated a level of nuclear armament that would have led to complete annihilation if either power declared war on the other – thereby deterring direct conflict.

From a structural realist perspective, Kenneth Waltz (1979) argued that bipolarity is the most stable form of power distribution. A bipolar system reduces uncertainty because each superpower relies solely upon its own resources. In contrast, unipolarity is the least durable of international configurations, whilst multipolarity greatly increases the level of uncertainty.

If we apply his argument to the Cold War, it is true that there was no direct confrontation between the two superpowers. For a period lasting well over four decades, a 'hot' war between the two rivals was avoided. However, there were a high number of proxy wars from the Angolan Civil War to the Vietnam War. In many cases, the proxy wars were instigated when a country gained national independence from its former colonial rulers. Given the dynamics of the Cold War era, a newly independent state often created a chain of events that pulled the superpowers into the orbit of the conflict.

Another issue raised within a bipolar system is the existence of an arms race. During the Cold War, both countries allocated extensive resources towards obtaining the latest weaponry. Not only was the acquisition of such weaponry costly, it also posed a number of security issues. On the basis of a simple miscommunication, the world came close to nuclear war during the stand-off between Kennedy and Khrushchev over Cuba in 1962. This problem of 'brinkmanship' is also present in ongoing tensions between nuclear-armed India and Pakistan.

A bipolar system also suffers from the problems posed by the security dilemma. The Cold War was an era marked by mutual suspicion and paranoia between the US and the USSR. Although not unique to a bipolar system, the security dilemma can result in a serious deterioration in relations between the two superpowers. In 1983, the world twice came perilously close to a full-scale nuclear war. In November of that year, NATO launched a military exercise called Able Archer. Given the planned arrival of Pershing II nuclear weapons into mainland Europe, the Soviet Politburo viewed Able Archer as preparation for an all-out attack. Before this event, a false alarm on the Soviet side could have easily set in motion a series of events that may have brought the superpowers into direct conflict.

Multipolarity

The third and final system to consider is that of multipolarity. As the term implies, it is defined as a distribution of power in which more than two states have roughly equal amounts of influence. Whilst this is often measured in a military manner, it is also applied on an economic basis. In a system based upon multipolarity, alliances tend to shift until two scenarios occur. The first is that a balance of power is established so that neither side has an incentive to attack the other for fear of reprisal. Alternatively, one side will attack the other because it can effectively defeat the other side (such as the Nazi Blitzkrieg during the early stages of the Second World War). These dependent factors must be considered for any reasonable assessment of the stability (or otherwise) of a multipolar system.

The argument that multipolarity results in peace and stability is a contentious one. During the Concert of Europe, in the nineteenth century, the great powers of Europe assembled on a regular basis to discuss international and domestic affairs. This was built upon the shared principle of collective responsibility for peace and stability within Europe. Although the system did bring some form of peace between the rival powers, the Concert of Europe came to an end due to the Crimean War. Equally, the multipolarity that characterised relations between the great powers during the 1920s and 1930s failed to prevent the rise of fascism and the resultant Second World War.

In a theoretical context, classical realists such as E.H. Carr (2016) argue that multipolar systems are relatively stable because the great powers are able to enhance their status via alliances and petty wars that in no way directly challenge other states. In contrast, neorealists claim that there is less chance of miscalculation under a bipolar system. To substantiate their argument, a distinction can be made between 'internal' and 'external' balancing. Under the former, states enhance their own capabilities. External balancing however occurs when they enter into an alliance to check the power of more powerful states. As there is only internal balancing in a bipolar system, there is less chance of a miscalculation. War between the superpowers is therefore avoided. In contrast, the great powers within a multipolar system might misjudge the intentions of others and engage in external balancing that eventually leads to warfare.

The academic Joseph Nye further alludes to the changing nature of power with his argument that global politics increasingly resembles a three-dimensional game of chess. In the military arena, power is concentrated into the hands of the United States. Economic power however is distributed in a multipolar manner whilst transnational issues such as climate change require a multitude of actors. It therefore makes little sense to view the world solely through realist prism as this would exaggerate the potential for conflict. Equally, the liberal perspective is flawed in its prediction of cooperation on the basis of mutual dependence. Viewed from a three-dimensional basis, states adopt a smart strategy to deal with different distributions of power in different domains. Nye's argument (2011, 213) that 'the world is neither unipolar, multipolar nor chaotic – it is all three at the same time' remains a salient and perceptive conclusion as to the consequences of polarity within the world order.

The Changing Nature of World Order Since 2000

At the turn of the century, the United States was so dominant it was described by some as a 'hyper-power'. It was *the* hegemonic power in a system based upon unipolarity. However, the hierarchy of states is in a constant state of flux and few expected the US to retain its position unchallenged. Since the year 2000, world order has been disrupted by the emergence of the BRICS (particularly China). American prestige has also been damaged due to the controversial intervention in Iraq, the 2008 financial crash and a growing willingness amongst emerging economies to challenge Washington. The hegemony of the United States has thereby come under attack in terms of both hard power and soft power.

In seeking to assess the changing nature of international relations, it is important to differentiate the various dimensions of power – as the picture is a highly uneven one. Militarily, the US remains without question the world's only superpower. It has a global presence, and it has no peer competitor in the way that the Soviet Union once was. According to the International Institute for Strategic Studies (2020, 21), in 2019 the United States spent $684.6 billion on defence – accounting for over a third of all global military spending. The US has personnel in dozens of countries and a naval and air capability that can be deployed to multiple theatres of conflict. Such figures underline the global capabilities of the world's only military superpower.

The picture is however more mixed when we consider the economic dimension. On the basis of nominal GDP, the US is still the world's largest economy. However, in terms of purchasing power parity the US has already lost out to China. This image is also made more complex by the relative slowdown in the American economy compared to the rapid growth of emerging economies. If current trends continue, the US will, more than likely, lose its economic dominance.

Finally, in terms of soft power, the United States still has an international reach. It provides a considerable amount of international aid in various regions and has the most diplomatic missions of any country in the world. Yet having said this, quantitative measures do not in themselves mean that the world order is necessarily dominated by the US. Even with its considerable military arsenal, the United States has not always managed to translate hard power into a satisfactory outcome. There are several case studies that can be used to analyse this line of argument.

Since the beginning of the century, the United States has intervened in several areas of the world. Most of these interventions have been to ensure a specific objective (e.g., the US deployed a patrol craft in the year 2000 to support evacuation operations from Sierra Leone), or on the basis of drone strikes (as in Pakistan between 2004 and 2018). In relative terms, these interventions have been small-scale. The two most significant long-term interventions were based in Iraq and Afghanistan.

In 2001, the US launched the Orwellian-sounding 'Operation Enduring Freedom' when it dispatched armed forces to invade the failed state of Afghanistan. Without a military presence from the US, it seems inconceivable that a coalition of over forty countries would have defeated the Taliban. American troops finally began to leave the war-torn state in 2014. Nonetheless, around half of all military personnel that were deployed in order to guarantee security derived from the US. Intervention in Afghanistan was the longest war in American history. However, with the full withdrawal of all NATO troops and missions in the summer of 2021, the Taliban regained control within a matter of days – bringing a greater sense of instability back to the region.

In 2003, the United States led a 'coalition of the willing' with the goal to disarm Iraq and ensure regime change. American troops finally withdrew eight years later at a total cost running into several trillion dollars. Although a number of other countries were involved, most of the ground troops were from the US. No other country in the contemporary era could likely fight two major wars simultaneously. It therefore seems reasonable to conclude that the global world order is underpinned by American hegemony.

In contrast, the balance of power has shifted considerably within the economic realm. The credit crunch and the 2008 financial crisis inflicted a major blow upon its international standing, and the US cannot dominate an international organisation comparable to say NATO. It must also negotiate on a bilateral basis with a number of emerging economies and seek some form of accommodation (particularly with the Chinese government).

There are also unmistakable signifiers of the multipolarity that characterises the global economy. For instance, the five countries that make up the BRICS have established the New Development Bank to rival the World Bank (which they claim is biased towards Washington). China is also flexing its economic muscles via the 'Belt and Road initiative' which involves infrastructure development and investments in nearly 70 countries. China has also engaged in currency manipulation and protectionism despite repeated complaints from the United States.

On a bilateral basis, it is abundantly clear that the US must reach some form of compromise with other major powers. For instance, the US had to reach a compromise with the Indian government over agricultural subsidies and faced stiff opposition from the developing nations during the 2003 WTO conference in Cancún, Mexico. In the contemporary world order, policymakers in Washington have to accept that they cannot dictate the rules of the game. Despite its economic might, the United States must negotiate with other actors and accept the constraints of complex interdependence.

Regime Types

Democratic, Semi-Democratic, Non-Democratic and Autocratic States

After the collapse of the Soviet Union, there was a sense of triumphalism within Western circles. Francis Fukuyama captured the spirit of the time with his argument that we had reached the conceptual 'end of history'. Liberal democracy had won the ideological battle against communism. Fukuyama (1989, 1992) predicted that countries throughout the world would embrace liberal values such as universal human rights alongside a political system built upon democratic accountability.

Since the end of the Cold War, the number of democratic states in the world has grown exponentially. According to metrics produced by Polity IV and Freedom House, around half of all regimes can be classed as democratic systems. Many of those once rated as dictatorial or autocratic have made some progress towards democracy. However, in more recent times, there has been a shift towards authoritarianism, illiberal democracy and a surge in nationalist populism. The unipolar moment that characterised the aftermath of the Cold War has also been challenged by the rise of the BRICS (especially China) and the damage done to the credibility of the liberal world order in recent years.

In order to more properly assess this in relation to global order, it is important to highlight the various characteristics of a democratic state. A democratic state is one that combines a multi-party electoral process with a range of civil liberties (such as freedom of assembly). The power of elected figures is constrained by democratic norms, an independent judiciary and a free media. The political culture of a democratic system is supportive of basic freedoms and fundamental principles. Democracies are relatively common within North America, Europe and Australasia. In terms of population, the world's largest democracy is India.

By contrast, a semi-democratic state combines both democratic and authoritarian elements. Such regimes are usually characterised by a mix of political stability and media censorship. In a semi-democratic state, democratic values and practices exist alongside authoritarian measures. For these reasons, a semi-democratic state is often classed as a hybrid system. One of the most significant examples of a hybrid system is Russia. Given its considerable natural resources and military might, the Russian Federation is one of the major powers on the world stage.

The very existence of semi-democratic states casts valuable insight into the appropriateness or otherwise of democratic values. As a result of their history and political culture, certain countries may be better suited to a form of semi-democracy. A number of Asian states have done exceptionally well in terms of economic growth and political stability on a hybrid basis (such as Singapore and Indonesia). The shift in the global balance of power towards the East may well lead to a greater examination of Eurocentric assumptions that shape our understanding of democracy and its desirability. In particular, the increased political and economic significance of China offers a challenge to liberal assumptions concerning the desirability of democracy.

In a non-democratic state, elections are held without a choice provided to the electorate. In an autocratic state, such as North Korea, the leader holds absolute power, whilst in a non-democratic state power is concentrated into the hands of the ruling party. In historical terms, the number of autocratic regimes reached its peak in the mid-1970s. Since then, such a regime has seen a rapid decline globally. That said, certain autocratic regimes can remain significant due to their geostrategic position. For instance, Saudi Arabia is embroiled in proxy wars within the Middle East and allocates the largest percentage of national income in the world to military expenditure.

Given these various typologies, it is often useful to measure the level of democracy. According to the Economist's Intelligence Unit's Democracy Index, the state of democracy is based upon five measures (the functioning of government, political participation, electoral process, democratic political culture and civil liberties). According to the Economist Intelligence Unit (2021), democracy is currently in retreat with the global score at its lowest since measurements were first taken. Just over twenty countries were classed as full democracies whilst nearly a third of all countries surveyed were 'flawed democracies' (including the US). The study also found that more than a third of the world's population live under authoritarian rule.

Failed States

In the contemporary world order, failed states pose a genuine dilemma for the international community. Given the potential impact of its disintegration, a failed state often holds geostrategic implications that go beyond its immediate neighbouring states. Having said this, the international community largely ignores failed states in which intervention yields little economic or political benefit; the 1992 intervention in Somalia evidencing this claim.

Although an inherently subjective term, the think-tank 'Fund for Peace' identifies a number of characteristics by which to define a failed state. Firstly, there is a loss of control over its territory. The state can no longer satisfy the Weberian definition of holding a monopoly upon the legitimate use of coercion. A failed state is also unable to perform the basic functions of the state (such as collecting taxes). In addition, it may be incapable of exercising legitimate authority within its territorial boundaries and in relations with other states. Whereas a weak state may have some degree of functionality, a failed state is neither functioning nor legitimate. The Fund for Peace (2021) publishes an annual fragile states index (formerly known as the failed states index) with Yemen ranked as the country with the highest level of alert in 2021.

Since the turn of the century, a number of states have met (and continue to meet) the definition of a failed state. However, in the world of realpolitik there is no universally agreed criteria by which to define a failed state. As such, the identification of a failed state is open to interpretation. This can mean that the hegemonic power imposes its own definition for their own particular interests. For instance, the United States has a clear geostrategic interest in Afghanistan and Iraq. The Afghanistan-Pakistan border, known as the 'Durand Line', is a recruiting ground for Islamic fundamentalists, and there are significant oil reserves in Iraq.

There are a number of interesting case studies of failed states throughout the world. In 1991, a civil war broke out in Somalia when armed opposition groups ousted the government. In 1992, UNOSOM I (UN Operation in Somalia) was launched in order to re-establish order. Shortly afterwards, the Unified Task Force was dispatched following the failure of the UN's monitoring mission. A later mission entitled UNOSOM II marked the follow-up phase of foreign intervention in Somalia with a mandate to encourage nation-building. Each intervention aimed at establishing a secure environment for humanitarian operations in the absence of a central government. Unlike other military interventions within failed states, the initial involvement of the international community did not present any real controversy. Around forty countries sent military and civilian personnel.

The main issue that faced military intervention in Somalia was the failure to gain ground support from warring factions. American involvement was curtailed after the Battle of Mogadishu, in which images of dead soldiers being dragged through the streets were broadcast. As a result of changing public opinion, President Clinton withdrew American forces (shortly followed by the UN doing the same). Since the mid-1990s, emphasis has been placed upon reconciliation talks between leaders of various factions. The UN estimates that over two and a half million people now live in protracted internal displacement and face serious human rights abuses (Human Rights Watch 2019).

Although intervention in Somalia helped save lives, the inability of the international community to maintain its resolve is a repetitive narrative. During the Rwandan genocide in 1994, the international community refused to intervene once the genocide took place and abandoned the people of Rwanda when they most needed protection. A report carried out by the UN found that the organisation and its member states failed to prevent a civil war between Hutus and Tutsis, undermining its own purpose as set forth in the UN Charter.

In one of the worst illustrations of ethnic cleansing, the UN force in Rwanda was sent without a mandate to use all necessary force. Their purpose was limited to peacekeeping based on an accord signed between the warring parties, but as there was no peace to keep their presence was ineffectual. Despite requests from the UN peacekeeping force, led by Roméo Dallaire, for increased military support, the UN Security Council scaled back intervention out of   a reluctance to be dragged into another quagmire similar to Somalia. In the perceptive words of the journalist Lindsey Hilsum (1994) 'the UN is only as effective as the great powers want it to be. In Rwanda's case, they did not choose to care until it was too late.'

Whilst the experience of Somalia and Rwanda paints a broadly similar picture, the increasingly contemporary failed state of Syria is markedly different. In contrast to the states discussed above, a number of powers have a clear political interest at stake. The US, Russia, Iran, Saudi Arabia, Qatar, Israel, NATO and Turkey have all been involved in the Syrian Civil War since its beginnings in 2011. The Assad regime is supported by Iran, Russia and the Lebanese militant group Hezbollah. In contrast, the neighbouring Turkish government is opposed to the Assad regime. Turkey also occupies parts of North-Western Syria due to concerns about an influx of Kurdish refugees. The US-led coalition has conducted air strikes against Islamic State and areas seen as supportive of the Assad regime. NATO sides with the United States, and although its position is officially neutral; the Israeli government has launched attacks on Iranian and Hezbollah militants.

The situation in Syria is a highly delicate one, especially due to: the prospect of Islamic extremists spreading their influence in northern Iraq, the potential escalation of conflict between Turkey and the Kurds, the prospect of the war crossing over into Lebanon, the on-going refugee crisis and the abuse of human rights within the war-torn country. Despite attempts to broker peace, fighting has continued with no obvious or immediate prospect of a resolution in sight.

Since the turn of the century, the two most important military interventions in failed states have occurred in Afghanistan and Iraq. In 2001, an invasion led primarily by the United States sought to remove the Taliban from power in retaliation for the terrorist attacks of 9/11. The Taliban had also seized control of Kabul in 1996 and imposed a fundamentalist interpretation of Islam. Although the American-led alliance quickly drove the Taliban from power, the task of repairing the failed state proved more protracted. In order to ensure stability, the UN Security Council established an International Security Assistance Force (ISAF) to train and assist National Security Forces, which ended its mission in 2021. One of the most intractable problems in dealing with a failed state is the potential for insurgent groups to reform, as seen clearly with the Taliban's re-ascendance to power in 2021 with the withdrawal of the ISAF.

The international community's involvement in Iraq was always more controversial than intervention in Afghanistan. Opponents of the invasion argued that the United States was motivated solely by economic benefits. The manner in which military action was justified did a great deal of damage to the credibility of American hegemony. It has also made it more difficult for a US president to mobilise public and congressional support for subsequent foreign interventions.

Perhaps the most important lesson from the invasion of Iraq is the inability of the international community to 'fix' a failed state. Despite considerable military resources and financial expense; the US-led alliance has failed to repair the state of Iraq. Being an invention of colonial powers with no shared national identity, sectarian divisions have posed a major problem. Secondly, the historical traditions of a failed state often tend to be of a non-democratic character. Democracy can only really be effective when the domestic environment is amenable. It has also proved problematic to resolve deep-rooted problems surrounding corruption within the Baghdad-based regime.

Rogue States

As with the term failed states, a rogue state is another somewhat subjective phrase. The definition of which countries should be classed as rogue is skewed towards the worldview adopted by great powers within the global world order. Those allied to the United States are therefore highly unlikely to be classed as rogue. It is also possible for a powerful state to act in a manner contrary to international law without being classed as rogue. Moreover, there are some situations in which great powers may disagree over which states should be labelled in such a manner. For instance, the US and Russia hold opposing views of the Assad regime in Syria. Similarly, the Chinese government has political ties with North Korea whilst the rest of the world views the North Korean regime as a rogue state.

There are some fundamental observations that could be applied to the term rogue state. Firstly, a rogue state is a threat to global peace and stability. This may entail possession of Weapons of Mass Destruction (WMDs), state-sponsored terrorism or a regime that acts in a manner contrary to international norms. Given these characteristics, it is clear that some countries are able to change their classification. For instance, the United States removed Libya from its state-sponsored terrorism list during the mid-noughties. Equally, the Trump administration described Venezuela as a 'dangerous narco-state' due to human rights violations and international drug trafficking.

The term rogue state has also been subject to changing developments. Under the Clinton administration, the term was replaced by the phrase 'states of concern', whilst the Bush administration used the term 'Axis of Evil' (referring primarily to Iran, Iraq and North Korea) after the terrorist attacks of 9/11. The phrase 'rouge state' has also been used by countries other than the US. For instance, Turkey has labelled Greece in this manner due to its alleged support for Kurdish groups. The Ankara-based government also declared Syria as a rogue state for shooting down a Turkish warplane. Somewhat fittingly, the term has been used against the Turkish government due to the authoritarian policies implemented by President Recep Erdogan.

The threat posed by a rogue state differs significantly throughout the world. Given its military arsenal and diplomatic isolation, the regime in Pyongyang poses a very real danger to the world. North Korea has already fired several short-range missiles into the Sea of Japan. However, there has at least been some rapprochement with South Korea in recent years. In contrast, the case of Iran is a more nuanced one. Since the turn of the century, the Iranian nuclear programme has raised understandable concerns and led to international sanctions. Yet unlike in Pyongyang, the regime in Tehran is more amenable to international diplomacy. In 2015, an agreement was reached with the P5 (plus Germany and the EU) to restrict the production of enriched uranium whilst weakening some of the sanctions imposed against Iran.

The Development and Spread of: Liberal Economics, The Rule of Law and Democratic Peace

The Development and Spread of Liberal Economics

The development and spread of liberal economics enable us to consider the liberal perspective on International Relations. According to a number of liberal thinkers, the spread of liberal democracy should create a more stable and peaceful world. There is a considerable body of literature within global politics that supports the spread and development of liberal economics. Sometimes known as the economic peace theory, classical economists have consistently argued that free trade generates a more peaceful world order. This is often allied to two other normative elements of liberalism, such as support for the rule of law and the spread of democratic values.

Economic peace theory stipulates that market-oriented economies will not engage in war with one another. This is based upon an assumption that states act via their own rational interests, and that we should adopt an optimistic view of human nature. Although the argument is a lengthy one, it has gained added relevance in an era of globalisation. In an integrated and mutually dependent global economy, countries will seek to avoid the heavy financial cost and loss of life attributable to warfare, deterring conflict.

Those who support the economic peace theory claim that 'the freer the market, the freer the people.' The forces of demand and supply enable individuals to make their own decisions. A market free from state intervention also leads towards the most efficient allocation of scarce resources. However, those on the left of the political spectrum point out that capitalism has long been upheld via agents of a repressive state. Secondly, decision-makers may reject the 'win-win' assumptions that lie behind the economic peace theory for a more zero-sum view of power. As a result, wars will always occur on the basis of economic gain for capitalist powers, linking to the world system and dependency theories discussed in Chapter one.

Liberal assumptions concerning the peaceful implications of capitalism and democracy are also criticised from within the realist perspective. Realists firmly reject the view that we should be optimistic about human nature. Regardless of economic and political ties, relations between states always hold the potential for a conflict to emerge. The normative tone of the liberal argument is entirely absent from the realist position.

During the eighteenth century, Immanuel Kant declared that the spirit of commerce was incompatible with war. It was a philosophical argument that captured the prevalent mindset of the time. In the contemporary era, the economic peace theory has been upgraded by Thomas Friedman (1989), who argued that when a country had reached a level of economic development with a strong middle-class it would become a 'McDonald's society'. His argument encapsulated the triumphalism of the end of the Cold War and proved a marker for the forthcoming era of globalisation. As with all theoretical arguments, the 'golden arches theory' has been subject to criticism. Most notably, there are exceptions one might consider such as the Kargil War in 1999 between India and Pakistan. There was also a short-lived conflict between NATO and Serbia in the same year.

In response to those conflicts, Thomas Friedman further developed his argument via the 'Dell theory' of conflict prevention. Friedman (2005, 421) argued that 'no two countries that are both part of a major global supply chain...will ever fight a war against each other as long as they are both part of the same global supply chain.' This is a theory that underlines yet further the significance of mutual dependence between countries. The Dell theory is an update of an earlier argument put forward by Sir Norman Angell in *The Great Illusion* (1909), reasoning that economic interdependence makes war unprofitable for all belligerents. Although not a cast-iron guarantee, both mature and developing economies will seek to maintain the trading benefits that come with globalisation, as opposed to descending into conflict.

Unsurprisingly, there is evidence to support and undermine the latest version of the economic peace theory. In terms of the former, the strained relationship between China and Taiwan is a useful illustration to consider. The level of economic ties between them prevents the possibility of actual warfare. Although diplomatic relations between Beijing and Taipei are often strained, a military stand-off has been avoided since the mid-1990s. However, there are also counter examples to highlight, such as the war between Russia and Georgia in 2008 or the annexation of Crimea by Russia in 2014. It should also be noted that Friedman conceded that his argument was offered in a somewhat 'tongue-in-cheek' manner.

The Development and Spread of The Rule of Law

Along with free trade and economic interdependence, liberals claim that a more peaceful world can be created via those institutions that maintain international law. Liberalism advocates an active role for international institutions in order to aid cooperation between states and ensure positive outcomes for all. This is based upon the assumption that states act in a rational manner and seek to maximise their utility. This is sometimes known as the institutional peace theory.

According to liberal institutionalists, democracy and capitalism create an international system which ensures long-term peace and provides beneficial economic opportunities for those countries involved. International institutions underpin both the global economic order and the spread of democratic values. International law itself is governed and maintained via a series of intergovernmental forums, and the framework provided by these institutions generates the conditions for peace and stability. Institutions can also provide the basis for global governance, as seen in earlier chapters.

There are of course flaws with institutional peace theory. Perhaps the most obvious is that institutions are only as powerful as states allow them to be. This often means that powerful countries avoid responsibility for their actions. For instance, the invasion of Kuwait by Saddam Hussein led to international condemnation and the mobilisation of multilateral forces to restore the sovereignty of the oil-rich regime. However, the invasion of Iraq by a US-led military alliance did not face anything like the same degree of condemnation over a decade later. Such institutions are also hampered by a lack of funding and non-compliance amongst certain states. As always, there is the thorny problem of enforcing international law.

Those who do not share the liberal mindset have also criticised the excessive and idealistic faith placed in global governance. For instance, the philosopher John Gray points out that 'global problems do not always have global solutions' (Gray 2020). It should also be noted that liberalism itself can be challenged for its double-standards and hypocrisy. From the perspective of the Global South, the institutions that uphold the liberal world order lack credibility, explaining much of the Global South's plight.

The Spread of Democracy and Democratic Peace Theory

It has long been a fundamental tenet of this normative body of liberal theory that democracies are more reluctant to engage in armed conflict with other democratic countries. This is more commonly known as the democratic peace theory. Dating back to the Enlightenment, the theory stipulates that the spread of democratic values will lead towards a more peaceful and stable world order.

The theory is based upon several interlinked assumptions. First and foremost, democratic leaders are directly accountable to the public for losses incurred during a war. In addition, democracies are more inclined to view other comparable systems as partners rather than enemies. Moreover, democratically elected politicians have a clear incentive to engage in cooperation and diplomacy with other democratically elected politicians. Democratic states are also more likely to accept third-party mediation when they are in dispute with one another. This is based upon a greater level of trust in the intentions and predicted behaviour of other democratic states. More importantly, democracies tend to be interdependent and are therefore highly reluctant to engage in the potentially system-wide disruption caused by conflict.

In terms of academic research, Dan Reiter (2017) found that there is enough evidence to conclude that democracy does lead to peace between democracies. Having said this, the last time two democracies fought against each other is a contested point. Some have claimed that the last inter-democracy conflict was the ancient Peloponnesian wars, whilst others argue that the NATO-led bombing of Belgrade in 1999 provides an example. Given the discursive nature of academic theories, contestability should always be expected, and this hinges on how we understand democracy.

Following on from this point, one of the most persuasive counterarguments is that the democratic peace theory confuses correlation with causation. Secondly, there is no universal agreement as to what classifies either of these terms. For instance, there have been militarised interstate disputes between democratic countries, and these could be classed as warfare. In order to actually prove the theory, the meaning of the terms democracy and war have, at times, been distorted.

In seeking to properly assess the democratic peace theory, there are some caveats to consider. For instance, it could be argued that the theoretical concept can only be applied towards mature democracies as sufficient time is needed for democratic procedures to become embedded (Rummel 1997). Evidence also suggests that countries in transition towards democracy are more likely to be engaged in warfare (Mansfield and Snyder 2002). Moreover, the number of democracies has until relatively recently been quite small. As such, even those who support the theory concede that it is going to take many more decades of peace to build our confidence in the stability of the democratic peace theory.

Another term to consider is the distinction between a 'dyadic' peace and a 'monadic' peace. The former refers to the argument that democracies do not fight one another. This is based on the argument that liberal democracies build up a habit of cooperation with one another that conflict would clearly undermine. The term 'monadic peace' however relates to the assumption that democracies are more peaceful. They are simply less inclined to engage in warfare than a non-democratic regime. The dyadic peace argument is more persuasive than the latter. For instance, Reiter and Stam (2003) found that autocracies initiate conflicts against democracies more frequently than democracies do against autocracies. However, Quackenbush and Rudy (2009) found that democracies initiate wars against non-democracies more frequently than non-democracies do with each other. In another study, it was shown that democracies are no less likely to settle border disputes peacefully than non-democracies.

Given this conflicting and contradictory evidence, it must be noted that there are several causal factors that have very little to do with the spread of democratic values. The outbreak of military conflict may occur due to a dispute over valuable resources or territorial boundaries. Most warfare in the contemporary world occurs in the form of civil war, as opposed to inter-state conflict. This requires some modification of the original democratic peace theory. The probability for a civil war is also enhanced by political change regardless of its eventual goal (Hegre et al. 2001).

On a final note, a cost-benefit analysis casts further insight into the debate. Since the net benefit to an autocrat exceeds the net benefit to a citizen of a liberal democracy, the autocrat is more likely to go to war. The disincentive to war is increased between liberal democracies via the establishment of political and economic linkages that further raise the actual costs of going to war. Liberal democracies are therefore less likely to go to war, especially against each other.

The Extent to Which the Changing Relations and Actions of States Address and Resolve Contemporary Global Issues

Regarding changing developments and the interplay of power politics between states, a fascinating case study is the political situation in the Middle East. Given its complex and multi-dimensional character, relations between Israel and Arab states have an impact upon conflict, poverty, human rights and the environment. Underlying the geostrategic and economic importance of the Middle East, a number of powerful actors have a clear and vested interest in the region.

The Arab-Israeli Conflict

Historically, the major powers have played a significant role in the search for stability between Arabs and Israelis. Most notably, the United States has provided considerable political and military assistance to Israel. Equally, the role of external powers has at times created barriers towards reconciliation. For instance, a number of Arab states still refuse to recognise Israel.

Right from the beginning, the international community was actively involved in seeking a solution. In 1947, the United Nations approved a proposal to partition Palestine into two separate states. Following the end of the British mandate, the vast number of Palestinian Arabs fled or were expelled from Israel, whilst thousands of Jews migrated to Israel. After a short-lived war, the State of Israel controlled the area specified by the UN for the proposed Israeli state, alongside over half of the proposed Arab state.

In 1956, the second Arab-Israeli war occurred over the nationalisation of the Suez Canal by the Egyptian leader, President Nasser. Along with the UK and France, troops from Israel invaded Egypt to secure regime change against his pan-Arab ideology. However, foreign troops were forced to withdraw after diplomatic pressure from the UN and the two superpowers. As a concession, the State of Israel gained assurance that the Straits of Tiran would remain open. Yet, by the time of the third Arab-Israeli war in 1967, President Nasser announced that the Straits of Tiran would be closed off to Israeli vessels.

In response to the mobilisation of Egyptian forces under Nasser, Israel launched pre-emptive air strikes against Egyptian airfields. After gaining air supremacy, Israeli forces launched a ground offensive that established control over the Gaza Strip, the Sinai Peninsula, the West Bank and the Golan Heights. The UN Security Council called for Israeli troops to retreat from their territorial gains, but, despite international condemnation, Israel continued to violate international law. This is made possible by financial and diplomatic support from the United States.

The economic importance of the dispute was graphically brought home during the 1973 Yom Kippur War. A coalition of Arab states, led by Egypt and Syria, sought to take back control of the Sinai and the Golan Heights. Although taken by surprise, Israel managed to push back the Syrians and advance towards the Suez Canal. The State of Israel had once again demonstrated its ability to defeat hostile neighbours. However, policymakers also recognised that there was no guarantee that they would always dominate Arab States in military terms. This shifted the focus towards the search for a peaceful long-term solution to the conflict. The OPEC oil price rise and the damaging impact upon the global economy gave yet further impetus towards the desire for a peaceful settlement.

Marking a new phase in relations between Israel and Egypt, negotiations surrounding the 1978 Camp David accords were spearheaded by the United States. The Israeli Prime Minister, Menachem Begin, secured recognition from an Arab state for the first time, whilst the Egyptian President, Anwar Sadat, gained back the Sinai Peninsula after the gradual withdrawal of Israeli troops. The American President Jimmy Carter had therefore managed to break-up the Arab alliance, marginalise the Palestinians and offer security to the State of Israel. However, tensions remained between the two rival camps.

Palestinian protests at the twenty-year anniversary of Israeli occupation of the West Bank and Gaza were launched in 1987. Known as the first 'intifada' - meaning 'shaking off' in Arabic – such protests were met with a military response from Israel and widely criticised as disproportionate. The Palestinian Liberation Organisation (PLO) and the Israeli government once again held talks supported by international efforts to broker peace between them. This culminated in the 1993 Oslo Accords, which awarded Palestinians a degree of autonomy in return for officially recognising the State of Israel. The peace process also aimed to establish a lasting agreement based on the right of the Palestinian people to self-determination.

Although there was some goodwill generated by their representatives, public opinion was largely hostile. Many Israelis viewed the PLO as a terrorist organisation responsible for both the intifada and the short-lived 1982 war in Lebanon, whilst Palestinians argued that the peace process gave Israel access to water from the West Bank. Although the peace process continued, the Camp David talks broke down over contentious issues such as Jewish settlements in the occupied territories, an issue that continues to stoke tensions today.

The second intifada (2000–05) began after Israeli Prime Minister Ariel Sharon made a visit to the Temple Mount. Palestinian protests were eventually brought to an end when Israel withdrew from the Gaza Strip in 2005. Despite the withdrawal of its troops, Israel exerted control over its airspace, maritime waters and land crossings. Gaza is also dependent upon Israel for its water, electricity and other utilities. Economic sanctions, travel restrictions and diplomatic sanctions against the regime are also in place.

Since the 2006 electoral victory of Hamas in the Palestinian National Assembly, the Gaza Strip has also been blockaded by Egypt. The Cairo-based government wants to prevent any additional Iranian influence within the region (who are widely thought to be funding Hamas). The role of the Egyptian government is supported by the President of the Palestinian National Authority Mahmoud Abbas. Israel, however, is more concerned with protecting its citizens from Hamas. Along with Iraq, Iran, Libya and Syria, the organisation Hamas does not recognise the State of Israel. The fundamentalist group is also opposed to the conditions for peace as laid down by Israel and the Quartet on the Middle East (the UN, the US, the EU and Russia).

Throughout the conflict, the role of the US as a protector of the Israeli state has been absolutely vital. For instance, the State of Israel has been allowed to occupy land based on self-defence, whilst building Jewish settlements contrary to international law. Moreover, the Biden administration advocates a two-state solution to the Arab-Israeli conflict. As the term implies, both countries would recognise each other's sovereignty and co-exist in a peaceful manner. As envisioned by the Oslo Accords, a two-state solution could result in greater stability between Israeli Jews and Palestinian Arabs. The only other practical alternative is a one-state solution. However, this would present a major headache for Israel regarding the status of Palestinians currently residing in the West Bank. The one-state approach would almost certainly result in Muslims outnumbering Jews, which would materially change the national identity of the self-styled Jewish state.

In terms of the environment, Israel has signed bilateral agreements that provide a framework for the exchange of information and expertise with Egypt, Jordan and Turkey. These agreements cover environmental protection, desertification and climate change. The implementation of these agreements entails exchange visits of professionals and researchers. Moves towards the protection of the environment underline the extent to which rivals can work together to ensure a mutually beneficial objective. There is even an agreement to share water access between Israelis and Palestinians. The latter agreement also serves to underline the salience of soft power in one of the most contentious areas of the world.

From the opposing angle, the on-going tensions between Arabs and Israelis presents several environmental problems. For instance, access to the Golan Heights will always be difficult because the area provides a substantial portion of the water from the Jordan River. Only Israel and the US recognise Israel's claim to sovereignty over the Golan Heights. The provision of water and other services essential for everyday survival underlines the difficulty in maintaining the human rights of those living in the Middle East. For instance, the Palestinian civil war between Fatah and Hamas has caused deep and lasting disruption to the lives of ordinary people living in Gaza.

In terms of human rights, the Westphalian system implies that territorial boundaries should hold some relationship to the wishes of the people. Clearly, this is not the case in the disputed territory surrounding Israel. For instance, the West Bank (including the symbolic city of East Jerusalem) has been under Israeli occupation since the late-1960s. Having said this, Israel is not the only occupying force within the region. For instance, Syria occupied parts of Lebanon from 1976 to 2005. It could also be acknowledged that the State of Israel would have never survived if not for its highly effective military arsenal and intelligence services. Human rights within the Jewish state have been under threat for several decades from Islamic militants and neighbouring Arab states.

Perhaps the most problematic issue presented by the Palestinian-Israeli dispute is its zero-sum character. When one side gains territory, the other side loses out. This in turn holds major implications for living standards. For instance, access to the supply of freshwater is of major importance within the region. It must also be recognised that both sides in the conflict have a persuasive religious claim over the city of Jerusalem. Mistrust and rivalries between warring groups makes compromise extremely difficult to achieve in the region. Indeed, it is also worth noting that figures who have pushed hardest for peace (such as Anwar Sadat, Bachir Gemayel and Yitzhak Rabin) have been assassinated by extremists from their own side.

It is, perhaps, no surprise that the Middle East region is one of the most significant areas of focus within International Relations. It helps us consider the theoretical context of power and development within global politics. There is undoubtedly some salience to both the realist and liberal perspectives in terms of the Middle East. Moreover, the implications of politics within the Middle East will always hold a great deal of importance towards other actors within global politics.

Saudi Arabia and Iran

Another significant inter-state relationship for the security of the Middle East is the rivalry between Saudi Arabia and Iran. Whilst they have never fought directly against one another; they have engaged in proxy wars within Syria, Iraq and Yemen. There is also a degree of sectarian division to consider, as the Saudi population is majority Sunni whilst most Iranians are Shia Muslims.

The tension between the two regional powers dates to the Islamic revolution of 1979 when the spiritual leader Ayatollah Khomeini rose to power following mass protests that toppled the regime of the US-backed 'Shah' of Iran. Saudi Arabia had long viewed itself as the prominent Muslim state in the region, but Iran subsequently claimed that mantle based upon theological purity. Iran also sought to spread revolution towards other Arab countries in a move bitterly opposed by the ultra-conservative Saudi monarchy. During the Iran-Iraq War, the Saudis provided financial and military assistance to Saddam Hussein's troops. Whilst Saudi Arabia remained aligned to the West, Iranian political discourse routinely portrays the US as 'the Great Satan.'

The US-led invasion of Iraq also heightened tensions between the Saudis and Iranians. In the resultant civil war, both Shia and Sunni groups took control of Iraqi territory. Consistent with their predilection towards proxy wars, both countries supported their own side in a war that neither really wanted. Up until that point, Iraq acted as a buffer zone between Tehran and Riyadh. During the Arab Spring, the two countries also found themselves on different sides. As a status quo power based upon an absolutist form of government, the Saudis opposed the wave of democratic protests in the Middle East and Northern Africa. In stark contrast, Iran endorsed those groups calling for change.

Not surprisingly, the situation is more complex within Syria. The Saudi regime supports the Sunni militia whilst the Iranians favour the Assad regime. The Tehran administration also supports the militant group Hezbollah, which is based in Lebanon. Founded as part of an effort to bring together Shia extremists under one umbrella organisation, Hezbollah acts as a proxy for Iran in their long-standing conflict with the State of Israel. For instance, Hezbollah fought against Israeli troops in Lebanon during 2006, and Iran does not recognise the Jewish state.

An understanding of the political situation within the Middle East holds ramifications for several elements of international relations. In seeking to comprehend the ways and extent to which changing relationships and the actions of states affect the political situation, we are forced to consider the impact upon issues ranging from security to human rights. In doing so, we are reminded that global politics will always be shaped by the actions of states and the importance of concepts such as the balance of power and the security dilemma.

Conclusion

In summary, the aim of this chapter has been to provide a thorough analysis of power within global politics. This has been related to the notion of polarity and its broader consequences. A number of relevant concepts have been considered alongside the various types of governments. The case study provided by the Middle East casts considerable light on power and developments. It also provides an insight into the broader debate between realists and liberals.

BOX 5.1 – KEY TERMS FROM CHAPTER FIVE

Hard Power

The academic Ernest Wilson (2008, 114) describes hard power as the capacity to force another 'to act in ways in which that entity would not have acted otherwise.' Hard power derives from the mobilisation of military resources and economic sanctions. Unlike soft power, hard power consists of tangible resources. Hard power is based upon a combination of the 'stick and the carrot' in order to shape the behaviour of others. In the contemporary era, the use of hard power can actually undermine the standing of a country abroad. Certain countries have a reputation for hard power (such as Russia) whilst others prefer the more persuasive nature of soft power (such as the Scandinavian countries). This may well depend upon the resources available to that particular country. Yet having said this, even the most powerful military states utilise soft power in order to promote their interests abroad.

Soft Power

Joseph Nye (2004, ix) defined soft power as 'the ability of a country to persuade others to do what it wants without force or coercion.' Unlike hard power, it relies upon the voluntary actions of others in order to be successful. The existence of soft power needs to be recognised as legitimate by those directly or indirectly affected. Soft power also consists of the ability to attract others as opposed to an emphasis solely upon compulsion. The salience of soft power has increased since the end of the Cold War and incorporates several related dimensions (such as culture and diplomacy). Perhaps the clearest illustration of the successful use of soft power is the European Union. Since its inception, the EU has sought to brand itself as a supporter of human rights. As one of the world's largest single markets with an extensive diplomatic presence, the EU projects considerable soft power to enhance the status of the organisation. The EU is also involved in a number of cultural exchanges that further enhance its prestige on the international stage (such as Erasmus).

Great Power

A great power can be identified as a sovereign state able to exert its influence on a global scale. To become a great power a country needs to be in possession of various power capabilities, spatial aspects and status dimensions. The emphasis upon power capabilities derives from an unmistakably realist emphasis upon hard power. A great power must be able to exercise genuine influence within the international system of states. In terms of status dimension, there has to be some formal or informal recognition from other great powers. This also means that the status can be taken off them. For instance, Russia was suspended from the G8 for its annexation of Crimea in 2014. It should also be noted that a state must be treated (and willing to act) in a manner befitting a great power. Gaining such elevated status comes with a set of obligations within an institutionalised structure.

Superpower

The term superpower is used to categorise those countries with overwhelming military resources. In terms of hard power, a superpower is far superior to any other comparable nation. Given the significance of coercion, the emphasis tilts towards military capacity. Unlike other actors within the international system, a superpower is a state that simply cannot be ignored. The management and resolution of global affairs requires meaningful cooperation with a superpower. The term is also applicable in the context of soft power because a superpower can persuade others to consent to their particular viewpoint. This is commonly linked towards its role as a hegemonic power. During the zenith of the British Empire, scholars referenced the term Pax Britannica (a Latin term for 'British peace'). Its role was gradually overtaken by the United States, and since the end of the Cold War American hegemony has underpinned the international world order – a 'Pax Americana'.

Emerging Power

An emerging power is a term loosely applied to those states recognised as rising powers on the world stage. In terms of the hierarchy of states, an emerging power aspires to achieve an even more powerful position within international relations. There is no agreed classification as to which states should be classed as an emerging power. That said, the fundamental shared characteristic of all emerging powers is that of a rapidly developing economy. The emphasis upon economic status is conventionally thought to be a preliminary step towards growing political power. Emerging powers may decide to work together to advance an agenda favourable to their interests. For instance, the BRICS have met formally on an annual basis since 2009. An emerging power may have little or no chance of gaining the status of a great power due to the limitations that derive from the seven dimensions of state power. These are geography, population, resources, military, diplomacy, national identity and economy. Such dimensions are a useful means by which one might properly assess the power of any given state.

Polarity / Unipolarity / Bipolarity

The term polarity refers to the various ways in which the poles of power are distributed within international relations. Although commonly applied on a global scale, it can also be used in a regional context. Unipolarity is a term used to describe a situation in which one state is dominant in an economic, cultural and/or military sense. In a system built upon the dominance of one power, the hegemonic state may adopt the unofficial role of the world's policeman. Bipolarity entails a distribution of power in which two states are dominant in terms of economic, military and/or cultural influence. In a system characterised by bipolarity, two distinct spheres of influence tend to emerge. In a system based upon bipolarity, there are two superpowers engaged in an arms race. As an aside, bipolarity can also be applied to alliances and organisations. During the Cold War, many countries sided with either NATO or the Warsaw Pact, reinforcing the claims of bipolarity. However, it can be argued that applying the term to the Cold War marginalises the role played by the Non-Aligned Movement – which remains the largest group of states outside of the United Nations.

Multipolarity

As the term implies, multipolarity consists of a dispersal of power in which more than two countries have an equitable amount of influence. Classical realists such as Hans Morgenthau (1948) contend that multipolar systems offer greater stability than a system built upon bipolarity. This argument rests upon the realist assumption that stability is grounded upon the balance of power. Neorealists, however, claim that states in a multipolar system may miscalculate others' intentions. In contrast, a bipolar system is more stable because it is only possible to misjudge the intentions of one other power. Under bipolarity, the logic of mutually assured destruction prevents all-out conflict. It is an argument that may explain why there has never been a full-scale war between India and Pakistan since the turn of the century.

Democratic State

Democracy derives from the Greek words for 'people' (demos) and 'power' (as power potential: '-kratos'). In a democratic state, the people exercise power via periodic multi-party elections in which representatives are elected to the legislature. In a democracy, elections also occur at the local and regional level. In a presidential system, the people even elect the head of the executive branch of government. Since 2006, the Economist magazine has compiled an index that measures the state of democracy within most of the world's sovereign states. The index categorises countries as full democracies, flawed democracies, hybrid regimes (sometimes known as a semi-democratic state) and authoritarian regimes. In a full democracy, civil liberties are respected and reinforced by a political culture conducive to democratic principles. Such countries have an independent judiciary system, a system of checks and balances and a media free from censure. Scandinavian countries score highly on the Democracy Index, whilst North Korea is routinely at the bottom of the scale (Economist Intelligence Unit 2021).

Semi-Democratic State / Non-Democratic State

A semi-democracy can be defined as a state that holds both democratic and authoritarian elements. In a semi-democratic state, democratic values and practices are combined with authoritarian measures. Such regimes are usually characterised by a degree of political stability alongside an illiberal form of 'democracy.' Semi-democratic states are also known by the term 'anocracy'. Part-democracy and part-dictatorship, anocracies combine political participation alongside a politicised judiciary and a highly-restricted media. Although an inherently subjective term, there are some prominent examples of a semi-democratic state. Most notably, Vladimir Putin has regularly described the Russian political system as a form of managed democracy (Mandel 2005). A non-democratic state is a system of representative government in which elections take place without a choice of political parties. In a non-democratic state, political parties may be prevented from participating in elections.

Autocratic State

An autocratic state is a system of government in which a single leader or party is in possession of supreme and absolute power. Unlike a democratic or semi-democratic state, there is no constitutional limitation upon the power of the ruling party or autocratic leader. The basis of an autocratic regime tends to be either a totalitarian ideology or an absolute monarchy. In the contemporary era, autocratic regimes based upon a totalitarian set of ideas are quite rare, whilst absolute monarchies are concentrated within the Arab Kingdoms. The term autocracy is often conflated with dictatorship. Whilst there are considerable similarities between the two, the phrase dictatorial regime is value-laden in a negative manner whilst an autocratic leader may be viewed in a positive light by its citizens. For instance, an autocratic leader may be able to provide an increase in living standards or sufficient protection against foreign threats. An autocrat might also govern in a benign manner over their people. In contrast, a dictatorial regime is rarely seen as legitimate within their own borders and must therefore rely heavily upon propaganda and the cult of personality.

Failed States

A failed state is one that cannot provide a functioning system of governance. This leads to major economic and humanitarian problems for those unfortunate enough to reside within its borders. There are several examples of failed states within contemporary international relations such as Somalia, Yemen and Libya. The international community's focus upon failed states has increased in recent years due to an alleged link with the spread of terrorist organisations. Alongside enabling a space for terrorists to organise, there are other problems posed by a failed state. Amongst neighbouring countries, there will be an influx of refugees. As the displacement of people often entails an ethnic dimension, a sudden rise in the number of refugees may exacerbate tensions within a neighbouring country. Given the geostrategic complexities of the situation, a failed state may even drag others into the conflict and lead to the formation of alliances amongst rival blocks. There are few better illustrations of these observations than the situation in Syria.

Rogue States

A rogue state consists of a regime that fails to conform to the norms and rules of the international community. Such regimes tend to be characterised by state-sponsored terrorism, authoritarian leadership and weapons of mass destruction. Rogue states such as North Korea are widely considered to be a threat to world peace. As there is no objective categorisation under international law, the classification of a rogue state is largely determined by powerful countries. This can result in glaring double-standards. For instance, Israel would never be classed as a rogue state by the US despite its repeated violations of international law. It is also revealing to note that the United States decides if and when a country should no longer be classified as a rogue state (as in the case of Cuba and Libya). Some of the most vocal critics of American foreign policy depict the US itself as a rogue state. The historian William Blum (2000) argues that interventions spearheaded by the US have repeatedly threatened world peace, whilst the famed activist and academic Noam Chomsky (2000) has equally claimed that the US matches the criteria laid down to be considered a rogue state. There is certainly a great deal of evidence to support this charge. For instance, Washington supported several right-wing dictatorships during the Cold War. Under Donald Trump, US foreign policy was shaped by a degree of unpredictability and personalisation commonly associated with leaders of rogue states (such as his phone call to the Ukrainian President Zelensky in order to investigate his Democrat rival Joe Biden).

BOX 5.2 – KEY POINTS FOR CHAPTER FIVE

1. There is a distinction between hard power, soft power and smart power.

2. There are three main types of polarity: unipolarity, bipolarity and multipolarity.

3. There is a debate over which type of polarity offers the most degree of stability.

4. States are often categorised on the basis of great powers, superpowers and emerging powers.

5. There are different classifications of regime types, ranging from full democracies (whose people elect their leaders) to autocracies (dictatorships, non-elected leaders etc.).

6. Stability is often threatened by failed states, failing states and rogue states.

7. The liberal perspective claims that democracy, capitalism and institutions can create a more stable international system.

6

Regionalism and the EU

This final chapter examines the magnitude of regionalism as a force within global politics. This chapter seeks to analyse the causes of regionalism, evaluate its relationship with globalisation and outline the development of regional organisations. A primary focus will centre on the European Union (EU), an organisation which continues to provide something of a blueprint for deeper integration. The chapter also considers the significance of the EU as an actor on the global stage, before concluding with the manner and extent to which regionalism attempts to resolve issues such as the avoidance of conflict.

Regionalism

Different Modes of Regionalism: Economic, Political and Security

Regionalism can be defined in the context of international relations as the expression of a shared identity and purpose. It is combined with the creation and implementation of institutions that manifest regional identity and shape activity within that particular region. There are a wide number of regional organisations to consider with varying levels of integration. For instance, the depth of integration within the Arab League or the Association of Southeast Asian Nations (ASEAN) is considerably weaker than the EU.

It should be recognised that regionalism is the process through which larger geographical or even continental areas emerge as political organisations through integrated international institutions. This may provide a forum for cooperation between various states. The formation of regional blocs has often been driven by the growing impact of economic globalisation. As borders have become more porous, states have sought to co-operate more closely in order to deal with the consequences of interdependence. However, it could also be argued that regional free trade agreements function contrarily, against the process of globalisation.

The driving forces behind regionalism can derive from economic, security and/or political grounds. The European Economic Community (EEC), the forebearer to the EU, is a clear example of economic regionalism. The whole justification for the EEC was to enhance economic growth and development within the European continent. The economic success of the organisation in its early years managed to attract countries around it who soon sought membership. For instance, the United Kingdom was drawn towards the European project partly due to the relative economic success of the EEC.

The creation of the European Union in 1993 was emblematic of regionalism. As a result of the Maastricht Treaty, the EU adopted three separate pillars. These pillars consisted of the European Communities, the Common Foreign and Security Policy (CFSP) and cooperation in the field of Justice and Home Affairs. This was later abandoned when the Treaty of Lisbon came into force in 2009, and the EU obtained a legal personality. By contrast, NATO is an organisation based entirely upon security concerns. The principal justification for NATO is contained within Article Five of the North Atlantic Treaty, in which an attack on one is interpreted as an attack upon all, ensuring collective security. The European Union has also sought to develop its security dimension via a joint foreign and security policy. The emphasis is upon soft power, such as developmental cooperation, humanitarian aid and the EU's diplomatic presence.

Allied to the three-dimensional character of regionalism is the distinction between old regionalism and new regionalism. Old regionalism is rooted in the experience of interwar nationalism, and as such held a tendency towards protectionism in the economic realm. The formation of the EEC is a clear illustration of the former. Contrastingly, 'new regionalism' entails a more spontaneous process that emerges from within the region itself. In doing so, the process of regionalism adopts towards the dynamics of the region in question. Inevitably, some regions are more conducive towards regional integration than others. The extent to which a particular region accommodates regionalism will also differ considerably over time. For instance, the process of European integration developed from economic to political regionalism. New regionalism is a more complex process that may take place simultaneously at a variety of levels.

The Relationship Between Regionalism and Globalisation

Regionalism is consistent with globalisation in three ways. First and foremost, regional economic blocs have formed due to the adverse impact of globalisation on national sovereignty. States have therefore been more inclined to work closely with other states in the same region, as borders have become porous as a result of normative adaptation within the wider discourse of international politics. This has been striking economically, due to financial markets and multinational corporations (MNCs) having such an impact upon the character of national sovereignty. It is worth noting that even the wealthiest and most powerful economies have been affected by the seemingly unstoppable trend towards globalisation. Membership of a regional bloc does provide at least some level of political influence for the member state in question.

A second reason for the formation of regional economic blocs is that they enable nation-states to resist pressure from external global competition. A regional bloc acting as a customs union can therefore act as a fortress against the pressures from the wider global economy. Perhaps the clearest illustration of this argument is the European Union (EU). The organisation has often been accused of creating trade barriers against states outside of the organisation. This argument is particularly salient towards many of the poorest economies within the Global South. Similarly, the EU can adopt a negotiating position that enables members to resist the competitive forces unleashed by globalisation. For example, the EU can adopt a common position in a trade agreement with China or the United States. It is more likely that a nation-state will have their voice heard as a part of one of the largest single markets in the world than if they were outside of such an organisation. In this manner, the power such a unit may hold will be greater than the sum of its parts, retroactively adding to the perceived power of its member-states.

Thirdly, member states rationalise that the path towards prosperity is by gaining greater access to regional markets. In an increasingly globalised economy, membership of a regional bloc firmly committed towards free trade is a positive. Membership of a free trade area provides access to a larger market. In doing so, it facilitates economies of scale for firms within the regional bloc. Furthermore, regional trade agreements enable the free flow of capital and labour. It is perhaps worth noting that the number of regional trade agreements has risen from just 50 in 1990 to well over 300 today (Fernandes et al.. 2021).

From the opposing angle, the relationship between regionalism and globalisation can be considered a contradictory one. Carving up the global economy on the basis of regional integration is clearly at odds with the actual meaning of globalisation. The rapid growth in the scope and scale of regional agreements is inconsistent with the creation of a truly global economy. Regionalism could therefore be described as the very opposite of the supposed global interconnectedness of states and non-state actors, centring focus on the regional as opposed to the global.

In order to substantiate this argument, the creation of regional organisations generates intra-regional trade rather than globalised trade. The existence of free trade areas, customs unions and common markets on a regional basis fosters trade amongst its members rather than with non-members. Regional integration also enables those organisations to place restrictions on those states outside of the organisation.

In economic parlance, regional integration fosters both trade creation and trade diversion. The motivation behind regional trade agreements is to enable increasingly free trade amongst the member states. However, it also leads towards trade diversion. This can present a major issue if protectionist measures are imposed against non-members. The practice of trade diversion contradicts the aims of the World Trade Organisation and the broader Washington Consensus. It is therefore inconsistent with the process of globalisation as it is usually grasped.

Whilst the terms are often presented on a binary basis, it is certainly plausible to claim that regionalism is intrinsically linked to globalisation. If globalisation is widely thought to be the mutual dependence of states, regionalism can be said to enable such dependence. This is a more nuanced understanding of international relations and one that arguably offers an increasingly convincing explanation of the actual reality of global politics.

The Prospects for Political Regionalism and Regional Governance

The prospects for political regionalism and regional governance are driven by a combination of internal and external factors. The former relates to those factors that characterise the region itself. External factors, however, relate to events that originate from outside of the region (such as the 2007–08 Global Financial Crisis). The internal forces that shape regional governance may be far greater in one area of the world than another. For instance, the devastation caused by the Second World War undoubtedly provided the impetus behind early moves towards European integration. In addition, the impact of external forces may be significantly greater in one area of the world compared to others.

In order to identify the prospects for regional governance and political regionalism, it is perhaps necessary to consider the issue on a region-by-region basis. In doing so, it is possible to highlight the prospects for political integration and governance. Within the European Union, the prospects for deeper integration appear to be negligible. Due to a combination of forces both inside and outside of their immediate control, the European Union failed to implement an effective convergence criterion. The European Union has also been affected by the decision of the United Kingdom to leave the organisation in 2016. Given the depth of Eurosceptic feeling within many countries, the prospect of deepening regional governance seems limited.

Unlike the European Union, integration within East Asia has been primarily of an economic character. The impetus behind recent political integration was provided by the dramatic impact of the financial crisis during the late 1990s. The financial contagion that swept throughout such relatively open economies required a co-ordinated response from the member states affected. The crisis exposed the dramatic nature of globalisation and the need for some level of political integration to mitigate the overall impact. This led to the Chiang Mai Initiative (CMI). The CMI began as a series of bilateral swap arrangements after the ASEAN plus Three (China, Japan and South Korea) held a meeting of the Asian Development Bank. This provided an Asian solution to the crisis, rather than the region becoming reliant upon the IMF. Having said this, progress towards regional governance remains slow, due to a lack of institutional integration.

In South America, regional governance has been limited by a number of familiar issues. These include the absence of economic convergence, a shift in the balance of global economic power and of course state sovereignty. The present situation consists of incremental attempts towards political regionalism in order to bolster democracy and regional security. The main impetus in recent times has centred upon liberalisation of trade. There are a number of complementary organisations within the region ranging from the Andean Community of Nations to the Southern Common Market – Mercado Común del Sur (MERCOSUR). The region also has a parliament acting as a consultative assembly similar to the early format adopted by the European Parliament. There are also plans to establish the institution as the legislative branch of the Community of Latin American and Caribbean States (CELAC). Created in 2010, the organisation reflects a decade-long push for deeper integration. In addition, the Pacific Alliance was created in 2012 amongst countries that border the Pacific Ocean. The aim of the Alliance is to establish the four freedoms in a manner comparable to European integration.

The path adopted by the European Union has also provided a blueprint for the African Union. The organisation has embedded several of the political elements of integration adopted within Europe. There are also signs that economic integration within the region is gathering pace. Although such institutions have not yet been established, there are moves to establish a single currency. This will entail the creation of a central bank based in Nigeria and a monetary fund within Cameroon. There are also plans to adopt an investment bank in Libya. In contrast, integration within North America seems unlikely due to the indifferent approach adopted by Washington. The United States is such a powerful country that integration with their neighbours does not offer anything like the same benefits as integration does for weaker states.

The Impact of Regionalism on State Sovereignty

The process of regionalism is widely viewed as having a negative impact upon state sovereignty. As states cede their authority towards regional organisations, they lose most of their ability to shape their own destiny. This was brought home in stark manner during the UK Brexit referendum, when a majority of the British public voted to leave the European Union. However, the picture is more nuanced than it might first appear.

There has long been a debate over the impact of regionalism on state sovereignty. There are those who claim that regionalism undermines the sovereignty of the state. This is based upon a zero-sum view of sovereignty. As a member of a regional bloc, decisions reached upon the basis of unanimity must be implemented by all the signatory states. This may be supported via the existence of supranational institutions. For instance, the African Union (AU) has recently strengthened its capacity to impose sanctions against member states who fail to meet their financial obligations. The Court of Justice of the European Union is another common illustration of this argument.

From the opposing angle, it could be convincingly argued that states merely pool (or share) sovereignty within any given regional organisation. In doing so, they are better able to shape their own destiny. They are also free to leave at any time. Crucially, this means that the sovereignty of the state has not been compromised. The salience of this argument is supported further by the broader process of globalisation. Issues within international relations tend to be of a cross-border nature (e.g. protection of the environment). Inevitably, this provides a persuasive reason for states to join regional blocs.

In recent years, it should be noted that certain countries have been able to reassert their sovereignty. Despite the combined forces of regional integration and globalisation, predictions about the demise of the nation-state and its associated sovereignty are overstated. Under the Trump administration, a number of decisions were consistent with isolationism. For instance, in 2017, the newly elected President decided to take the US out of the Trans-Pacific Partnership (TPP). The United Kingdom has also decided to counter the trend towards regional integration by leaving the European Union. Conversely, it must be recognised that these decisions have not slowed down the process of regional integration and globalisation. For instance, it is notable that when the United States withdrew from the TPP, in 2017, the remaining countries simply negotiated a new trade arrangement that incorporated most of the provisions from the former agreement. Equally, the European Union has continued with the process of deeper integration despite a major power leaving the organisation.

The Development of Regional Organisations (Excluding the EU)

The North American Free Trade Association (NAFTA)

The North American Free Trade Association is a trilateral trading bloc that consists of the United States, Canada and Mexico. NAFTA aims to reduce or eliminate barriers in the field of trade and investment between those three economies. One of the largest trading blocs in the world, the agreement came into effect during the mid-1990s.

In terms of its positives, the agreement ensures a more open trading system that represents just under 30% of the world's Gross Domestic Product (GDP). Free trade has also contributed to a series of knock-on effects, such as lower transaction costs and a more efficient allocation of resources consistent with market forces. However, the impact has been controversial in terms of employment and the environment. In the US, NAFTA has been depicted as a source of job losses and lower wages. This criticism has been echoed by figures from both sides of the political spectrum. During the US electoral campaign in 2016, both Democrats (such as Bernie Sanders) and Republicans (such as Donald Trump) voiced anxieties felt within the 'Rust Belt' over the loss of jobs to lower-cost producers in Mexico. Trump, whilst president-elect, even referred to the agreement 'the single worst trade deal ever approved in the US.'

During initial negotiations over the trade agreement, there was significant vocal opposition within the US over the potential impact on American employment. Supporters however claimed the economic benefits of the agreement would be significant. Revealingly, a recent congressional report into the economic impact of the agreement confirms that 'NAFTA did not cause the huge job losses feared by the critics or the large economic gains predicted by supporters' (Villarreal et al.. 2017). Overall trade with their two immediate neighbours is relatively modest by US standards. Whilst in office, President Trump sought to replace NAFTA with a United States-Mexico-Canada Agreement (USMCA) which took effect in July 2020. Given the similarities with the previous agreement, USMCA is often characterised as NAFTA 2.0.

The environmental impact of NAFTA has also been a source of controversy within Mexico. On the day the agreement came into force, the Zapatistas declared war on the Mexican government for its endorsement of NAFTA. The left-wing political organisation is aligned to the wider alter-globalisation movement and seeks indigenous control over agricultural land. The trade liberalisation that lies at the heart of NAFTA is contrary to their ideological platform. Whilst the USMCA enhances environmental and working regulations, the impact upon the environment remains subject to criticism.

The African Union (AU)

The African Union (AU) represents just over one billion people and includes all states that form the African continent. The AU replaced the Organisation of African Unity (OAU) which was regularly criticised as the 'dictators club'. Since its founding in 2002, the African Union has sought to defend human rights in a more effective manner than its immediate predecessor. One of the inherent weaknesses within the OAU was the manner in which national sovereignty was placed above concerns about human rights violations. The African Union has taken firm action in this area. For instance, Sudan was suspended from the organisation due to violence used against protestors in 2019.

The long-term objective of the organisation is the creation of an economic and monetary union. Following the approach adopted by the EU, the AU seeks to create a single market underpinned by a central bank and a common currency. The aim is to establish an African Economic Community with a common currency by the year 2023. The African Continental Free Trade Area (AfCFTA) came into effect with trade commencing on 1 January 2021. The AfCFTA is the largest in the world in terms of the number of participating countries since the formation of the WTO. This would represent the process of deeper regional integration amongst the member states.

The highest decision-making body within the AU consists of its member-states' premiers. Given its status within the organisation, the Assembly has the authority to act upon proposals sent by the African Court of Human and Peoples' Rights (ACHPR). There is also a representative body of the African Union called the Pan-African Parliament. In contrast, the Commission of the African Union adopts the role of an executive and administrative branch. The organisation also consists of an executive council, a committee of permanent representatives, and a consultative body that considers economic and cultural issues. There is also a quasi-judicial institution responsible for interpreting the African Charter on Human and Peoples' Rights. The governance of the AU is therefore comparable to the structure adopted by the EU.

Law-making within the organisation derives from a number of sources, such as constitutional documents, treaties and soft laws. Examples of the former consist of those documents that protect the welfare of the child and outline the conduct of democratic elections. The Abuja Treaty (signed in 1991) established the African Economic Community, whilst soft law tends to cover the issues concerning human rights. In common with the EU, the organisation has also developed a military dimension. Its first military intervention occurred in 2003 when peacekeeping forces were dispatched to Burundi. Troops from the African Union have since been deployed in failed states like Somalia on the basis of humanitarian concerns. Integration has also been fostered through various documents (most notably the New Partnership for Africa's Development) that have enhanced levels of governance. There has also been progress amongst the member states in terms of improving education and infrastructure. However, there are still issues to resolve, such as discrimination against minority groups.

The Arab League

Formed in 1945, the principal objective of the Arab League is to foster cooperation between member states and promote the common interests of Arab states. Over its lengthy history, the Arab League has provided a forum for member states to deliberate on matters of interest, settle disputes and construct a united voice.

One of the main achievements of the organisation is the development of a common security or military dimension. In 1950, an agreement was reached that committed the signatories to coordinate defence measures. In more recent times, the Arab League launched the Joint Arab Force (JAF) in order to combat the growing threat posed by Islamic extremism within the region. Participation is voluntary and the Army will only intervene at the request of one of the member states. Unlike the EU, the Arab League places a firm emphasis upon national sovereignty and independence.

In the absence of supranational institutions, decision-making is based upon cooperation and negotiation. Although the Arab League does have elements of a representative parliament, it would be highly misleading to make any comparison with the European Parliament. Without supranational institutions to draft and supervise policies, the Arab League has been hamstrung by the need to reach a unanimous position. The governance of the organisation has often been criticised as inefficient.

In contrast to European integration, Arab states have proved resistant to share economic wealth. Members have also found it problematic to resolve ideological differences between them. In particular, the ruling elites within the Gulf region have been reluctant to embrace the concept of Arab nationalism. Equally, vested interests with external powers have proved a major obstacle to the Arab League adopting a system that would compare with the depth of integration achieved by the EU.

In terms of the Middle East conflict, the Arab League has long been supportive of a homeland for the Palestinians. The framers of the initial Pact included the Palestinian Arabs from the very outset and, in 1964, the Arab League created a group designed to represent the Palestinian people. The group later became known as the Palestinian Liberation Organisation (PLO). At the Beirut Summit in 2002, the Arab League adopted the Arab Peace initiative at the behest of Saudi Arabia. The proposal offered a normalisation of relations with Israel in exchange for the withdrawal of Israeli troops from occupied territories. Under the plan, Israel would recognise Palestinian independence in the West Bank and Gaza with East Jerusalem as its capital. The initiative was later promoted by representatives from Jordan and Egypt in 2007.

The Arab League has also reached a common position vis-a-vis the politics of the region. For instance, the League supported the Saudi-led intervention in Yemen and passed a resolution calling for Turkish forces to withdraw from northern Syria. The Arab League also condemned Benjamin Netanyahu's plans to annex the Jordan Valley in 2019. Yet having said this, smaller organisations within the Arab world have often been more effective in terms of securing economic objectives. For instance, the Organisation of the Petroleum Exporting Countries (OPEC) often uses its valuable resources to exert global political pressure, as it has done in the past.

The Association of Southeast Asian Nations (ASEAN)

The Association of Southeast Asian Nations is an intergovernmental organisation that consists of ten countries within South-East Asia. The organisation aims to promote cooperation and facilitate political and economic integration amongst its members. ASEAN is one of the most important political organisations within the region alongside the Asia Pacific Economic Cooperation (APEC).

ASEAN has made considerable progress in terms of establishing an area of free trade and political stability. In terms of the former, the ASEAN Free Trade Area (AFTA) is one of the most important in the world. Unlike the EU, AFTA does not impose a common external tariff on imported goods. Back in 2008, member states launched the ASEAN Charter, committing the organisation to move towards 'an EU-style community'. The Charter aims to establish a trading area encompassing around 500 million people. It marks progress within a region of the world that – like Europe – was once riven by warfare. However, there are doubts as to the ability of certain economies to meet the requirements of closer economic integration. In terms of political stability, the organisation has also managed to ensure a nuclear weapons-free zone within the region, despite marked differences between the member states on the issue.

The organisation has also made some progress in the field of human rights. In 2009, the ASEAN Intergovernmental Commission on Human Rights (AICHR) was established in order to promote human rights within the region. However, the AICHR lacks the ability to impose sanctions against those countries that violate the rights of its citizens. Criticism has been made over the inability of the organisation to address ethnic cleansing within Myanmar. Corruption also remains an issue within the region, as do several border disputes.

ASEAN works closely with states from outside of the region. Since 1997 'ASEAN plus three' has provided a forum for cooperation with China, Japan and South Korea. As a result of the late-1990s financial crisis, the Chiang Mai Initiative has sought to establish greater financial stability within Asia. 'ASEAN Plus Six' incorporates India, Australia and New Zealand and provided the framework for the planned East Asia Community and the Regional Comprehensive Economic Partnership. ASEAN has also played an active role in the Shanghai Cooperation Organisation.

On a final note, the phrase 'ASEAN way' describes an approach to resolving issues that reflects the cultural norms of South-East Asia. Decision-making is informal, consultative and characterised by the desire for consensus. Quiet diplomacy amongst the member states enables leaders to communicate effectively without resorting to bellicose jingoism. However, this method has been criticised for contributing towards wording based upon the lowest common denominator. It also makes it very difficult for the organisation to take effective action in the face of a serious problem. ASEAN is sometimes viewed as a talking shop that's big on words but small on action.

The European Union

Factors That Fostered European Integration

There are several factors that are readily identifiable as having driven forward the process of European integration. Although the significance of these factors has fluctuated over time, the two constant themes throughout have been economic and political. From the very outset, European integration was designed to provide tangible economic benefits and prevent conflict within the continent.

After the disruption caused by the Second World War, a number of continental countries sought a new pathway towards a more peaceful and stable Europe. France and Germany had engaged in three major wars in the space of just seventy years. In order to break the cycle of conflict, it was agreed that the industries of war would be placed under the control of a supranational institution. In doing so, the ability to create a war machine would be removed. The European Coal and Steel Community (ECSC) was a success, and it paved the way for deeper integration. By the end of the 1950s, both the European Community and the European Atomic Energy Community (Euratom) – a single market for nuclear materials and technology – had been established.

In an economic sense, the original six member states of the European Community sought to improve trading links via the removal of trading barriers. France, Germany, Italy and the BENELUX countries all recorded high levels of economic development as a result of trade liberalisation. It is no exaggeration to say that the lure of economic benefits persuaded countries within the second enlargement (such as the UK) to join. During the 1980s and 90s, a framework for economic and monetary union was outlined amongst the member states. The eurozone was established and the European Central Bank (ECB) in Frankfurt sets a common monetary policy within participant states. The eurozone consists of 19 EU member-states and the euro is one of the major global trading currencies on the foreign exchange markets. Given the tradition of state sovereignty over an area of considerable importance, the depth of integration achieved within the economic realm is remarkable.

Alongside political and economic factors, the process of integration has also been driven by a habit of cooperation amongst the member states. Former rivals have placed their differences to one side and embarked upon a European project that has transformed inter-state relations within the continent. Out of the depths of the deadliest military conflict in history, the member states of the European Union have forged a genuine zone of peace. The process of integration within Europe has established a significant actor on the world stage. The European Union is a hybrid of both supranational institutions, such as the ECB, and intergovernmental forums such as the European Council. The existence of both types of institution reflects the debate about supranational versus intergovernmental approaches.

In a theoretical context, the concept of 'spillover' has played a key role within the development of European integration. The founding fathers of the European project sought to provide a practical path towards an ever-closer union. Alongside Altiero Spinelli and Robert Schuman, Jean Monnet outlined a blueprint for a European federation. The Monnet plan entailed taking control of the German coal-producing areas and redirecting production towards the French. The aim was to weaken Germany and strengthen the French economy. Monnet and his allies later put forward the idea of a European Community. Prophetically, it was said that 'this proposal represents the first concrete step towards a European federation'. Jean Monnet also prophesied that 'Europe will be forged in crises', and that the bloc would end up being 'the sum of the solutions adopted for those crises.' Whether this depiction of the European Union remains a valid one is open to deliberation.

From an initially negative mindset (in the sense that countries were focused upon avoidance), integration amongst the European states has adopted a more proactive approach. Integration in one area has also created a momentum towards integration in other policy areas. Over time, deeper integration has enabled the European Union to perform the role of a major global power. The European Union now boasts a Common Foreign and Security Policy, harmonisation over policymaking and a diplomatic presence throughout the world. It also co-operates extensively with partners – such as its relationship with NATO which is depicted as 'separable, but not separate'.

Formation, Role, Objectives and Development of the European Union

The core aim of the European Union is to make progress towards 'an ever-closer union'. The unmistakable tone of this phrase is very much towards further integration. Right from the very outset, the direction of European integration pointed towards the creation of a United States of Europe in the notion of 'an ever-closer union'. From an original community of just six states, the organisation is now one of the most important non-state actors in global affairs with twenty-seven members. During the historical development of the European Union, the organisation has created a quasi-federalist system.

Another key objective of the EU is the existence of the four fundamental freedoms. Since the early-1990s, the EU has been pledged towards free movement of: (1) goods, (2) services, (3) capital and (4) people. This is an integral element of the single market and associated moves towards closer economic integration. The four freedoms are maintained by the role of member states and the various institutions (particularly the Commission). Consistent with the principle of spillover, the organisation has developed from the common market towards a single market with freedom of movement.

Implementation of the four freedoms has not been without controversy. Freedom of movement for goods and services tends to benefit the wealthier economies at the expense of those on the periphery. However, this is to some degree offset by the provision of regional funding. The main problem has undoubtedly been that of immigration. The influx of immigrants from the twelve new member states in the noughties caused anxiety amongst the wealthier states. Cheap labour from Central and Eastern Europe was one of the main causes behind the defeat of the proposed EU constitution during the French referendum. Concern over uncontrolled and unprecedented levels of immigration has also been highlighted by several populist parties and politicians. Furthermore, it was a decisive factor in the result of the 2016 Brexit referendum in the United Kingdom.

Establishment and Powers of its Key Institutions and the Process of Enlargement

When seeking to comprehend the various institutions of the European Union, the first point to consider is the distinction between supranational and intergovernmental institutions. In basic terms, supranational bodies take decisions above the nation-state. An intergovernmental institution, however, retains the sovereignty of the state. The former tends to drive forward the development of a federal Europe, whilst the latter emphasises the importance of unanimity and the protection of national interests.

Another point to grasp is that the various institutions approximate the three branches of government. In terms of the executive branch, the European Commission consists of appointees from each member state. It is responsible for implementing decisions, upholding the treaties and managing the administrative functions of the EU. The Commission also proposes legislation and operates on the basis of a cabinet government. As with other executive branches, the term 'Commission' is used in a collective sense towards the civil servants in the *de facto* capital – Brussels. They work within departments known as 'Directorates-General'.

The European Parliament (EP) is the main law-making branch of the EU. Alongside the Council of the European Union, the EP adopts legislation proposed by the Commission. The EP consists of members directly elected from the member states. The European Parliament has grown in terms of competence and now shares equal legislative and budgetary powers with the Council. The legislative branch also holds the Commission to account. For instance, the EP approves the appointment of the Commission and can force the entire executive body to step down.

The Court of Justice of the European Union (CJEU) interprets EU legislation to ensure that rules are implemented in the same manner across all twenty-seven member states. National courts may require clarification from the CJEU in terms of how to interpret existing law. This supranational body also adjudicates upon legal disputes between national governments and EU institutions. Individuals, companies, and organisations can also bring cases to the attention of the court provided it relates to EU law. The judicial body enforces the law when an infringement has taken place. Finally, the CJEU can annul any EU law when there is a violation of existing treaties or fundamental rights. The CJEU is sometimes confused with the European Court of Human Rights (ECtHR). However, it must be recalled that the ECtHR is *not* an EU institution but rather enforces the ECHR and is attached to 'The Council of Europe', not to be confused with any EU body, and is the institution formed after the Second World War to uphold human rights on the European continent.

The main intergovernmental body of the EU is the European Council. Given that it consists of member-states' premiers, the European Council is well-suited to debates over major projects. For instance, the practicalities of enlarging the EU during the noughties were discussed in depth at the Council level. As a collective body, the European Council shapes the overall direction and priorities of the organisation. Although it has no law-making power, it does provide a forum by which strategic planning can be achieved. Decisions taken within these EU summits are taken on the basis of consensus unless the existing treaties provide otherwise.

The Council of the European Union (sometimes referred to simply as the Council, or sometimes 'The Council of Ministers') is also an intergovernmental institution. It consists of representatives from member states to create a particular policy area. Alongside the European Parliament, the Council serves to amend and approve proposals made by the executive branch via its legislative role. The presidency of the Council rotates every six months amongst the national governments. Unlike the European Council, decisions are usually made on the basis of qualified majority voting (QMV), whereby each state is given a plurality of votes in relation to population density. Employed within intergovernmental forums, qualified majority voting (QMV) enables the decision-making process to move forward without the need for unanimity within the European Council and Council of the EU. QMV is arguably the inevitable consequence of an organisation that has expanded significantly since its inception. Less important decisions are made via simple majority, although in some cases the national veto is retained.

The accession process is formally launched when a country submits their application. This is addressed to the Council of the European Union, which then asks the Commission to assess the application. On the basis of agreed criteria, known as 'The Copenhagen Criteria', the Commission issues its recommendations for further steps that the applicant must take. Depending on these details, the Commission may recommend that the Council grant the applicant candidate status. On the basis of the opinions provided by the Commission, the Council has to agree on a unanimous basis whether to accept the application and whether accession negotiations should begin. The Council also decides whether or not the applicant should be given candidate status.

The lengthy process of negotiation focuses upon when the candidate country is to adopt the rules and obligations of membership, and under what conditions. Since the 2004 enlargement, the negotiating framework entails a suspension clause if the candidate makes a serious and persistent breach of the principles of the organisation (such as democracy, respect for human rights and the rule of law). The negotiating framework also contains a clause that considers the EU's capacity to absorb a new member. These two areas have proved to be a stumbling-block regarding Turkey's potential membership of the EU.

Key Treaties and Agreements

Ratified by all of the member states, the EU treaties outline the role of the institutions alongside its remit and objectives. The EU acts within the competences granted via these treaties (and subsequent amendments ratified by the member states). However, the actual constitutional basis of the European Union derives from the Rome Treaty and the Maastricht Treaty.

The Treaty on the functioning of the European Union (more commonly known as 'The Rome Treaty') was signed in 1957 by the six original members. The Rome Treaty established the European Economic Community (EEC) and laid the foundation for integration amongst member states. In 1992, the Treaty on European Union signed at Maastricht was primarily responsible for the creation of the single currency, the euro. It also renamed itself as the 'European Union' in recognition of the expanded competences of the organisation, and established a pathway towards further integration within high politics (such as foreign policy and home affairs).

Since the passage of the Maastricht Treaty, there have been three further agreements. The Treaty of Amsterdam (1997) transferred certain powers from national legislatures to the European Parliament alongside institutional changes to accommodate planned enlargement. The Nice Treaty (2001) agreed to further institutional reform in order to accommodate the planned expansion towards Central and Eastern Europe, which took place in 2004. From a similar angle, the Lisbon Treaty (2007) moved from unanimity voting to QMV in several areas. It also expanded the powers of the European Parliament, created a legal personality for the EU and made the Charter of Fundamental Rights legally binding. Finally, it gave member states the right to leave the EU and outlined the means to do so.

The EU also has a number of agreements that match its multi-speed approach. Although not a formal part of EU law, since 1995 the Schengen agreement enables visa-free travel amongst its participants. Most member states participate within the Schengen zone; 22 member-states currently fully participate, with Bulgaria, Croatia, Romania and Cyprus holding a legal obligation to join in the future, and Ireland opting out. The EU has managed to bypass the problem of gaining unanimity via securing agreements regarding the creation of Eurocorps, the European Gendarmerie Force, and the European fiscal compact. This serves to underline the overall importance of agreements reached within a multi-speed Europe.

Economic and Monetary Union

Economic and monetary union (EMU) is one of the major achievements of the European Union. In accordance with the incremental nature of European integration, EMU has been established at various stages. The latest stage is the creation of a eurozone, which is characterised by a common monetary policy and a single currency. In order to become a member, participant states need to meet the convergence criteria. With the exception of Denmark, all EU member states must comply with the convergence criteria with the expectation of eventual membership of the eurozone.

During the 1950s and 1960s, the process of European integration provided tangible economic benefits to its members. This was an era of stable economic growth within and between the original six members. The practical path offered by the founding fathers of the European project seemed to deliver genuine economic benefits. However, the record of the eurozone is more mixed. There are several reasons for this, not least the slowdown in the global economy that was out of the direct control of the EU. That said, the lack of convergence within the organisation is partly due to unrealistic targets. Poorer performing economies such as the Mediterranean PIGS (Portugal, Italy, Greece and Spain) were allowed to join the eurozone by including the hidden economy within the figures. The level of public sector debt recorded within these economies has meant bailouts funded by the more efficient economies and significant political unrest within those affected by the sovereign debt crisis, the events in Greece during the 2008 financial crash illustrating this case in point.

Another problem specific to the eurozone is the inflexible nature of monetary policy. Within such a vast economic unit, it is difficult for the central bank to adopt the correct measures. Adopting a level of interest rates suitable for the German economy may not match the interests of those economies on the periphery (such as those in Southern Europe). This may relate to other economic problems such as high levels of unemployment. The degree of youth unemployment within the eurozone is a particular concern for the long-term prospects of the European project. The inability of European integration to provide the economic benefits associated with its previous success continues to cast a considerable shadow over EMU.

Debates about Supranational Versus Intergovernmental Approaches

The debate concerning supranationalism versus intergovernmentalism concerns the thorny issue of how to proceed with European integration. This reflects a difference of opinion that was present at the very beginnings of the European project between those who wished to retain national sovereignty, and those who believed in the formation of a, so-called, United States of Europe. During the historical development of the organisation, the influence of these two distinct perspectives has fluctuated.

To clarify the distinction between supranationalism and intergovernmentalism, the Maastricht Treaty introduced the 'principle of subsidiarity', which was the notion that decision making capabilities are retained by member-states if EU intervention is unnecessary. Since then, the EU is obliged to take action at the most appropriate level of decision-making. For example, there are certain areas of policymaking that are more properly dealt with on the basis of unanimity. In such cases, the intergovernmentalist approach is adopted. However, there are other areas in which a supranational institution such as the Commission should make the decisions. In recent years, the powers of the European Parliament have also increased, for example to include supervising EU budgetary and institutional matters.

The founding fathers of the European Union could see the necessity for supranational institutions to drive the project forward. From the very outset, it should be recognised that integration was never intended to be wholly democratic in the manner that political action would be on the domestic level of the nation-state. Instead, there was a recognition that the forces of nationalism should be suppressed in order to prevent the outbreak of warfare, as had cursed Europe for centuries. For instance, during the Second World

War, Altiero Spinelli and fellow prisoner Ernesto Rossi compiled a draft manifesto for a united Europe (Union of European Federalists 2019). They claimed that the war against fascism would have been pointless if it re-established a discredited system based upon shifting alliances. The proposal for a European federation of states with supranational bodies offered a tangible path towards a lasting peace. In tying all European nations so closely together, the possibility for any future wars would disappear, following a liberal grasp of International Relations.

The intergovernmentalist approach stipulates that member states are the primary actors within the process of integration. Intergovernmentalism marks an attempt to defend the national interest against communality and harmonisation driven by supranational bodies. The European Council and the Council of the European Union can halt those projects put forward by the supranational institutions. The institutional structure of the EU therefore provides a brake upon the process of political, social and economic integration. Equally, the intergovernmental forums within the EU have provided the right environment for planning major European projects like the single market.

The Significance of the EU as an International Body and Global Actor

The importance of the EU presents a fascinating case study to consider within global politics. Often identified as *sui generis*, any assessment of the EU and its agency must recognise that it holds a unique set of characteristics. For instance, it would be unhelpful to make a direct comparison with great powers in terms of political and military influence. Given its structure, there are obvious limitations placed upon the EU that are distinct from that of a nation-state. Yet, having said this, the EU exerts considerable influence within global affairs on the basis of its soft power potential within the economic and diplomatic realm.

Over its historical development, the EU has facilitated the spread of democracy and respect for human rights. This has been achieved via encouraging former dictatorial regimes to join the organisation and therefore accept the rules and obligations of membership, transforming these previously non-democratic societies into open, democratic states. Many of the member states from Southern and Eastern Europe were at one time characterised by their dictatorial systems. The EU has also fostered liberal values in terms of the rule of law alongside free, fair and regular elections – upholding the liberal democratic peace thesis.

In diplomatic terms, the European External Action Service performs the role of the EU's diplomatic service with delegations and offices throughout the world. The EU is represented at the high table of global governance with a seat at the G20 and the WTO. It also holds observer status in the IMF, the UN General Assembly and G7 summits. The EU is a signatory to 50 free trade agreements with other countries, and works in partnership with emerging and regional groups on the basis of mutual interests. The level of humanitarian assistance provided by the organisation is second only to the United States. For an organisation initially created out of the wreckage of warfare, it seems symbolic that the EU was once awarded the Nobel Peace prize, in 2012. The success of the EU as a political organisation is tacitly underlined when other regional organisations seek to implement a comparable structure (most notably the African Union and ASEAN).

The political capacity of the EU has expanded alongside the enlargement of the organisation itself. Membership of the EU could be said to foster a zone of stability in a continent with a troubled history of conflict. It could be argued that the most significant political achievement of the organisation is its expansion from the original six to twenty-seven members, covering just under 4.5 million square kilometres and housing the third largest population in the world, if taken cumulatively. This has led to an increasing number of states applying to join the union. At the time of writing, there were five official candidate countries: Montenegro, the Republic of North Macedonia, Serbia, Turkey and Albania. It is worth noting that as recently as the 1990s some of these applicants were ravaged by warfare and instances of ethnic cleansing. Membership of the EU remains an attractive pull in terms of regional funding, global standing and access to the single market.

There are of course several constraints and obstacles that limit the EU's political influence. In terms of its relative importance, the EU is undoubtedly weaker than the United States. Whilst there is a debate over how to characterise the power balance within international relations, it cannot be denied that the US is the dominant political power.

The EU also finds it problematic to adopt an effective unified position. The EU is an organisation forged through compromise and consensus. In the search to speak with one voice, the European position can at times be something of a whisper. The complexity of its internal structure is one obvious limitation to consider here. In an organisation built upon a hybrid of intergovernmentalism and supranationalism, the EU cannot always act in a rapid and effective manner. Ultimately, it lacks the federal structure and political weight of a potential hegemon such as the United States, and as such is limited by its internal structural fractures, divisions and debate.

In economic terms, the EU is undoubtedly a significant actor within global affairs. Measured by the share of global GDP, the EU is the second largest economy in the world with a population size of approximately 450 million. This alone enables the EU to utilise its economic resources to exert influence. This is perhaps to be expected given that the project itself began essentially as an economic union. As the common market proved to be a success, countries sought membership for its economic benefits. The process of economic and monetary union has created a distinct European market that operates in a similar manner to any domestic economy. The single currency is the second largest reserve currency and the second most traded currency in the world, following the US Dollar in both cases. Moves towards implementing the four freedoms make it far easier to move abroad for work, and the Schengen Agreement even allows for largely unrestricted free movement of labour.

Having said this, the process of economic and monetary union has faced major problems since the sovereign debt crisis of the late 1990s. It could be argued that the lack of convergence between the more developed economies such as Germany and the less efficient economies of Southern Europe was always going to present a problem. The institutions of the EU fudged the issue of convergence – and the resultant difficulties were to some extent a problem of their own making. Attempts to resolve the issue (such as debt restructuring) have only partially addressed the economic difficulties facing the organisation. For instance, there is a clear limitation presented by the divergent levels of public debt within the EU. In the context of economic and monetary union, those who support deeper integration may have placed political rhetoric over economic reality.

In structural terms, the EU has developed a highly developed and unique system of governance. This has enabled the organisation to act effectively and drive forward the process of integration. In relative terms, the progress made via European integration is indeed considerable. The EU has a common fisheries policy, a common agricultural policy and has harmonised over thirty separate policy areas. The laws, court decisions and directives passed by the institutions of the EU (otherwise known as the 'Acquis Communautaire') are of undoubted political importance.

However, the main constraint upon the EU is its democratic deficit. This refers to a lack of democratic legitimacy within the organisation. The main source of criticism centres upon the executive branch. It is undeniable that an unelected number of bureaucrats lie at the very heart of European decision-making, placing the accountability of the EU in the line of critique. Another related element to consider is the lack of public support for European integration. It is revealing to note that turnout in European Parliamentary elections has tended to decline, whilst the powers awarded to the institution have increased.

Pro-Europeans argue in favour of institutional reform in order to make decision-makers more accountable. Eurosceptics however believe that the project is inherently undemocratic. They point out that EU institutions have a habit of gaining powers over time despite the lack of public support for such measures. Powers should therefore be transferred to the national level in order to restore a sense of accountability. The UK's 2016 referendum and subsequent withdrawal from the organisation in 2020 has undoubtedly changed the contours of debate over this matter. Eurosceptic parties and politicians have gained support in several member states as a reaction against federal overreach from Brussels.

In terms of its military influence, the EU is relatively weaker than in the case of its economic might. The Common Security and Defence Policy (CSDP) involves military or civilian missions. Troops are deployed in order to preserve peace, prevent conflict and maintain security in accordance with the requirements of the international community. Military missions are carried out by EU forces established from the member states. Similar to Article Five of NATO, the CSDP consists of the principle of collective self-defence amongst the member states.

For an organisation that is often characterised as a civilian actor with soft power, the military capacity of the EU is worth noting. Headed by the EU's High Representative, the European Defence Union (EDU) is smaller than NATO's command structure. Given the amicable relations between the EU and NATO, the Allied Command Operations of the latter may be used for the conduct of EU missions. Having said this, the Military Planning and Conduct Capability is the actual military Headquarters of the EU. The European Defence Fund, created in 2017, marked another step towards a more effective military dimension.

The first deployment of EU troops under the CSDP occurred in 2003 in North Macedonia. Since then, the EU has deployed missions for policing and monitoring purposes to countries such as Sudan, Chad, Central African Republic and Indonesia. EU troops have also been sent to the Democratic Republic of Congo under a UN mandate. In terms of its maritime engagement, the EU has sent forces in order to combat piracy off the coast of Somalia. Closer to home, it has also sent troops to address migration issues in the southern Mediterranean.

Having said this, there are significant constraints in terms of its global military role. Perhaps the main problem facing European foreign policymakers is that the member states do not share a common platform. Historically, there are significant differences in terms of national interests and engagement with the outside world. Whilst France has a seat on the P5 and a history of engagement with the outside world, the Baltic states are primarily concerned with the desire to deter Russian overstretch via NATO membership. Attempts to create a common security and defence policy have been curtailed by the reluctance of certain states to establish a European alternative to NATO. The EU therefore remains somewhat reliant upon NATO (and in particular the United States). Of all the areas considered, the limitation upon its military role is the most problematic.

There are few better illustrations of the inability of the European Union to resolve a military conflict than the breakup of Yugoslavia in the 1990s. Faced with a problem on its own doorstep, the EU was initially hopeful that it could operate effectively without American assistance. This was rhetoric that seemed to match the optimism of the post-Cold War era and the integration agreed upon during the Maastricht Treaty. However, the conflict was only resolved with a significant role from the Clinton administration and NATO involvement. In a unipolar world, the role of the world's only superpower proved absolutely vital in bringing the conflict to a peaceful resolution.

As a final note, it could be argued that the EU remains the leading model for regional integration. The fundamental concepts of European integration, such as pooled sovereignty, supranational bodies and the single currency, have been adopted in several areas of the world. The sheer force of globalisation further emphasises the need for successful regional integration along the basis of the EU. The manner in which European integration has accommodated the process of globalisation provides a useful blueprint for other regions of the world. That said, the circumstances behind European integration were unique to a particular context. The European project may have also reached its natural end. This is particularly noticeable within the political dimension. It should also be noted that the economic performance of the European Union has been relatively poor in recent years. This perhaps undermines the desirability of European integration, and in part explains why regional blocs such as ASEAN have gone their own way, trailing a somewhat differing path of regionalism.

The Extent to Which Regionalism Addresses Contemporary Global Issues

Conflict

In the case of preventing conflict, the concept of regionalism and the establishment of regional blocs is designed to mitigate potential disputes between states. The leading illustration of this point is the EU. The initial purpose of the European Coal and Steel Community was to make war 'not only unthinkable but materially impossible' in the words of the former French foreign minister, Robert Schuman. The practical benefits of the organisation provided a blueprint for deeper integration amongst former enemies (most notably France and Germany).

The argument that regional blocs can be utilised in order to prevent conflict is built upon the theory of neofunctionalism. According to this perspective, integration in one area inevitably creates a dynamic towards deeper integration overall. Over time, member states will make progress towards a federalist structure comparable to the United States. Neofunctionalism advocates rule by technocratic experts housed in supranational institutions.

Another important concept within neofunctionalism is that of spillover. This reflects an assumption that moves towards a more federal Europe must be achieved on a gradual basis. The creation of an ever-closer union with three discernible branches of government requires a level of legitimacy that can only be achieved on an incremental basis.

Since the 1950s, the European Union has managed to prevent conflict amongst its own members via creating a zone of peace and stability within the continent. For instance, it is a prerequisite of membership that members must be committed to democracy. In the 1980s, three countries joined the organisation after a period of dictatorial rule. In addition, several of the countries that joined in the noughties were former communist regimes. The European Union has since expanded its external presence within the field of conflict prevention. The EU has a standing army, a foreign policy and a security policy. Although primarily a civilian actor, the EU is in possession of a military capacity that seeks to ensure peace. These operations are usually conducted in cooperation with other international organisations.

Regional blocs also provide a method by which potential disputes can be resolved with meaningful dialogue and a mediated forum. In some regions of the world, these forums have actively prevented conflict. For instance, the AU is pledged to secure a peaceful continent via a dialogue-centred approach to conflict prevention and resolution amongst its members. Another example to consider would be ASEAN representatives dispatched to Cambodia in order to negotiate a settlement following the 1997 coup. In these and several other cases, regional blocs act in order to resolve or prevent conflict. As one might expect, the record of such organisations is somewhat mixed.

Poverty

Regionalism also plays a role in terms of mitigating the impact of poverty. In the EU, regional funds are directed towards deprived areas such as southern Italy (known as the 'Mezzogiorno'). The cohesion fund aims to improve economic well-being and avoid regional disparities. Over a third of the EU's budget is allocated towards this particular objective. The broader aim of European integration (a Europe of the Regions) could also be said to empower regions. In doing so, initiatives associated with greater regionalism *within* the European Union help to alleviate its poorest areas. Since the mid-noughties, the main emphasis within the organisation has been to increase living standards in the relatively disadvantaged parts of Eastern Europe.

The general aim of regional blocs is to increase the level of prosperity and thereby reduce levels of poverty. The reduction of trade barriers within such organisations undoubtedly stimulates economic growth and development. This should help to raise living standards on the basis of trade creation. In certain aspects of integration this is a central objective. For instance, the creation of the African Economic Community has helped to increase trading opportunities amongst the member states. However, it must also be acknowledged that economic integration creates both winners and losers. In terms of the former, consumers should benefit from lower prices and enhanced choice. However, less efficient producers will be forced out of the market. It could also be claimed that the process of economic and monetary union within the EU has exacerbated poverty. This is particularly striking amongst those economies who struggled to meet the convergence criteria laid down at Maastricht.

Human Rights

Regionalism seeks to protect human rights via internal and external measures. Membership of regional organisations often requires an adherence to fundamental human rights. This is particularly obvious in the case of the European Union. Turkey first applied to join the organisation in a formal sense during the late-1980s. However, its human rights record presents a barrier towards joining. Indeed, the states which are admitted require unanimous support amongst existing member states. They also require approval from the supranational bodies in terms of their adherence to an accession agreement. In an external sense, the EU routinely condemns those countries that violate human rights. They may also utilise their considerable soft power in order to exert pressure upon countries outside of the organisation to uphold universal human rights.

A similar observation applies to other regional blocs. Member states can be prevented from joining an organisation due to their poor human rights record. In some cases, they can even be removed from the organisation, for instance as Venezuela was in its suspension from MERCOSUR in 2016. Having said this, some regional blocs take the issue more seriously and therefore have a better record on human rights. In the Middle East, a number of states have been accused of violating human rights. Controversially, the Cairo Declaration of Human Rights in Islam was adopted by member states of the Organisation of Islamic Cooperation in 1990. The declaration undermined the universality of those rights guaranteed under the UDHR. It is also worth noting that the Organisation of African Unity (OAU) which dates back to 1963 did little to protect civil liberties. Often called the 'dictators club,' the OAU has since been replaced by the African Union (AU).

In the specific context of the European Union, access to its lucrative single market is problematic for those outside of the organisation. There have been several criticisms from civil society organisations about the level of protectionism adopted by 'Fortress Europe.' This presents a very real barrier towards export-led growth from less developed countries. It also presents an issue in regards to migration and human rights. A high number of asylum seekers flee from human rights abuses in regimes such as Syria, Afghanistan and Somalia. Although European states pay lip service to universal human rights, they have also been criticised for their reluctance to accept refugees fleeing from human rights violations. The response to the Migration and Refugee Crisis from 2014 onwards has illustrated precisely this.

The Environment

Finally, regionalism also seeks to protect our shared environment. Given the transnational character of the issue, regional blocs provide a particularly suitable forum by which to address common problems. For instance, the EU's environmental policy has a major impact upon its member states. According to one estimate EU environmental law is now in excess of 500 directives, regulations and decisions. It has even been argued that the EU has the most extensive environmental laws of any international organisation in the world (Jordan and Adelle 2012).

The significance of the European Union's environmental programme can be assessed upon the international stage. The EU is a signatory to all the major multilateral environmental agreements. However, there is also a gap between capabilities and expectations. The rhetoric employed by the European Union does not always mirror its results. Other regional blocs have sought to promote trade in environmental goods. For instance, APEC economies seek to bolster trade in those goods that promote green growth and sustainable development. The commitment to reduce tariffs on environmental goods dates back to 2012.

The existence of regional organisations would seem to imply that environmental issues can be addressed in a more effective manner. Given the habit of cooperation generated by membership of such organisations, there is a regular forum to deliberate upon transnational issues. However, this is not in itself enough to ensure that levels of pollution are reduced. To take one example, NAFTA places less emphasis upon the environment. Under the agreement, domestic environmental laws should not discriminate against trade. As a consequence, firms can challenge environmental regulations passed in the signatory states. This is an approach that has contributed towards a significant increase in greenhouse gas emissions according to research by the noted environmentalist organisation Sierra Club (Sierra Club 2018). It should also be noted that Chinese membership of regional blocs has done little to limit the level of emissions deriving from the world's largest polluter.

Conclusion

In summary, the aim of this chapter has been to place the significance of regionalism within the broader context of international relations. For instance, there are several factors to consider that drive the process of regionalism. The relationship between regionalism and globalisation is a complex one. In one sense, regionalism is a reflection of the process of globalisation. However, it could also be viewed as contrary to the ethos of globalisation. Of all the regional organisations to consider, the most significant remains that of the European Union. It has for instance provided a blueprint for other areas of regional integration (notably in Africa). The EU is also an increasingly important actor within global politics.

BOX 6.1 – KEY TERMS FOR CHAPTER SIX

Regionalism

Regionalism is a broad-based political principle that focuses upon the development of a political or social system based upon one or more regions. Regions are often distinguished on the basis of religion, cultural identity and even language. In a political context regionalism refers to those movements that campaign for territorial autonomy, the organisation of the state on a regional basis and greater regional autonomy. Regionalism is also applicable towards those organisations that seek to integrate states within any given geographical area of international relations (most notably the EU). In terms of globalisation, trade between countries is conducted on a regional basis. There are several regional blocs within the world such as the European Union, NAFTA and the AU. The degree of regional integration amongst these blocs differs considerably.

European Union (EU)

The EU is an organisation with both supranational and intergovernmental elements. It is one of the most significant non-state actors within international relations dating back to the 1950s. Shortly after the end of the Second World War, the European Coal and Steel Community was established in order to ensure that any future war would be materially impossible. It was also based upon the concept of 'spillover', in which integration in one area leads towards further integration in other areas. The change in name from the European Community to the European Union was highly symbolic of a determination within the organisation to push forward a federalist agenda. The European Union was created in 1993 as a result of the Maastricht Treaty. The process of European integration has often been forced along due to agreements reached amongst the heads of state and government during negotiations over treaties. In 2007, the Lisbon Treaty sought to make the EU more democratic, more efficient and more able to address global issues with one voice.

European integration

The process of European integration has developed along the basis of 'Europe a la carte'. The depth of integration is therefore a highly uneven process due to its multi-speed character. The more federalist-minded states (notably France and Germany) have sought to integrate at a faster rate than countries on the periphery of the organisation. Since the 1990s, European integration has been particularly marked in both the economic realm and in terms of foreign policy. Moves towards a Common Foreign and Security Policy have been particularly noteworthy given the sheer diversity of national interests within the organisation. One of the member states is a nuclear power with a permanent seat on the UN Security Council, whilst five states are officially neutral (Austria, Ireland, Finland, Malta and Sweden). Some countries in the EU have a lengthy tradition of military engagement, whilst others are the very epitome of soft power. In an ever-expanding organisation, a multi-speed Europe has been maintained via the use of opt-outs. In doing so, the process of integration is maintained in an organisation of over 450 million people.

Sovereignty

In one sense, sovereignty should be viewed as a zero-sum concept in which supranational organisations can pass laws and directives that member states must adhere to. If they do not, member states may be liable to face sanctions from the Court of Justice of the European Union. Those who favour a more federal Europe claim that membership enables member states to implement effective policies. This is particularly important in regards to those issues that require a cross-border response. The logic of pooled (or shared) sovereignty also applies to a variety of international agreements and institutions. However, the extent to which integration has occurred within these institutions is relatively limited when compared to that of the EU. The controversy generated and issues raised by membership of the EU is of a very different character to that of any other international organisation.

Supranationalism

Supranationalism consists of institutions that can impose decisions above the member state. A supranational institution is of a higher authority in their specific remit or area than those of the nation-state. It therefore holds implications in terms of sovereignty and a deepening of European integration. An increase in the powers of supranational institutions is widely interpreted as a shift towards a more federal Europe. Originally, the European project was devised as an attempt to combat the destructive forces of nationalism. The Rome Treaty enabled the creation of supranational institutions in order to drive forward the process of 'an ever-closer union' and ensure the four freedoms (goods, services, capital and persons) throughout the regional bloc. Each supranational institution within the European Union has the ability to make decisions and impose binding sanctions upon the member states. This is conventionally interpreted as a loss of sovereignty. However, there are those who claim that the process of European integration can be viewed as shared (or pooled) sovereignty. The institutions of the European Union approximate the three conventional branches of government, but naturally are still distinct in a number of respects.

Intergovernmentalism

Intergovernmentalism is the polar opposite of supranationalism. Intergovernmental institutions, such as the IPCC and the World Bank, maintain the sovereignty of the nation-state. Member states therefore retain their ability to make decisions within their own territorial boundaries. In one sense, this limits the effectiveness of the organisation. This is particularly evident when countries are able to exercise their powers of veto. The dependent factor to consider here is the degree of political integration within that particular organisation. This holds major implications for the sovereignty of the nation-state. Intergovernmental institutions are the most common basis for the various avenues of global governance. Given the centrality of the Westphalian system, this is to be expected. Moves towards a truly world government would require governments to relinquish their national sovereignty, or at the very least fundamentally overturn their understanding of the concept. This seems highly unlikely as any change in the status quo would require a dramatic and possibly drastic chain of events. The only manner in which nation states might surrender sovereignty is when the necessary political will or economic benefit exists. The existence of regional blocs reminds us that the world economy is shaped by the dynamics of regionalism. It also challenges the widespread assumption that international relations is characterised by the process of globalisation.

Federalism

In the context of European integration, federalism consists of moves towards a United States of Europe. A federal Europe would therefore adopt the structure of a federal system with power shared between the European and national level. The founding fathers of the European project were committed to deeper integration rather than the American objective of a more perfect union. The federalisation of the European Union is the institutional process in which the EU becomes a single federal state with a central government. This may be contrasted to a confederation, in which member states maintain their sovereignty. Since the formation of the European Coal and Steel Community (ECSC), European integration has developed on the basis of a compromise between those who favour a federal Europe (such as the former Commission President Jacques Delors) and those such as Margaret Thatcher who support a Europe of wholly sovereign states. Given the tension between these two competing visions, the extent to which the European Union could be described as a federal system is debatable. In a legal sense, the EU is not a federation. However, academics such as R. D. Kelemen (2003) point out that the EU is sui generis (a Latin term meaning 'of their own kind') incomparable to a federal state. Although there are three branches of government in existence, the overall structure is different to that of a federal system.

The development of European integration has occurred in a multi-speed manner in order to accommodate divisions as to the desirability or otherwise of a federal Europe. As the member states retain the ability to amend the treaties, it seems unlikely that the EU would ever evolve into a truly unified federal state. That said, moves towards a more quasi-federal system may gain added momentum with the UK leaving the organisation.

Global Actor

The European Union is an important global actor within world affairs. However, it consists of a number of unique characteristics that do not fit easily under the conventional understanding of the subject matter. It must be acknowledged that the main capabilities of the EU derive from its soft power. In economic terms, the EU represents one of the world's largest single markets. The imposition of trade restrictions on those countries outside of 'fortress Europe' underlines the economic clout of the organisation. The EU also has a diplomatic presence throughout most of the world and provides an extensive level of humanitarian aid. In terms of hard power, the EU has established a European Security and Defence Policy (ESDP) which has deployed resources to the Middle East, the Balkans and the Caucasus. The presence of the EU has helped to resolve conflicts and build peace throughout many troubled areas of the world. The European Union has also formulated a common policy within the realm of social policies, taxation and the environment. However, the main illustration of agency has been within the process of economic and monetary union. The majority of countries within the organisation are part of the eurozone with a shared currency and a common monetary policy. States with a lengthy tradition of sovereignty over their territorial boundaries have transferred a great deal of economic decision-making to the European Central Bank in Frankfurt. Taken together, this would suggest that the EU is a significant global actor with a major presence within international affairs. The inherent difficulty for the EU to act in an effective manner concerns the absence of consensus. In short, it cannot answer the riddle first posed by Henry Kissinger when he mischievously asked: 'who do I call if I want to speak to Europe?'. For example, there are five Presidents in total (the European Commission, the European Parliament, the European Central Bank, the Euro Summit and the Euro group). In an organisation of twenty-seven member states with sometimes conflicting interests, the ability of Europe to speak with one voice will always be somewhat muted.

Widening-deepening

There is a stark contrast to be made between widening and deepening. The former refers to an enlargement in the number of member countries within the European Union. Deepening however entails further moves towards a 'United States of Europe'. Federalists favour a continued process of deepening in order that the EU satisfies the original goals of its founding fathers. Widening tends to weaken the process of integration, and an increase in membership constraints the ability of the organisation to adopt a common path. The European Union has widened on a number of occasions. In theoretical terms, the process of European integration has been driven by the concept of neofunctionalism (Haas 1958). Many of the founding fathers sought to integrate different sectors in the hope of achieving the positive effects of spillover. Neofunctionalism is shaped by three causal factors – economic interdependence, organisational capacity to resolve disputes and supra-national institutions. As a result, the EU has engaged in a lengthy process of further integration in several areas. However, intergovernmentalists point out that national governments still control the level and speed of European integration. The debate between neofunctionalists such as Ernst B. Haas (1975) and the intergovernmentalists such as Stanley Hoffman (1966) provide a theoretical context to the dichotomy between widening and deepening.

BOX 6.2 – KEY POINTS FOR CHAPTER SIX

1. International relations have been affected by the process of regional integration.

2. The main distinction to consider is that between widening and deepening.

3. Regionalism takes on different forms (such as economic, security and political).

4. The process of regional integration holds implications for the sovereignty
of the state.

5. There are many factors that drive the process of European integration.

6. The European Union is a significant actor on the global stage but not without critique.

7. Regional integration seeks to address and resolve issues such as conflict, poverty, human rights and the protection of the environment.

Conclusion

By way of a conclusion, I want to address what the reader might be moving onto and how this book may help guide them on their future pathway. First and foremost, it is always necessary to recognise that the same event can be interpreted very differently from an alternative perspective. This is more than simply a question of semantics. In the modern era, there is a need to consider how something may appear to others. We live in a noisy world of clickbait, fake/false news and misinformation. We need clarity and calmness in order to comprehend the complexity of situations that face us.

Secondly, all theoretical perspectives offer the hope of peace and stability. Despite its inherently pessimistic view of human nature, even realism offers a roadmap towards a more stable orderly system. The balance of power considerations that characterise realism provide a pathway towards a kind of peace. Equally, a number of rival perspectives are couched within an unmistakably normative tone. This is most clearly expressed within the ideology of liberalism and its adherence to the three Ps (peace, prosperity and progress). Those perspectives outside of the two dominant paradigms also offer the prospect of something better than what we currently have. It could even be argued that the study of International Relations is at its most empowering when there is an attempt to create a better society around us. This is of central importance towards an understanding of perspectives such as feminism, postcolonialism and liberalism. It is my wish that the reader will go beyond the mere functionality of a textbook and have begun to develop their own insights into a better way of approaching the world. The hope of a better tomorrow is contained with all the perspectives available.

After two decades of teaching within the social sciences, there are two main themes (classification and bickering) that reappear from one year to the next. Most notably, theorists working in any of the social sciences have a tendency to categorise. This can at times give the impression that thinkers are more concerned with cataloguing terms and concepts. Whilst this is an understandable conclusion, it is also a misleading one. There is a need to go beyond these limitations, and there are often practical and effective solutions to the problems of the global system.

In addition, a considerable level of heat is generated on the basis of finger pointing. Allied to this, the subject very often gives the appearance of academics bickering amongst themselves. To some extent, this problem is a self-imposed one. I remember the advice given by a former colleague: 'you cannot point the finger without that finger pointing back at you'. On reflection, this was good advice. The phenomenon seems to have been exacerbated by the instant gratification offered by the internet. We need to remind ourselves that global politics is subject to both change and continuity, and it is the task of the student to unify these themes together under the most convincing narrative. It is also imperative that we become part of the solution, rather than part of the problem itself. Even the construction of a persuasive grievance narrative can offer a convenient disguise for scapegoating others.

Regardless of these themes, International Relations teaches us that the system around us is never entirely stable. There is a constant potential of new developments, creating new realities and ever-changing landscapes. Global politics is forged under a perennial current of social change. This whirligig of change gives the study of the subject matter so much of its academic stimulation, providing students with an exciting subject and one at the vanguard of change. There will always be something to debate and explore within your studies and in the words of the Buddhist proverb: 'nothing is forever except change'.

We are all to some degree products of the era of our age and the dominant ideology. It shapes our mind map in ways that we may be unconscious of. On reflection, I was blissfully unaware of my own Western-centric assumptions until they were pointed out to me. I became a better person for having those deep-seated assumptions subject to a robust intellectual challenge. This unconscious bias in our thinking may lead us towards a view of the world trapped by ignorance, stereotypes and misinterpretation. Greater awareness of these distortions will present us with a clearer picture of the world around us. There is always the need to go beyond cultural relativism, patriotic correctness and false consciousness in order to see the world from a different perspective.

Each theoretical perspective has its own language and range of specific terms, and language itself is couched within certain assumptions about the subject. The main areas of contention entail human nature, the motivation for the behaviour of states and the importance (or otherwise) of non-state actors. There is also considerable reflection on issues such as the colonialism of language, the subordination of the female and the construction of identities and interests. In each case, there is a direct relationship between language used and assumptions made. In seeking to identify these linkages, we can better understand the world around us. In considering all the perspectives available, I hope this book has enabled the reader to escape the all-pervasive problem of paradigmatic prisms.

We are very much encouraged by modern capitalism and the internet to perceive ourselves as competitors in a global race. We are also encouraged to seek and maximise instant gratification over thoughtful reflection. That is why the time allocated to your studies is so crucial to your development. You have the time to consider the future and your place within it. In your studies, political ideas will bounce back and forth along the intellectual landscape. Your palate will be broadened at a time in your life when the constraints of the workplace have yet to shackle your mind. This book is just the start of your journey into International Relations. With hope it has provided a solid grounding for what can at times be a demanding subject and left you in a better place than when you began.

ABBREVIATIONS

AfCFTA	The African Continental Free Trade Area
ASEAN	Association of South East Asian Nations
AU	African Union
BRICS	Brazil, Russia, India, China and South Africa
CJEU	Court of Justice of The European Union
CFSP	Common Foreign and Security Policy
COP	United Nations Conference of the Parties
ECHR	European Convention of Human Rights
ECOSOC	United Nations Environmental and Social Council
ECSC	European Coal and Steel Community
ECtHR	European Court of Human Rights
EEC	European Economic Community
EFP	Enhanced Forward Presence
EU	European Union
EP	European Parliament
FAANGs	Facebook, Apple, Amazon, Netflix and Google
G7/8/20/77	Group of Seven/Eight/Twenty/Seventy-seven
GATT	General Agreement on Tariffs and Trade
GDP	Gross Domestic Product
ICC	International Criminal Court
ICJ	International Court of Justice
INGO	International Non-Governmental Organisation
IPCC	International Panel on Climate Change
IS	Islamic State
LEDCs	Less Economically Developed Countries
MAD	Mutually Assured Destruction
MDGs	Millennium Development Goals
MEDCs	More Economically Developed Countries
MERCOSUR	The Southern Common Market
MINTs	Mexico, Indonesia, Nigeria and Turkey
MNCs	Multinational Corporations or Companies
MPI	Multidimensional Poverty Index
NAFTA	North American Free Trade Association
NAM	Non-Aligned Movement
NATO	North Atlantic Treaty Organisation
NGO	Non-Governmental Organisation
NPT	Non-Proliferation Treaty
OPEC	Organisation of the Petroleum Exporting Countries
OPHI	Oxford Poverty and Human Development Initiative
P5	Five Permanent Members of the UNSC
PfP	Partnership for Peace
PLO	Palestinian Liberation Organisation

PRSPs	Poverty Reduction Strategy Papers
QMV	Qualified Majority Voting
R2P	Responsibility to Protect
SAPs	Structural Adjustment Programmes
SDGs	Sustainable Development Goals
UDHR	Universal Declaration of Human Rights
UK	United Kingdom
UN	United Nations
UNAMIR	United Nations Assistance Mission for Rwanda
UNFCCC	United Nations Framework Convention on Climate Change
UNEP	United Nations Environmental Programme
UNGA	United Nations General Assembly
UNSC	United Nations Security Council
UNOSOM	United Nations Operation in Somalia
UNTAET	United Nations Transitional Administration in East Timor
US	United States
USSR	The Soviet Union (or 'Union of Soviet Socialist Republics')
VJTF	Very High Readiness Joint Task Force
WHO	World Health Organisation
WMDs	Weapons of Mass Destruction
WTO	World Trade Organisation

GLOSSARY OF KEY TERMS

Abraham Accords – A joint agreement between Israel, the UAE and the US signed in 2020. The Abraham Accords marked the first normalisation of relations between Israel and a neighbouring Arab state since the mid-1990s.

Absolute gains – The overall benefit of a decision for a state or non-state actor regardless of the gains made by others. Actors therefore determine their actions on the basis of absolute rather than relative gains. The concept of absolute gain is rooted within the liberal perspective on International Relations.

Accountability – A situation in which those in power are held responsible for their decisions. There is a distinction to be made between horizontal and vertical accountability. The former requires a system of checks and balances between the three branches of government. Vertical accountability entails a role for citizens in acting as a limit upon the powers of government.

Adaptation – Changes made in order to accommodate different circumstances (such as living with the consequences of climate change). Strategies consistent with adaptation include the relocation of settlements in areas most at risk from climate change. Adaptation therefore entails changes within the processes, practices and structures dealing with environmental degradation.

African Continental Free Trade Area – A free trade area amongst members of the African Union. Established in 2021, the aim is to remove tariffs and increase intra-African trade. The agreement seeks to create a single market along similar lines to European integration.

African Monetary Union (AMU) – The process of deeper monetary integration within the African Union. The AMU will be administered by a central bank and result in the creation of a single currency.

African Union (AU) – An organisation consisting of member states from the African continent. The African Union was founded in 2002 and replaced the Organisation of African Unity. The regional bloc has created the Pan-African Parliament, the Commission and a semi-annual meeting of state premiers. The AU has also established a Peace and Security Council in order to implement decisions.

Anarchy – A condition in which states are free to pursue their own interests regardless of any wider obligations towards other members of the international community. Ultimately, there is no governing institution with the authority to resolve disputes between states and non-state actors. The realist school of thought tends to emphasise the importance of anarchy on the behaviour of states, whilst liberals claim the effects are somewhat exaggerated.

Annexation – The acquisition of another state's territory by force. Annexation is a unilateral act in which territory is seized rather than via cession (given or sold via a Treaty). Annexation can be legitimised via general recognition by international bodies (such as intergovernmental institutions).

Anocracy – A type of government that combines democratic and dictatorial features. Anocracies enable some form of democratic participation within a broader dictatorial framework. The number of anocracies has increased since the end of the Cold War.

Anthropocentrism – A worldview associated with the belief that humans are custodians of the Earth's resources. Anthropocentrism emphasises the elevated status of humans within the animal kingdom.

Anti(alter)-globalisation – A political movement that campaigns for an alternative form of globalisation to that of the Washington Consensus. Pressure groups, academics and civil society favour another world built upon concepts such as equality and social justice. The anti (or alter)-globalisation movement also seeks to promote an environmentally-friendly approach to economic development.

Arms Race – A situation in which two or more nations increase their military expenditure due to a shared mistrust. The arms race is a direct consequence of the security dilemma (or spiral of insecurity).

Association of Southeast Asian Nations (ASEAN) – ASEAN is a regional inter-governmental organisation that encourages political, economic, and security cooperation among its members. The group has held a key role in Asian economic and, to a certain extent, political integration. Equally, ASEAN has led negotiations amongst Pacific-Asian nations to form one of the largest free trading blocs the world has ever seen.

ASEAN Way – An informal and consensual approach adopted by leaders of the ASEAN states. The emphasis is upon compromise, consultation and the avoidance of conflict. The ASEAN way is also characterised by quiet diplomacy and coordination amongst member states.

Assimilation – A process in which different cultures are absorbed within the broader culture of that society. Assimilation places social harmony above the diversity championed by integration, and therefore offers a counter to the clash of civilisations thesis.

Asymmetrical development – The disparity in economic development between the industrialised 'North' and the underdeveloped 'South.'

Authority – The legitimate right to author decisions and rule over others. When power is exercised without legitimate authority, it can lead to conflict.

Autocracy – A system of government in which a single leader or party is in possession of supreme and absolute power. Once viewed in a favourable manner, the term autocracy is often considered in a negative sense due to its association with dictatorial regimes.

Balance of power – A concept which stipulates that states secure their survival via forging alliances with other states. In doing so, an equilibrium can be maintained between rival groups. The balance of power seeks to ensure a degree of stability compared to a system in which a hegemonic power could dominate its weaker neighbours.

Bandwagoning – A situation in which a state is aligned with a stronger adversary. Bandwagoning occurs when the weaker state decides that the cost of opposing the stronger power exceeds the benefits.

Bangkok Declaration on Human Rights – Signed in 1993, the Bangkok Declaration offers an alternative narrative to the Eurocentric approach. The Bangkok Declaration emphasises communal obligations rather than the rights of the individual. The document also emphasises the importance of sovereignty and the principle of non-interference.

Beijing Consensus – The political and economic policies adopted by China following the free-market reforms instigated by Deng Xiaoping. The phrase was coined by Joshua Cooper Ramo to highlight an alternative approach towards the Washington Consensus. The Chinese approach is sometimes referred to as a 'birdcage economy'.

Belt and Road Initiative – A global infrastructure development strategy adopted by the Chinese government. It is the centrepiece of contemporary Chinese foreign policy with a target date for completion by the middle of the century.

Billiard ball model – A realist conception in which the state is analogous to an independent and unitary billiard-ball. According to this state-centric assumption, domestic politics ends at the water's edge and engagements with other states may be calculated. In contrast, liberals claim that International Relations is characterised via the cobweb model.

Bipolarity – The distribution of power within international relations characterised by two superpowers each with their own sphere of influence. The term can be applied in a global or regional sense. Bipolarity often entails proxy wars rather than direct confrontation.

Bourgeoisie – A Marxist term used to describe the owners of capital. According to the Marxist perspective, those who own the means of production exploit those who sell their labour for a wage (the proletariat). Dependency theorists adopt a neo-Marxist understanding of the global economic system.

Brazilification – The hollowing-out of the middle class combined with an increase in the level of inequality. According to Ulrich Beck, 'Brazilification' can be attributed to the process of globalisation.

Brandt line The demarcation between the developed 'North' and the underdeveloped 'South.' The line was proposed by the former West German Chancellor Willy Brandt.

Bretton Woods System – An economic system of governance created shortly before the end of the Second World War. The Bretton Woods system was based upon a fixed exchange rate system.

Buck passing – A situation in which a state assumes that another state (or group of states) will deal with an emerging threat.

Buffer state – A relatively weak and neutral state situated between two larger hostile countries. The buffer state therefore prevents the outbreak of regional conflict (such as Iraq acting as a buffer between Iran and Saudi Arabia).

Bush doctrine – The foreign policy strategy of George W. Bush (2001 - 2009). The main feature of the Bush doctrine was the use of pre-emptive strikes. The Bush doctrine was also characterised by a singular pursuit of American interests rather than the globally-minded multilateral approach of Bush's predecessor (Clinton) and successor (Obama).

Capitalism – An economic system based on market forces, private ownership and minimal state intervention. The end of the Cold War marked the triumph of Capitalism over Communism.

Carter Doctrine – The pledge from the Carter administration (1977-1981) to employ military force in order to defend American interests in the Persian Gulf. The aim was to deter the Soviets from seeking hegemony in a region of strategic importance to Washington.

Cession – An understanding under international law by which territory is transferred from one state to another with the consent of both parties (such as the Louisiana purchase).

Chain Ganging – A term used to describe how, in a balance of power scenario, alliance partners must follow the lead when another goes to war. If a partner does not participate, it endangers the security of its allies.

Chauvinism – An exaggerated sense of national superiority. It is associated with jingoist rhetoric and an aggressive pursuit of the national interest(s).

Civil War – An intra-state conflict between groups, be they ethnic, political, religious, etc. Unlike conventional warfare, it is conflict within rather than between states.

Clash of Civilisations – A term associated with the American political scientist Samuel Huntington. He predicted that conflict in the twenty-first century would be characterised via tensions between rival cultures. Having said this, most contemporary warfare occurs between members of the same civilisation.

Class conflict – A Marxist term used to describe the political struggle between the bourgeoisie and the proletariat.

Classical realism – A theoretical perspective which offers an explanation of International Relations based upon assumptions concerning human nature. Classical realists adopt a pessimistic view of human behaviour and the primordial forces that shape us. Classical realism gained in popularity during the post-Second World War era, but has been eclipsed by the emergence of Structural (Neo)Realism.

Cleft Countries – States which contain large groups of people who identify with other civilisations (such as Ukraine, Sri Lanka and Sudan). This forms part of the broader clash of civilisations thesis.

Climate Change – Man-made changes to the natural environment that result in global warming and consequently global climate adaptations. Although there have been moves to address climate change, global governance has proved problematic.

Climate Change Denial – Those who refuse to acknowledge the scientific evidence behind climate change. Donald Trump once called climate change a 'hoax'.

Clinton Doctrine – The philosophical and strategic basis of foreign policy directed by the Clinton administration (1993–2001). The Clinton doctrine was characterised as liberal interventionism on a selective basis. Clinton's administration intervened in the former Yugoslavia, Kosovo and Somalia in order to promote humanitarian aims and defend American interests.

CNN factor – A phenomenon by which the media compels decision-makers to intervene in order to address a particular issue. The CNN factor creates a mindset amongst decision-makers in which 'something must be done.' The term can also be applied towards the proliferation of new media.

Cobweb Model – A liberal notion that claims global politics can be understood on the basis of complex interdependence. The cobweb model explicitly rejects the realist contention of the Billiard Ball model. Liberals claim that relations between states and non-state actors reflect a system of mutual dependence.

Cold War – A situation in which two rival states engage in proxy wars rather than direct conflict. The term is commonly applied towards the ideological dispute between the United States and the Soviet Union from 1945 to 1991. However, the term can also be applied towards current tensions between Washington and Beijing.

Colonialism – The settlement of a foreign country via an imperial power. Colonialism is characterised by exploitation of resources, and the separation of the indigenous population from settlers. The term is often used interchangeably with imperialism.

Commercial Peace Theory – A liberal perspective which claims that the spread of capitalism creates a more peaceful global system. There is a clear economic incentive for states to avoid warfare.

Communism – An economic and political system which is based on the common ownership of the means of production. During the Cold War, the Soviet Union implemented a state-centric economic system based upon common ownership.

Communitarian View – A perspective on human rights which claims that social cohesion and communal norms should take a higher priority over the rights of the individual. The communitarian approach is more prevalent within Asian and Muslim-majority countries.

Complex Interdependence – A liberal notion which claims that states and non-state actors are interconnected via commerce and global norms, such as human rights. Whilst states remain the most significant institutions, intergovernmental and supranational bodies also play a role. Decisions are therefore reached via a process of interaction between various officials shaped by a shared space and a habit of cooperation.

Constructivism – A theoretical perspective built upon the assumption that elements of International Relations are historically and socially constructed. According to Alexander Wendt (1992), even the realist concept of power politics is a social construct. In other words, anarchy is itself a social construct of the state system and can therefore be transformed. Constructivism has emerged as a major school of thought within International Relations with a number of different strands.

Containment – A foreign policy objective implemented by the United States during the Cold War. The aim was to prevent the spread of communism. Associated often with Truman, containment was based on the assumption that the Soviet regime was expansionist (Kennan 1947).

Conquest – The acquisition of territory on the basis of force.

Core States – According to the World Systems Theory, the global economy is divided into three distinct areas: Core, Semi-Periphery and Periphery. The exploitative economic system is structured in order to maintain the dominance of core countries such as the United States over those within the periphery.

Corruption – Dishonest and fraudulent behaviour amongst those in a position of power who use their position for personal benefit. Corrupt leaders often divert economic resources towards a privileged few in order to strengthen their own grip on power.

Cosmocracy – A world government characterised by the three branches of governance (legislature, executive and judiciary). The term Cosmocracy may be contrasted with global governance in which a quasi-system of governance operates.

Cultural Backlash – Opposition towards the Western-bias of cultural globalisation.

Cultural Flattening – The process in which information, commodities and images produced in one part of the world enter into a global village. Cultural flattening is associated with a homogenising monocultural set of Western values that tends to undermine cultural differences.

Cultural Globalisation – The transmission of ideas, meanings and values around the world in a manner that extends the scope and scale of transnational relations. The process is characterised by the consumption of a common culture via the media.

Cultural Homogenisation – The decline in cultural diversity through the popularisation of cultural symbols. Cultural homogenisation has contributed towards a cultural backlash, a rise in ethnic nationalism and the spread of religious fundamentalism.

Cultural Imperialism – A process by which dominant states impose their own values and mindset. As a consequence of cultural imperialism, cultures are presented in a hierarchical manner.

Cyberwarfare – The use (or threat) of cyber weapons against another with the intention of causing digital harm. Cyber hostilities may lead towards conventional warfare between two or more states. For instance, Israel and Iran have been victims (and perpetrators) of cyberwarfare operations.

De Facto – A Latin term meaning 'in fact'.

De Jure – A Latin term meaning 'in law'.

Defensive realism – The strand of realist thought which claims the anarchic structure of global politics encourages states to prioritise their own national security. Defensive realism is associated with theorists from the neorealist perspective such as Kenneth Waltz. Defensive realism emphasises the centrality of the security dilemma and that military expansionism undermines the primary objectives of the state.

De Lege Ferenda – A legal phrase meaning 'what the law ought to be'. The term is often contrasted with what the law is.

De Lege Lata – A legal term meaning 'what the law is', in contrast to *de lega ferenda*.

Dell Theory of Conflict Prevention – An updated version of the commerce (or capitalist) peace theory. According to Thomas Friedman (2005), no two countries that are both part of a major global supply chain (like Dell's) will ever fight a war against each other. Although not a complete guarantee, mutual dependence within the economic sphere tends to maintain peaceful relations between the countries involved.

Democratic Peace Theory – A liberal perspective that claims that the spread of democratic values leads towards a more peaceful, stable and harmonious international system. This is based on the assumption that democratic leaders are held to account by the electorate. Democratic countries are therefore incentivised to establish and maintain diplomatic institutions in order to resolve disputes between them.

Dependency Culture – A situation in which recipients of aid become reliant upon the provision of aid. Critics claim that the provision of financial assistance undermines individual responsibility and self-reliance.

Dependency Theory – A theoretical perspective which claims that the global economic system is characterised by the exploitation of those living in the periphery. It is a neo-Marxist perspective which claims that the imperialism of the past has been replaced by a form of neocolonialism implemented via the Washington Consensus.

Diplomatic Immunity – The legal principle in which a diplomat is exempt from certain laws within the state in which they are working.

Double Standards – Where one group (or state) is treated differently to another. Western nations ignore crimes committed by strategic allies whilst punishing those whose interests are contrary to their own. The hypocrisy is particularly evident in the context of American foreign policy in the Middle East. The US has defended Israel from the charge of violating international law and traded with authoritarian regimes that undermine human rights.

Doves – A term used to describe an individual who favours peaceful means by which to resolve a dispute. A dove is traditionally portrayed as a symbol of peace. The term is usually contrasted with a hawk who favours a militaristic approach.

Dyadic Peace – The liberal argument that democracies tend not to fight one another. Dyadic peace is a key element of the democratic peace theory.

Ecocentrism – A belief-system associated with the environmental movement that advocates an equal relationship between human beings and the environment. According to their outlook, humans are part of a wider whole with no particular elevated status. Ecocentrism is associated with deep green ecology.

Economic Globalisation – The process by which national economies have, to a greater or lesser extent, been absorbed into an interlocking global economy. Economic globalisation is characterised by mutual dependence amongst state and non-state actors.

Emerging power – Those states recognised as rising powers on the world stage (such as the BRICS).

Erga Omnes – The principle upon which legislation is applicable towards everyone regardless of social background. Within international law, the term depicts the legal obligations of states.

Ethnic Cleansing – The forced removal of ethnic, racial and religious groups from any given territory by another ethnic group. Ethnic cleansing may occur on the basis of forced migration, ethnic dilution and intimidation. The term has become more prevalent since the mid-1990s.

Exploitation – A situation in which a dominant group manipulates another. The term is associated with dependency theorists who emphasise the role of a transnational social class, and the world systems perspective which highlights the role played by powerful states within the global economy.

Facts on the Ground – A term often employed within diplomatic circles to denote the situation as it really is. The phrase is rooted in pragmatism rather than abstract notions of justice, equity and morality. One illustration of the term is the existence of Israeli settlements in the West Bank (including East Jerusalem) and the Golan Heights.

Failed State – A state in which there are no political institutions that can claim sovereignty within that territory. Failed states often provide a haven for terrorist organisations and other extremist groups. Humanitarian intervention may be justified within a failed state such as Somalia in 1992.

Failing State – A state in which the government finds it highly problematic to maintain social order. This may eventually lead towards the country being classed as a failed state. Such countries are either emerging from a disruptive conflict or on the brink of an actual conflict.

Federalism – A political system in which legal and political structures distribute power between two or more distinct levels of government. The United States and Russia are both based upon a federalist system of governance. In relation to regional integration, the EU is committed to the federalist aim of the United States of Europe.

Four Freedoms – A set of goals articulated by Franklin Roosevelt during the 1940s. They include freedom of speech and religious worship alongside freedom from want and fear. The four freedoms formed the basis for the Universal Declaration of Human Rights.

Functionalism – A theoretical perspective which recognises the common interests of states and non-state actors towards the process of integration. The term is commonly used in the context of globalisation.

Fundamentalism – An ideological doctrine which demands total obedience from its members. The term is usually applied in the context of extremist groups, terrorist activity and totalitarian regimes.

G2 – A term used to denote the political and economic ties between Washington and Beijing.

G4 – The four countries who campaign for a permanent seat on the UN Security Council. The G4 consists of Germany, Japan, Brazil and India. The G4 is opposed by the uniting for consensus movement under the leadership of Italy.

G5 – The group of five nations who seek to promote dialogue and understanding between developing and developed countries. The G5 consists of the emerging economies of China, India, Brazil, Mexico and South Africa.

G7 – An informal series of meetings between seven of the most developed economies. The G7 relies upon the goodwill of its members as its decisions are non-binding. The G7 is notable for the exclusion of China and as a body that represents the 'West.'

G20 – An international forum of the most advanced economies in the world, the EU and representatives from the IMF and World Bank. The aim of the G20 is to address issues surrounding global financial stability. The G20 is widely seen as a more proactive and effective institution than the G7.

Game Theory – A theoretical model which highlights the manner in which decision-makers interact to take into account the choices of other decision-makers. Conflict and cooperation can be understood via the application of game theory.

Gaza Strip – A densely-populated territory claimed in a legal sense by the State of Palestine (along with the West Bank). In 2006, the electoral success of Hamas provoked an Israeli-led economic and political boycott. In a de facto sense, the State of Israel also restricts the movement of people residing within Gaza.

Geneva Conventions – A set of treaties and protocols that provide an agreed standard for humanitarian treatment in warfare. The Geneva Conventions outline the fundamental rights of wartime prisoners, protections for the wounded and safeguards for civilians.

Genocide – The deliberate destruction of a large number of people from a particular nation or ethnic group. The 1948 UN Genocide Convention defined genocide as 'acts committed with intent to destroy...a national, ethnic, racial or religious group'.

Global Commons – Those parts of the planet to which all nations have access. The global commons lies outside the jurisdiction of any national government. There are several examples of the global commons such as the High Seas and Outer Space.

Global Governance – The process of decision-making at the global level aimed at solving problems that affect more than one state (or region). Liberals argue that there has been progress towards global governance driven by the Bretton Woods system, international criminal courts and the G20. However, realists challenge this assumption given the continued importance of statism and sovereignty.

Globalisation – A political system characterised by mutual dependence within the political, cultural and economic realm. The significance of globalisation is a source of disagreement between the dominant theoretical perspectives within International Relations. The impact of globalisation has been greatest upon the concept of sovereignty due to the growing salience of non-state actors, and the extent to which states are interdependent.

Golden Arches Theory – A modern variant upon the commerce (or capitalist) peace theory. Associated with Thomas Friedman, the golden arches theory claims that no two countries with a McDonalds would fight against one another. Friedman argued that when a country reaches a sufficient level of economic development it becomes a 'McDonald's country'. The golden arches theory is undermined by the 2006 war between Israel and Lebanon, Russia-Georgia (2008) and Russia-Ukraine (2014 and 2022).

Good Governance – A condition in which foreign aid is provided to those countries that seek to address problems such as corruption. The provision of financial assistance is therefore conditional upon improvements made to governance within recipient countries.

Great Power – A country with considerable influence within international relations. The term is used interchangeably with major powers.

Gridlock – An inability to take united and decisive action within an organisation. For instance, the UNSC has been gridlocked over the Syrian Civil War due to divisions amongst the P5.

Guantanamo Bay – An area of Cuban territory claimed by the United States. The Cuban government regards American presence as an illegal occupation on the basis that the original agreement was a violation of international law.

Hard Power – The use of force (or coercion) to meet a political objective of some kind. Unlike soft power, hard power entails the act or threat of aggression. According to Joseph Nye, the term reflects the ability of a state to utilise economic and military might. The significance of hard power may have declined in the contemporary era.

Hawks – A term used to describe a politician or academic favourable towards warfare and militarism. The term is sometimes preceded by 'chicken' or 'liberal.' The former refers to an individual who advocates a hawkish stance whilst avoiding military service. The latter denotes a liberal who adopts an aggressive approach towards the spread of democracy and capitalism.

Hegemonic Stability Theory – An argument which stipulates that the larger the concentration of power into the hands of the pre-eminent state, the more peaceful the international order will be. According to Charles P. Kindleberger, the instability of the 1920s and 30s was caused in part by the lack of a global hegemonic power.

Hegemony – Where a single state exercises structural dominance over the rules, norms, conventions and behaviour of a regional or international system. The existence of a hegemonic power is central towards an understanding of hegemonic stability theory. A hegemonic state is able to exercise leadership and its status is expressed in structural, military and economic terms.

Hierarchy of States – A term used to describe how states are stratified within international relations. The classification of states on the basis of hierarchy casts an insight upon concepts such as polarity and the balance of power.

Horizontal Nuclear Proliferation – The spread of nuclear weapons based upon acquisition by states and non-state actors. In terms of the latter, there is the possibility of a terrorist organisation acquiring some form of nuclear weaponry.

Human Rights – Those rights based upon an entitlement by virtue of being human. They are typically considered universal and can be the basis for humanitarian intervention. Since the turn of the century, there has been an increase in the number of institutions and agreements that seek to uphold human rights.

Humanitarian Intervention – Military intervention carried out in the pursuit of humanitarian (rather than geo-strategic) objectives. Humanitarian intervention is likely to be successful when a major global or regional power is prepared to take the lead (such as the French in Mali). Successful intervention also requires an exit strategy and some consideration of nation-building. Humanitarian intervention often reflects double standards and can at times make matters worse.

Hyperpower – A state that is dominant in every domain of international relations. As such, it is of greater importance than a mere superpower. The United States has been described as a hyperpower, although this has in part been undermined by the emergence of China.

Hyper-globalisation – A theoretical perspective which claims that globalisation represents a fundamental and transformative development within international politics. The emergence of a global society may well mark the death knell of the nation-state.

Idealism – A forerunner of liberalism, idealism within International Relations assumes that states are rational actors who recognise the benefits of mutual cooperation. Idealism prescribes a normative foreign policy. According to figures such as Woodrow Wilson, idealism provides a basis for foreign policy, such as the fourteen points and the League of Nations. The academic Michael W. Doyle depicts idealism as a belief that states can trust the positive intentions of others.

Imperialism – Extending power and dominion over territories via acquisition. The three main forms of imperialism are: colonies, protectorates and spheres of influence.

Intended Nationally Determined Contributions – An intended reduction in greenhouse gas emissions as specified under the UNFCCC.

Institutional Peace Theory – A liberal argument that the establishment of international institutions help foster peace and stability. This is closely related to the creation of a global commons. According to liberal theorists, international institutions and organisations can be used to foster a habit of cooperation between states.

International Bill of Human Rights – An overarching term that incorporates the UDHR, the International Covenant on Civil and Political Rights (ICCPR) and the International Covenant on Economic, Social and Cultural Rights (ICESCR). None of these documents are legally binding.

International Court of Justice (ICJ) – The International Court of Justice aims to settle disputes between states in accordance with international law. The ICJ also offers advisory opinions and consists of a panel made up of 15 judges elected by the UN. The effectiveness of the ICJ, also known as 'The World Court', is however undermined by the fact that it cannot initiate cases and needs to gain support from the UNSC in order to enforce its decisions.

International Criminal Tribunals – Institutions established to prosecute war criminals in certain war-torn areas. For instance, the international tribunal into the former Yugoslavia brought high-profile prosecutions against Slobodan Milosevic and Radovan Karadzic. The former was the first Head of State to be placed on trial for war crimes. The International Criminal Tribunal for Rwanda also convicted its former Prime Minister Jean Kambanda.

International Monetary Fund (IMF) – An international financial institution that lies at the epicentre of the Washington Consensus. The chief objectives of the IMF are to facilitate international trade and provide financial assistance. Funding for the IMF derives from quotas and loans.

Intra Legem – A Latin term meaning 'within the law'.

Ipso Facto – A legal term meaning by the act (or fact) itself.

Iron Curtain – The ideological division within Europe between the American and Soviet spheres of influence. The term was used during the Cold War and coined by Winston Churchill. In the Far East, the phrase 'Bamboo Curtain' was also employed to denote the division between capitalism and communism.

Isolationism – The doctrine of isolating a state from international alliances and agreements. Isolationism is characterised by non-intervention and unilateralism. It seeks to place the national interest above those obligations derived from the broader international community.

Juria Jus Non Oritur – A Latin term translated as 'law does not arise from injustice'. Illegal acts (such as annexation) do not therefore create international law.

Jus ad Bellum – A Latin term outlining the circumstances in which a state is justified in using military force. For instance, according to the philosopher Thomas Aquinas, warfare must be justified by the appropriate authority. It could be argued that humanitarian intervention is based upon the notion of right intention or just cause.

Jus Cogens – The principle on which no derogation (or exemption) is permitted amongst sovereign states. Whilst there is no universal agreement as to its application, obvious examples include a ban on genocide and enslavement. The concept of *jus cogens* provides a foundation for international law.

Jus Gentium – A legal phrase meaning 'law of nations'. It is a body of customary law held in common by nations.

Jus in Bello – A Latin term that relates to the conduct of warfare. According to the philosopher and theorist Hugo Grotius, *jus in bello* is characterised by moderation. There are six main principles to consider. These include just cause, warfare as last resort, proper authorisation, right intention, a reasonable chance of success and proportionality. A disproportionate response to a violation of international law by a non-state actor would therefore be contrary to the conduct of warfare.

Jus Inter Gentes – A legal phrase meaning 'law among peoples'. It consists of a body of treaties, conventions and other international agreements.

Jus Soli – The legal principle that an individual's nationality is determined by place of birth. The term is often contrasted with *jus sanguinis* (the law of descent) in which an individual acquires the nationality of their parents.

Kyoto Protocol – An environmental agreement adopted in 1997 that committed transitional economies to limit and reduce greenhouse gas emissions. Kyoto also placed an obligation upon developed countries based on the notion of differentiated responsibility and respective capabilities.

Laissez-faire Economics – An economic system based upon market forces and minimal state intervention. In theory, the Washington Consensus is built upon a laissez-faire approach towards economic management.

Legitimacy – The right and acceptance of proper authority to rule. Legitimacy is a fundamental element of Joseph Nye's concept of soft power, and enables us to better understand the importance of international institutions. For instance, judicial bodies and regional organisations are often undermined by a lack of sufficient legitimacy.

Liberal Democracy – A synergy of liberal freedoms alongside a democratic method of electing representatives in which almost all adults are entitled to political participation. A liberal democracy is therefore liberal in the sense that the power of decision-makers is constrained, and democratic in relation to free competition for power between politicians and political parties.

Liberalism – A theoretical perspective which claims that international relations is characterised by complex interdependence, global governance and rational behaviour. In contrast to Realism, the liberal perspective adopts a normative tone. For instance, liberal figures advocate the democratic peace and the commercial (capitalist) peace theories. Liberals are also supportive of international institutions and globalisation. The liberal approach is therefore centred upon peace, prosperity and progress.

Lisbon Treaty – A Treaty signed in 2007 that sought to make the EU more democratic. It gave more power to the European Parliament, introduced a citizens' initiative and created the EU's diplomatic service.

Long Cycle Theory – A theoretical approach which depicts connections between war, economic supremacy and world leadership. George Modelski (1987) argues that there is a cyclical order that should frame our understanding of International Relations. The long cycle theory challenges the predominant view in which the international system is characterised by anarchy.

Maastricht Treaty – A Treaty signed in 1992 that prepared the pathway towards European Monetary Union, created a CFSP and instigated the co-decision procedure.

Madman theory – An attempt by the Nixon administration to persuade leaders of the Communist bloc that the President was irrational and prone to volatile behaviour.

Mandate – In the context of international relations, a mandate relates to the concept of legitimacy. States and organisations often need a clear mandate in order to confer legitimacy upon humanitarian intervention.

Millennium Development Goals (MDGs) – A series of interlinked development goals agreed upon by the UN in the year 2000. The MDGs were the first internationally agreed goals in relation to economic and social development.

Mitigation – A process by which countries seek to moderate the impact of greenhouse gases in order to tackle climate change (such as a shift from non-renewable to renewable energy sources).

Modernisation Theory – A theoretical perspective which emphasises the need to follow a particular path of economic development (such as Rostow's model of economic growth). Modernisation theory argues that traditional societies will only develop when they adopt practices associated with more advanced economies.

Monadic Peace – The proposition that democracies are more peaceful than non-democratic regimes. Within academia, there is less support for the concept of monadic peace than that of dyadic peace.

Montreal Protocol – An international treaty signed in 1987 aimed at protecting the ozone layer. The Montreal Protocol has undergone a number of revisions, and remains one of the most successful environmental agreements due to a relatively equitable share of the burden. The Protocol also offered effective solutions.

Multilateralism – Where states pursue foreign policy objectives via a constructive engagement with other actors. Even a military superpower may adopt some semblance of multilateralism (such as the 'coalition of the willing' during the Iraq War). Regional powers are also inclined to adopt a multilateral approach (e.g., intervention in Yemen launched in 2015 led by Saudi Arabia).

Multipolarity – The distribution of power in which more than two states have roughly equal amounts of military, cultural and economic influence.

Mutually Assured Destruction (MAD) – An assumption that the devastation caused by nuclear weapons ensures that neither side has any incentive to launch a first-strike. Nuclear annihilation therefore provides a sufficient deterrent. There is no incentive to engage in a first-strike, which thereby ensures stability between two superpowers.

National Identity – An identification with one's nation. The extent to which members of society feel an emotional attachment towards their nation offers a counter-balance to the forces of globalisation.

Nation-Building – The construction of national identity via the agents of the state. The aim is to unify the people within a nation-state. The term has become more applicable towards humanitarian intervention in a failed (or failing) state.

Nation – A community of people who typically share a common national identity, history, religion and language.

Nation-State – A theoretical concept in which nations hold defined territorial statehood. The concept dates back to the Treaty of Westphalia in 1648. The nation-state is a fundamental concept within international relations which continues to shape independence movements throughout the world.

Neocolonialism – The process by which the developed world exerts economic control over LEDCs via exploitation. Neocolonialism is upheld by governments, multinational companies and the Washington Consensus. The term is sometimes used interchangeably with neoimperialism.

Neoconservatism – Neoconservatives advocate the promotion of democracy and capitalism via an interventionist foreign policy. Neoconservatives, who are most prevalent in the United States, tend to adopt a hawkish stance.

Neofunctionalism – A theoretical blueprint for regional integration based upon the logic of spillover. The development of the EU is consistent with neofunctionalism.

Neoliberalism – An updated version of liberalism which claims that the behaviour of states is shaped via absolute gains rather than relative gains. Neoliberals also tend to promote the spread of democratic values as a means to create a more peaceful global world order. They are also favourable towards institutions that generate the conditions necessary to ensure peace and stability. Neoliberalism is built on an assumption that states are rational entities in which cooperation will emerge via norms, institutions and mutual trust.

Neo-Neo Debate – The debate within contemporary International Relations between the neorealist and neoliberal schools of thought.

Neorealism – A strand of realist thought centred on the assumption that the international system is structurally anarchic and it is this structure that determines state behaviour. States are in possession of some offensive military capability and can never be entirely certain about the intentions of another state. The primary motive behind the behaviour of states is that of structural survival.

New Wars – A term associated with Mary Kaldor in order to characterise warfare in the post-Cold War era. New Wars are centred on identitarian politics between competing groups. It is claimed that the nature of warfare has shifted due to the process of globalisation.

Non-democratic State – A system of representative government in which elections take place without a choice of political parties. They are sometimes referred to as no-party democracies.

Non-Refoulement – A principle within international law that prevents a country receiving asylum seekers and then returning them to their country of origin if they would be in danger of persecution.

North Atlantic Treaty, Article 4 – A clause within the North Atlantic Treaty which enables consultation whenever the territorial integrity, political independence or security of any of the signatories is threatened.

North Atlantic Treaty, Article 5 – The famous clause within the North Atlantic Treaty that commits member states to the principle of collective defence, i.e. an attack on one is an attack on all. NATO first invoked Article 5 in 2001 after the terrorist attack of 9/11.

North Atlantic Treaty Organisation (NATO) – An intergovernmental organisation charged with implementing the North Atlantic Treaty, signed in 1949. NATO is centred upon the concept of collective defence in which an attack on one is considered to be an attack upon all. Members therefore accept the principle of mutual defence in response to an external attack. Since the end of the Cold War, the organisation has sought to rebrand itself as a more humanitarian organisation. The organisation has also expanded into the former Soviet sphere of influence and has implemented military action in response to a unanimous position adopted by the UNSC (e.g. enforcing a no-fly zone over Libya in 2011).

North-South Divide – The political and economic distinction between the developed 'North' and the underdeveloped 'South.' The interests of the former often differ to those of the latter on issues such as climate change.

Nuclear Proliferation – The global spread of nuclear weapons. The possession of nuclear weapons tends to hold certain political benefits (such as a deterrent). Furthermore, joining the nuclear club enables a country to become a great power.

Obama Doctrine – The guiding philosophy and strategy of the Obama administration (2009–2017). The principal emphasis centred on multilateralism. Although idealistic in tone, the Obama administration engaged in unilateral action in order to promote American interests where necessary. The Obama doctrine also sought to reduce overseas commitments (particularly in regards to Iraq and Afghanistan).

Offensive Realism – A realist perspective which states that the anarchic nature of global politics promotes aggressive behaviour. States therefore seek to achieve security via domination and hegemony.

Oslo Accords – Agreements reached between Israel and the PLO that were negotiated by the Clinton administration in 1993 and 1995. The PLO agreed to recognise the State of Israel whilst the Israelis recognised the Palestinian right to self-determination. The Oslo Accords also created the Palestinian Authority.

Pacta Sunt Servanda – A legal doctrine stating that agreements must be observed and obeyed.

Panda Diplomacy – The diplomatic practice of sending giant pandas from China to other countries. The term was popularised during the Cold War.

Paris Agreement – A UN agreement signed in 2015 that seeks to limit greenhouse gas emissions. Although there is no enforcement mechanism, the Agreement marked the first-ever comprehensive climate agreement.

Partnership for Peace (PfP) – A series of bilateral agreements between NATO and its partner states. The PfP aims to build up mutual trust between NATO and Eastern Europe, and thereby enhance the organisation's reach.

Peripheral States – According to World Systems Theory, peripheral states within the global economy are exploited by those at the core. This may be on the basis of resource extraction and the location of sweatshops. It is important to note that countries can change their status within the global economy, but the distinction between the two remains.

Plurilateral Agreement – A legal or trade agreement between a number of states. The term is applicable towards the WTO, in which an agreement requires unanimity. This makes the resolution of a bargaining round highly problematic.

Political Globalisation – The growing importance of international organisations within global politics. These organisations are transnational in that they exercise jurisdiction within a broader system of states. Political globalisation often entails moves towards a form of governance with an identifiable executive, legislature and judicial branch.

Positivism – A scientific approach towards a study of the subject matter. Positivism is built on the assumption that the social sciences should replicate the methodology employed within the natural sciences. In doing so, knowledge can be verified on a scientific and causal basis.

Postmodernism – Within International Relations, post-modernism is based on an incredulity towards grand theories. Instead, our understanding of global politics should focus on questioning rather than offering metanarratives (such as Marxism or liberalism). The key contribution of postmodernism is the observation that 'truth' is relative rather than absolute.

Post-Positivism – A reference to those theories that reject the epistemological basis of positivism. Sometimes referred to as reflectivist or interpretivist theories, post-positivism claims that the study of International Relations should include non-state actors and low politics. For instance, a study of ethnicity casts insight towards our comprehension of the subject matter (such as stateless nations). Unlike the predominant metanarratives, the focus of post-positivism is on how power is experienced. Post-positivism also claims that discourse can never be entirely free of power.

Power Vacuum – A scenario in which a government has no control, and no group has replaced them. Insurgents, extremists and organised militia may seek to fill the gap within a failed state. A power vacuum may also occur following a constitutional crisis.

Predatory Hegemon – Where the global hegemon adopts an aggressive pursuit of their own national interest(s) and disregards their obligations towards the international community. The term may be contrasted with a benign hegemon.

Precautionary Principle – A principle applicable towards environmental law. If an activity might have harmful consequences, it is better to control the activity rather than wait for scientific evidence. The precautionary principle was a core element of the Montreal Protocol.

Pre-emptive Strikes – According to the Bush administration, Washington had the right to take military action against the threat of terrorism. A pre-emptive strike was therefore presented as a defence against a perceived future threat. The concept was used as justification for wars in Afghanistan and Iraq.

Protectorate – A state that is controlled by another sovereign state. Protectorates are typically a dependent territory, albeit with a degree of limited autonomy. The protectorate accepts certain obligations depending on the arrangement (such as Puerto Rico in relation to the United States).

Proxy Wars – Those wars instigated by major powers without becoming directly involved. For instance, during the Cold War the two superpowers fought a number of proxy wars whilst avoiding direct confrontation with one another, such as in Angola.

Puppet State – A state that is independent in law, but not in fact. They are under the influence and control of another state due to the threat of military force (such as East Germany in relation to the Soviet Union).

Quasi-Federalism – An intermediate form of state organisation between a unitary state and a federation. It combines features of both federal and unitary government. The term is applicable in relation to the European Union.

Reagan Doctrine – A hawkish foreign policy stance characterised by an ideological and military confrontation with Soviet-backed communism. It combined a religious rhetoric with a significant increase in military expenditure. The Reagan administration provided covert support and funding towards those groups opposed to the spread of communism. The Reagan administration marked a clear departure from the détente of the 1970s.

Realism – A theoretical perspective which claims that international relations should be understood via reference to a number of central tenants. Firstly, the state remains the most significant actor. Secondly, the anarchic political system is characterised by a system of self-help. States also pursue their own national interests and are driven to doing so either as a result of human nature or the anarchic structure of the international system. The realist lens adopts a far more negative view of human nature than liberalism.

Realpolitik – A system of politics or principles based upon practical considerations. It is sometimes referred to as the pursuit of pragmatic policies.

Recognition – A process in which certain facts are accepted with legal and legitimate status. Statehood is a common illustration of recognition within international relations.

Regime Change – The replacement of one government by another. Regime change may be instigated via demands for social change, a revolution or a coup. It may also occur from the reconstruction following the collapse of a failed state. The United States has often been involved with the process of regime change (such as Operation Condor in Latin America).

Regionalism – The formal coordination of activities within a geographical region that comprises a number of states. The growth of regional bodies such as the EU both supports (and refutes) the concept of globalisation.

Relative Gains – The actions of states in respect of power balances and without regard for other relevant factors (such as economics). Relative gains is based on a zero-sum formulation of power politics. Cooperation may be necessary due to power balance considerations, but the focus of states is on relative gains. The concept is more closely associated with the realist perspective on International Relations.

Resolution – A declaration voted on by member states of the UN. A simple majority is required, although important issues require two-thirds support within the General Assembly (such as the admission or expulsion of a member state). Resolutions are non-binding within international law.

Resource Curse – An inverse relationship between a lack of economic development and an abundance of natural resources. It is also known as the paradox of plenty.

Revisionist States – A term used to categorise states that seek to change the present system. A revisionist state is dissatisfied with the current balance of power.

Rights – An entitlement held by an individual or group. The concept of rights is related in some manner to the notion of responsibilities or duties (such as the right to national self-determination).

Rio Summit – Held in 1992, the Earth Summit held in Rio addressed the issue of sustainable development. The main achievement of the Rio Summit was the Climate Change Convention (which later became the Kyoto Protocol and the Paris Agreement). The Rio Summit also instigated the Convention on Biological Diversity.

Rogue States – A term applied to those states that fail to adhere to the norms and conventions of international relations. Rogue states are usually characterised by authoritarian rule, state-sponsored terrorism and weapons of mass destruction. Withdrawal of the term can also be used as a bargaining chip. For instance, Sudan was taken off the list of state-sponsored terrorism in return for diplomatic support for Israel. The US also agreed to lift its veto upon assistance from the IMF and the World Bank.

Rome Statute of the International Criminal Court – The Treaty that established the International Criminal Court (ICC). Entering into force in 2002, the statute outlined four international crimes (genocide, crimes against humanity, war crimes and the crime of aggression). The majority of countries are members of the ICC albeit with notable exceptions such as the United States, Russia, China and Israel.

Rule of Law – In the context of international relations, the rule of law is a principle of governance applicable to a wide range of actors. Individuals, institutions and entities are held accountable within the boundaries of international law. The rule of law aims to impose a system of rules and regulations that are proportionate and non-arbitrary.

Strategic Arms Limitation Treaty – Two rounds of bilateral conferences between the US and the Soviet Union on the issue of arms control. Negotiations led to the Anti-Ballistic Missile Treaty and led to the strategic arms reduction talks of the early 1990s.

Satellite State – An independent state that experiences political, economic and military influence from another state. Countries under the Soviet sphere of influence within Eastern Europe were widely depicted as satellite states.

Security Dilemma – A situation in which actions by a state intended to heighten its security, such as increasing their military arsenal, leads to further instability. It is sometimes referred to as the spiral of insecurity.

Secretary General of the UN – The chief spokesman of the United Nations. Appointed by the member states of the General Assembly, the Secretary General will seek to express the opinions of the international community. The UN Secretary General can at times drive forward the process of global governance, such as Kofi Annan in regards to developing the R2P and the MDGs.

Selective Intervention – A common critique levied against the international community when human rights violations are ignored. Selective intervention routinely highlights the problem of bias and hypocrisy held by powerful states.

Self-Determination – A prescriptive concept in which a nation or imagined community is said to have the right to form its own political structure. Self-determination claims that a nation should achieve statehood and determine how they are governed. According to the ICJ, the right to self-determination is based on *erga omnes*.

Semi-Democracy – A state that holds both democratic and authoritarian elements. A semi-democracy may be classified as a partial democracy rather than a full democracy. They are also known as hybrid regimes with a guided form of democracy.

Shanghai Cooperation Organisation – An alliance amongst Eurasian and South Asian states (most notably Russia and China). Sometimes known as the Shanghai Pact, the aim is to promote cooperation in areas of a shared interest (such as the fight against terrorism). The Shanghai Cooperation Organisation is the largest regional organisation in the world in terms of land mass and population.

Smart Power – A combination of coercion and persuasion in order to promote the national interest. It seeks to underline the importance of military force with the need to establish legitimacy and linkages with others. According to Joseph Nye, the most effective strategies in regards to foreign policy necessitate coercion and persuasion.

Social Cohesion – Those factors which bind members of a society together. Social cohesion is based upon norms, values and mores. Institutions, symbols and national anthems may also be considered within the context of social cohesion.

Soft Law – A situation in which quasi-judicial institutions lack adequate powers of enforcement. The term is associated with international law. For instance, the ICC lacks the power of enforcement when issuing arrest warrants for those convicted of crimes against humanity.

Soft Power – The use of persuasion (rather than force) in order to exert influence over other actors, convincing other states to want the same ends as one's own state. Unlike hard power, soft power operates via intangible factors such as the moral standing of that particular country.

Sovereignty – The authoritative right of a governing body to be the ultimate decision maker and exercise power within its own borders without interference from external bodies.

Spaceship Earth – An ecological concept based on the argument that Planet Earth will eventually run out of fuel. According to ecologists, we are all choking on the exhausts of Spaceship Earth.

Sphere of Influence – A spatial division over which a state or organisation has a level of exclusivity. This may occur on a formal or informal basis. In some cases, a country located within a sphere of influence effectively becomes a satellite state.

Spillover – A fundamental concept within the theory of neofunctionalism. Within the process of European integration, the practical benefits provided by supranational institutions creates an impetus towards deepening the process of integration. Outside of the EU, the economic benefits of increased trade leads towards the formation of multilateral alliances (such as ASEAN).

Stare Decisis – The legal doctrine in which judicial precedent is followed. The courts will therefore abide by a previous decision made. The principle of stare decisis is not part of international law, although judicial members of the World Court may refer to previous decisions.

START – A Treaty signed between the US and the USSR (later Russia) aimed at reducing nuclear arsenals.

Stateless Nation – A single nation that is politically stateless or territorially divided amongst a number of states. It is a value-laden term as it implies that the group should have a state. Stateless nations are usually not represented within the United Nations. A number of stateless nations have a history of statehood, whilst others have always been stateless. Multiple stateless nations can also reside in the same geographical region or country.

Statism – The realist notion that states are the principal actors within international relations. Realism offers a state-centric approach whilst the liberal perspective acknowledges the importance of non-state actors.

Status-Quo Ante Bellum – A Latin phrase meaning 'the situation as it existed before the war'.

Status-Quo State – A state that seeks to uphold the current international system of states. As the term implies, status quo states wish to preserve the principal features of the present system (such as the balance of power). The more powerful a state, the more likely it is that they will seek to preserve the status quo. A high number of powers seeking to preserve the status quo may contribute towards a more peaceful international system.

Stimson Doctrine – The non-recognition of those states created as a result of military aggression.

Structural Power – The level of power exercised by certain states within the global political and economic system. For instance, the US holds significant structural power within a range of international organisations.

Stockholm Declaration – An agreement reached by participants at the 1972 UN Conference on the environment. The Stockholm Declaration marked a new approach to the issue of environmental degradation.

Superpower – A term first used by William Fox to indicate those countries with a reach greater than a traditional 'major power'. Superpowers typically possess a global reach, a predominant role within their respective sphere of influence and a massive military capacity (especially in terms of nuclear weaponry).

Sustainable Development Goals (SDGs) – A set of global objectives designed to establish a more sustainable future for all. The sustainable development goals specify targets that states must adhere to. In order to ensure transparency, performance indicators are published.

Sustainable Development – Levels of development that meets the needs of the present without compromising the ability of future generations to meet their own needs. Sustainable development entails an economic, environmental and generational dimension. The term has increased in salience due to climate change.

Terra Nullius – A legal term meaning 'land without an owner' (such as the uninhabited landlocked territory of Bir Tawil between Egypt and Sudan).

Territory – A geographical area usually outlined by the boundaries of a country (or nation). There are several territories throughout the world where two or more ethnic groups claim sovereignty.

Terrorism – The use or threat of action designed to influence a government or to intimidate the public. Terrorism also seeks to advance a political, religious or ideological cause. Terrorism therefore consists of the use of political violence to demand social change. As the name implies, terrorism aims to spread fear amongst the public in order to influence decision-makers.

Theocracy – A regime based upon a strong adherence to religious beliefs (such as Iran). In a theocracy, laws are divinely ordained. The creation of a theocratic regime is at times the long-term objective of some terrorist organisations, especially in relation to groups such as Islamic State and al-Qaeda.

Three C's – Conflict, competition and cooperation. The three C's are often used as a template towards an understanding of bilateral relations between states.

Tragedy of The Commons – The argument that rational actions by individuals can lead to irrational outcomes. In the words of Garrett Hardin 'freedom in a commons brings ruin to all.' The term is applicable towards an understanding of climate change.

Transformational Diplomacy – A phrase used during the Bush administration in order to promote democracy via military coercion. It may be contrasted with smart power, which seeks to combine elements of both soft and hard power.

Trans-Pacific Partnership (TPP) – A proposed trade agreement signed in 2016 amongst several states including the US, Japan and Australia. When the Trump administration withdrew from the TPP, the remaining countries negotiated a new agreement called the Comprehensive and Progressive Agreement for Trans-Pacific Partnership. In political terms, the partnership seeks to reduce the economic dependence of signatory states on China.

Trump Doctrine – The Trump administration was characterised by a mix of populist measures with a nativist 'America first' approach. The Trump doctrine was a blend of hawkish rhetoric and selective intervention. It therefore represented a rejection of globalism, multilateralism and liberalism. Examples of the Trump doctrine include the raid on Yakla, recognising Jerusalem as the capital of Israel and a drone strike killing the high-ranking Iranian official Qasem Soleimani.

Unilateralism – A foreign policy approach in which states pursue their own interests without any diplomatic or military involvement from others.

Unipolarity – An international system in which there is only one pre-eminent state. In a unipolar system, one dominant state has the capacity to act as a hegemon. Some theorists argue that unipolarity ensures stability. The dependent factor is the intentions of the dominant power; as a benign hegemon will act in a very different manner to a predatory hegemon.

United Nations (UN) – Founded after the Second World War in 1945, the United Nations is an intergovernmental organisation which chiefly endeavours to maintain international peace and security, international cooperation, and be the centre of the harmonisation of state activity – following the aims set out in its founding document, the UN Charter.

United Nations Charter, Article 42 – The clause within the UN Charter that allows the organisation to utilise military action. This may entail a role for peace-keeping operations.

United Nations Charter, Article 51 – The clause within the UN Charter that enables states to engage in military action on the basis of self-defence.

United Nations Framework Convention on Climate Change (UNFCCC) – An environmental treaty that seeks to address climate change. The UNFCCC has resulted in a number of salient environmental agreements such as the Kyoto Protocol and the Paris Agreement.

Universal Declaration of Human Rights (UDHR) – A document that enshrines a set of universal rights and freedoms. The UDHR recognises that all humans are born free and equal in dignity and rights regardless of social background. In historical terms, it marked the initial step towards the International Bill of Rights

Uti Possidetis – The legal principle that territory remains with its possessor at the end of the conflict unless otherwise provided for via a treaty. Each side retains whatever territory it holds at the end of the war.

Vertical Nuclear Proliferation – The accumulation of nuclear weapons by established nuclear states.

Veto – To vote against or refuse to ratify. In the UN Security Council, members of the permanent five hold a technical veto, as resolutions may only pass if the P5 vote unanimously. However, there is a so-called 'sixth veto' whereby the seven non-permanent members vote against a resolution.

Victor's Justice – A term that refers to the double standards often employed by the victorious side. Crimes committed by the defeated party are therefore subject to punishment, but those committed by the winning side are not. For example, the UN Tribunal into the Rwandan genocide only convicted Hutus.

War on Terror – A concerted attempt by the United States and other key allies to defeat those groups considered responsible for 9/11. The War on Terror differs from conventional warfare in that the latter was fought against a distinct state and a uniformed organisation, the former is not. It is also characterised by an attempt to deal with rogue states and to prevent the proliferation of nuclear weapons. However, critics claim that the War on Terror is almost exclusively directed at militant Islam.

Washington Consensus – A series of policy prescriptions promoted by institutions based in the American capital. It entails a package of measures such as privatisation, deregulation and marketisation. The Washington Consensus is often contrasted with the Beijing Consensus as a potential pathway towards economic development.

West Bank – A landlocked territory under Israeli occupation since 1967 (including the contentious area of East Jerusalem). The West Bank is divided between illegal Israeli settlements and the remit of the Palestinian National Authority. The Oslo Accords created administrative districts with varying levels of Palestinian autonomy.

Westernisation – A term often used by critics of globalisation to emphasise the extent to which Western governments and Western-based companies export a set of norms and values to other countries. Westernisation is closely associated with the process of globalisation.

Wisconsin School – A school of thought which claims that American foreign policy can be understood as the search for markets abroad. Economic factors are therefore more salient than other possible explanations (such as the balance of power).

World Bank – An international financial institution that provides grants and loans to governments of middle and low-income countries.

World Economic Forum – An international non-governmental organisation in which prominent political and economic stakeholders meet in Davos, Switzerland. The organisation provides a platform to promote a shared capitalist agenda with no democratic accountability or transparency.

World Trade Organisation (WTO) – An intergovernmental organisation created in 1995 in order to replace the GATT. The WTO seeks to regulate international trade in goods, services and intellectual property. It also provides a framework for negotiating trade agreements, resolving disputes and avoiding discrimination between trading partners.

World Systems Theory – A theoretical perspective which emphasises the world system (rather than nation-states) as the main focus of analysis. Associated with the work of Immanuel Wallerstein, the chief feature of the world systems theory is its focus upon the transnational division of labour between core, semi-peripheral and peripheral states. It also claims that the global economic system is highly exploitative.

Zone of Peace – A discrete geographical region of the world in which states have maintained peaceful relations amongst themselves for a period of time. The European Union has sought to create a zone of peace on a war-torn continent. Former rivals have placed their historical enmity aside in order to build a more peaceful continent.

References

Aisbett, E., Harrison, A.E., Levine, D.I., Scorse, J. and Silver, J. (2021). Do Multinational Corporations Exploit Foreign Workers?. In: Fritz-Foley, C., Hines, J.R. and Wessel, D. (Eds.). *Global Goliaths: Multinational Corporations in the 21st Century Economy*. Washington D.C.: Brookings Institution Press. 257–298.

Aksenov, P. (2013, Sept. 26). Stanislav Petrov: The man who may have saved the world. *bbc.co.uk*. Available at: https://www.bbc.co.uk/news/world-europe-24280831.

Allison, G. (2017) *Destined for War: Can America and China Escape Thucydides's Trap*. Boston, MA: Houghton Mifflin Harcourt.

Amnesty International. (2020, May 18). Guantánamo Bay: 14 years of injustice. *amnesty.org*. Available at: https://www.amnesty.org.uk/guantanamo-bay-human-rights.

Amnesty International. (2021, June 10). China: Draconian repression of Muslims in Xinjiang amounts to crimes against humanity. *amnesty.org*. Available at: https://www.amnesty.org/en /latest/press-release/2021/06/china-draconian-repression-of-muslims-in-xinjiang-amounts-to-crimes-against-humanity/.

Anderson, B. (1983). *Imagined Communities: Reflections on The Origin and Spread of Nationalism*. London: Verso.

Angell, N. (1909). *The Great Illusion: A Study of The Relations of Military Power in Nations to Theory Economic and Social Advantage*. London: William Heinemann.

Armitage, R.L. and Nye, J. S. (2007). *Smart Power and the U.S. Strategy for Security in a Post-9/11 World*. Testimony before the Subcommittee on National Security and Foreign Affairs, House Committee on Oversight and Government Reform. Washington, DC: Centre For Strategic and International Studies.

Ayoob, M. (2004). Third World Perspectives on Humanitarian Intervention and International Administration. *Global Governance*. 10(1): 99–118.

Baron, J. (2013). *Great Power Peace and American Primacy: The Origins and Future of a New International Order*. New York: Palgrave Macmillan.

Baylis, J., Smith, S. and Owens P. (Ed.).(2016). *The Globalization of World Politics: An Introduction to International Relations*. Seventh Edition. Oxford: Oxford University Press.

Beehner, L. (2007, Feb. 22). The 'Coalition of The Willing'. *cfr.org*. Available at: https://www. cfr.org/backgrounder/coalition-willing.

Bhagwati, J. (2007, Feb. 18). Made In China (Review of Hutton, W. (2007). *The Writing on The Wall: China and The West in the 21st Century*. New York: Free Press). *The New York Times Book Review*. p.25.

Binder, M. (2015). Paths to intervention: what explains the UN's selective response to humanitarian crises?. *Journal of Peace Research*. 52(6): 712–726.

Binder, M. (2017). *The United Nations and the Politics of Selective Humanitarian Intervention*. Basingstoke: Palgrave Macmillan.

Bloor, K. (2019). *Sociology: Theories, Theorists and Concepts*. London: New Generation Publishing.

Blum, W. (2000). *Rogue State: A Guide to the World's Only Superpower*. London: Zed Books Ltd

Brown, C. and Ainley, K. (2009). *Understanding International Relations*. Fourth Edition. Basingstoke: Palgrave Macmillan.

Bull, H. (1966). "Society and Anarchy in International Relations". In Butterfield, H. and Wight, M. (Eds.), *Diplomatic Investigations: Essays in The Theory of International Politics*. London: George Allen and Unwin, pp. 35–50.

Bull, H. (2012). *The Anarchical Society: A Study of Order in World Politics*. Fourth Edition. Basingstoke: Palgrave Macmillan.

Butler, J. (1988). Performative Acts and Gender Constitution: An Essay in Phenomenology and Feminist Theory. *Theatre Journal*. 40(4): 519–531.

Butler, J. (1990). *Gender Trouble: Feminism and The Subversion of Identity*. New York: Routledge.

Cairncross, F. (1997). *The Death of Distance: How the Communications Revolution Will Change Our Lives*. London: Orion Publishing Book.

Campbell, H. (2013). *Global NATO and the Catastrophic Failure in Libya*. New York: Monthly Review Press.

Climate Action Tracker. (2021). China. *climateactiontracker.org*. Available at: https://climate actiontracker.org/countries/china/.

Carr, E.H. (1945). *Nationalism and After*. London: Macmillan.

Carr, E.H. (2016) [1939]. *The Twenty Years' Crisis: 1919–1939*. Cox, M. (Ed.). London : Palgrave Macmillan.

Cassel, D. (2001). Does International Human Rights Law Make a Difference?. *Chicago Journal of International Law*. 2(1): 121–135.

Castells, M. (1996). *The Rise of the Network Society - The Information Age: Economy, Society and Culture - Vol. 1*. Oxford: Blackwell.

Centers for Disease Control and Prevention. (2021). What is Ebola Virus Disease?. *cdc.gov*. Available at: https://www.cdc.gov/vhf/ebola/about.html.

Chang, H.J. (2002). Breaking the Mould: An Institutionalist Political Economy Alternative to the Neo-Liberal Theory of the Market and the State. *Cambridge Journal of Economics*. 26(5): 539–559.

Chomsky, N. (1991). *Deterring Democracy*. London: Verso Books.

Chomsky, N. (2000). *Rogue States: The Rule of Force in World Affairs*. London: Pluto Press.

Cobden, R. (1903). *The Political Writings of Richard Cobden – Volume One*. London: T. Fisher Unwin.

Cohn, C. (1987). Sex and Death in the Rational World of Defense Intellectuals. *Signs*. 12(4): 687–718.

Cohn, C. and Ruddick, S. (2004). "A Feminist Ethical Perspective on Weapons of Mass Destruction". In Hashmi, S. and Lee. S.P. (Eds.). *Ethics and Weapons of Mass Destruction: Religious and Secular Perspectives.* Cambridge: CUP. 405–435.

Cooper, R. (2003). *The Breaking of Nations: Order and Chaos in The Twenty-First Century*. London: Atlantic Books.

Cosgrove-Mather, B. (2005, Jan. 11) Warmed Over. *cbsnews.com*. Available at: https://www. cbsnews.com/news/warmed-over/.

Cox, R.W. (1981). Social Forces, States and World Orders: Beyond International Relations Theory. *Millennium: Journal of International Studies.* 10(2): 126–155.

Deutsch, K.W. and Singer, J.D. (1964). Multipolar Power Systems and International Stability. *World Politics*. 16(3): 390–406.

Donnelly, J. (2000). *Realism and International Relations*. Cambridge: Cambridge University Press.

Dos Santos, T. (1970). The Structure of Dependence. *The American Economic Review*. 60(2): 231–236.

Dunne, Tim and Brian C. Schmidt. (2020). 'Realism' in John Baylis, Steve Smith and Patricia Owens (eds.) *The Globalization of World Politics*. Oxford: Oxford University Press.

Dukes, P. (2000). *The Superpowers: A Short History*. London and New York: Routledge.

Easterly, W. (2007). *The White Man's Burden: Why the West's Efforts to Aid the Rest Have Done So Much Ill and So Little Good*. Oxford: Oxford University Press.

Economist Intelligence Unit. (2021). *Democracy Index: 2020*. London: EIU.

Elcano Institute. (2021). Elcano Global Presence Index. Available at: https://explora.globalpresence.realinstitutoelcano.org/en/ranking/iepg/global/2020/2013/ES,DE,CA,CN,JP,IT,NL,US,GB,FR,XBEU,KR,IN/US/1.

Elliott, L. (2019, Jan. 21). World's 26 richest people own as much as poorest 50%, says Oxfam. *theguardian.com*. Available at: https://www.theguardian.com/business/2019/jan/21/world-26-richest-people-own-as-much-as-poorest-50-per-cent-oxfam-report.

Enloe, C. (2004). *The Curious Feminist: Searching for Women in a New Age of Empire*. Berkeley, CA: University of California Press.

Extinction Rebellion (2019). *This Is Not A Drill: An Extinction Rebellion Handbook*. London: Penguin Books.

Fanon, F. (1963). *The Wretched of The Earth*. Farrington, C. (Trans.). New York: Grove Press.

Fernandes, A., Rocha, N. and Ruta, M. (2021, 23 June). The economics of deep trade agreements: A new eBook. *Voxeu.org*. Available at: https://voxeu.org/article/economics-deep-trade-agreements-new-ebook.

Finnemore, M. (1996). *National Interests in International Society*. Ithaca, NY: Columbia University Press.

Friedman, M. and Friedman, R. (1980). *Free to Choose: A Personal Statement*. New York: Harcourt Brace Jovanovich.

Friedman, T.L. (1989). *From Beirut to Jerusalem*. New York: Farrar, Straus and Giroux.

Friedman, T.L. (1996, Dec. 8). Foreign Affairs Big Mac I. *nytimes.com*. Available at: https://www.nytimes.com/1996/12/08/opinion/foreign-affairs-big-mac-i.html.

Friedman, T.L. (2000). *The Lexus and The Olive Tree*. London: HarperCollins Publishers.

Friedman, T.L. (2005). *The World Is Flat: A Brief History of The Globalised World in The Twenty-First Century*. London: Allen Lane.

Fukuyama, F. (1989). The End of History?. *The National Interest*. 16: 3–18.

Fukuyama, F. (1992). *The End of History and The Last Man*. New York: Free Press.

Gallarotti, G.M. (2011). Soft power: what it is, why it's important, and the conditions for its effective use. *Journal of Political Power*. 4(1): 25–47.

Gartzke, E. (2007). The Capitalist Peace. *American Journal of Political Science*. 51(1):166–191.

Global Fire Power. (2021). 2021 Military Strength Ranking. *globalfirepower. com*. Available at: https://www.globalfirepower.com/countries-listing.php.

Gray, J. (2001, Sept. 24). The Era of Globalisation is Over. *newstatesman. com*. Available at: https://www.newstatesman.com/uncategorized/2001/09/the-era-of-globalisation-is-over.

Gray, J. (2020, Apr. 1). Why this crisis is a turning point in history. *newstatesman.com*. Available at: https://www.newstatesman.com/uncategorized/2020/04/why-crisis-turning-point-history.

Grieco, J.M. (1988). Anarchy and The Limits of Cooperation: A Realist Critique of The Newest Liberal Institutionalism. *International Organization*. 42(3): 485–507.

Guillaume, X. (2011). 'Resistance and the International: The Challenge of the Everyday'. *International Political Sociology*. 5(4): 459–462.

Gunning, J. and Baron, I.V. (2014). *Why Occupy a Square? People, Protests and Movements in the Egyptian Revolution*. Oxford: Oxford University Press

Haas, E.B. (1958). *The Uniting of Europe: Political, Social, and Economic Forces, 1950–1957*. Stanford, CA: Stanford University Press.

Haas, E.B. (1975). *The Obsolescence of Regional Integration Theory*. Berkeley, CA: Institute of International Studies, University of California Press.

Hafner-Burton, E.M. and Tsutsui, K. (2005). Human Rights in a Globalizing World: The Paradox of Empty Promises. *American Journal of Sociology*. 110(5): 1373–1411.

Hardin, G. (1968). The Tragedy of the Commons. *Science*. 162(3859): 1243–1248.

Hayter, T. (1971). *Aid as Imperialism*. London: Penguin Books.

Hegre, H., Ellingsen, T., Gates, S. and Gleditsch, N.P. (2001). Toward a Democratic Civil Peace? Democracy, Political Change, and Civil War, 1816–1992. *The American Political Science Review*. 95(1): 33–48.

Held, D. and McGrew, A. (2002). *Globalization and Anti-Globalization*. Cambridge: Polity Press.

Held, D. and McGrew, A.G. (Eds.). (2002). *Governing Globalization: Power, Authority and Global Governance*. Cambridge: Polity Press.

Held, D., McGrew A., Goldblatt, D. and Perraton, J. (1999). *Global Transformations: Politics, Economics and Culture*. Stanford, CA: Stanford University Press.

Heller, J. (2019, Dec. 22). Netanyahu accuses ICC of anti-Semitism in pursuit of war crimes probe. *reuters.com*. Available at: https://www.reuters.com/article/us-icc-palestinians-israel-idUSKBN1YQ0KC.

Herz, J. (1976). *The Nation-State and The Crisis of World Politics: Essays on International Politics in The Twentieth Century*. New York: McKay.

Hilsum, L. (1994, Dec. 5). What on Earth Were They Doing?. *New Internationalist*. Available at: https://newint.org/features/1994/12/05/doing.

Hirst, P. and Thompson, G. (1996). *Globalization in Question: The International Economy and the Possibilities of Governance*. Cambridge: Polity Press.

Hobbes, T. (2017) [1651]. *Leviathan*. Christopher Brooke (Ed.). London: Penguin Books.

Hobden, S. and Jones, R.W. (2016). Marxist Theories of International Relations. In Baylis, J., Smith, S. and Owens P. (Ed.). *The Globalization of World Politics: An Introduction to International Relations*. Seventh Edition. Oxford: Oxford University Press. pp. 129–143.

Hoffmann, S. (1966). Obstinate or Obsolete? The Fate of the Nation-State and the Case of Western Europe. *Daedalus*. 95(3): 862–915.

Hooper, C. (1999). Masculinities, IR and the 'Gender Variable': A Cost-Benefit Analysis for (Sympathetic) Gender Sceptics. *Review of International Studies*. 25(3): 475–491.

Howard, M. (2000). *The Invention of Peace: Reflections on War and International Order*. London: Profile Books.

Human Rights Watch. (1996). Shattered Lives: Sexual Violence during the Rwandan Genocide and its Aftermath. *hrw.org*. Available at: https://www.hrw. org/reports/1996/ Rwanda. htm.

Human Rights Watch. (2019). Somalia: Events of 2018. *hrw.org*. Available at: https://www. hrw.org/world-report/2019/country-chapters/somalia#.

Huntington, S. (1993). The Clash of Civilizations?. *Foreign Affairs*. 72(3): 22–49.

Huntington, S. (1996). *The Clash of Civilizations and the Remaking of World Order*. New York: Simon & Schuster.

Huntington, S. (1999). The Lonely Superpower. *Foreign Affairs*. 78(2): 35–49.

In.europa. (2017). State Power Index. *index.ineuropa.pl*. Available at: http:// index.ineuropa. pl/en/state-power-index/.

Intergovernmental Panel on Climate Change. (2021). *AR6 Climate Change 2021: The Physical Science Basis*. Geneva: IPCC. Available at: https://www. ipcc.ch/report/ar6/wg1/ downloads/report/IP CC_AR6_WGI_Full_Report.pdf.

International Institute for Strategic Studies. (2020). Chapter Two: Comparative Defence statistics. *Military Balance*. 120(1): 21–27.

Jackson, R. (2000). *The Global Covenant: Human Conduct in a World of States*. Oxford: Oxford University Press.

Jervis, R. (1978). Cooperation Under the Security Dilemma. *World Politics*. 30(2): 167–214.

Jezard, A. (2018, Apr. 23). Who and what is 'civil society?'. *weforum.org*. Available at: https:// www.weforum.org/agenda/2018/04/what-is-civil-society/.

Jordan, A. and Adelle, C. (2012). *Environmental Policy in The EU: Actors, Institutions and Processes*. Third Edition. London: Routledge.

Kagan, R. (2004). *Of Paradise and Power: America and Europe in The New World Order*. London: Atlantic Books.

Kaldor, M. (2013) *New and Old Wars: Organised Violence in a Global Era*. Third Edition. Cambridge: Polity Press.

Kant, I. (1991) [1796]. *To Perpetual Peace: A Philosophical Sketch*. Ted Humphrey (Trans.). Indianapolis, IN: Hackett Publishing Company.

Katzenstein, P.J. (1996). *The Culture of National Security: Norms and Identity in World Politics*. Ithaca, NY: Columbia University Press.

Kelemen, R.D. (2003). The Structure and Dynamics of EU Federalism. *Comparative Political Studies*, 36(1-2): 184–208.

Kennan, G.F. [X]. (1947). The Sources of Soviet Conduct. *Foreign Affairs*. 25(4): 566–582.

Kennedy, P. (1987). *The Rise and Fall of The Great Powers*. New York: Random House.

Keohane, R. (1984). *After Hegemony: Cooperation and Discord in the World Political Economy*. Princeton, NJ: Princeton University Press.

Keohane, R. and Nye, J.S. (1977) *Power and Interdependence*. New York: The Free Press.

Keynes, J.M. (2015). *The Essential Keynes*. London: Penguin Classics.

Khor, M. (2000). *Globalization and The South: Some Critical Issues*. Discussion Paper 147. Geneva: United Nations Conference on Trade and Development. Available at: https://unctad .org/system/files/official-document/dp_147.en.pdf.

Kindleberger, C.P. (1973). *The World in Depression, 1929–1939*. Berkeley, CA: University of California Press.

Klein, N. (2000). *No Space, No Choice, No Jobs, No Logo: Taking Aim at The Brand Bullies*. Toronto: Vintage Canada.

Klug, F. (2015). *A Magna Carta for All Humanity: Homing in on Human Rights*. Abingdon: Routledge.

Krasner. S.D. (1999). *Sovereignty: Organised Hypocrisy*. Princeton, NJ: Princeton University Press.

Kreuder-Sonnen, C. and Zangl, B. (2015). Which post-Westphalia? International organizations between constitutionalism and authoritarianism. *European Journal of International Relations*. 21(3): 568-594.

Locke, J. (1967) [1690] *Two Treatise of Government*. Laslett, P (Ed.). Cambridge: Cambridge University Press.

Lovelock, J. (1979). *Gaia: A New Look at Life on Earth*. Oxford: Oxford University Press.

Lowy Institute. (2019). Global Diplomacy Index. *globaldiplomacyindex. lowyinstitute.org*. Available at: https://globaldiplomacyindex.lowyinstitute. org/#.

Lubin, G. and Badkar, M. (2010, Dec. 17). 15 Facts About McDonald's That Will Blow Your Mind. *businessinsider*.com. Available at: https://www. businessinsider.com/amazing-facts-mc donalds-2010-12?r=US&IR=T.

Machiavelli, N. (1983) [1531]. *The Discourses*. London: Penguin Classics.

Machiavelli, N. (2008) [1532]. *The Prince*. Bondanella, P. (Trans.). Oxford: Oxford University Press.

Macias, A. (2018, Apr. 3). From Aruba to Iceland, these 36 nations have no standing military. *cnbc.com*. Available at: https://www.cnbc.com/2018/04/03/ countries-that-do-not-have-a-stan ding-army-according-to-cia-world-factbook. html.

Malik, M. (2011). *China and India: Great Power Rivals*. Boulder, CO: First Forum Press.

Mandel, D. (2005). 'Managed democracy': Capital and state in Russia. *Debatte: Journal of Contemporary Central and Eastern Europe*. 13(2): 117–136.

Mann, M. (1997). Has Globalization Ended the Rise and Rise of the Nation-State?. *Review of International Political Economy*. 4(3): 472–496.

Mansfield, E.D. and Snyder, J. (2002). Democratic Transitions, Institutional Strength, and War. *International Organization*. 56(2): 297–337.

Marin, G. and Calame, P. (2005). Main Points for the Discussion with The United Nations Secretariat. *alliance21.org*. Available at: http://www.alliance21.org/2003/article.php3?id_articl e=670.

Mayall, J (1990). *Nationalism and International Society*. Cambridge: Cambridge University Press.

Mayall, J (2000). *World Politics: Progress and Its Limits*. Cambridge: Polity Press.

McGlinchey, S. (2022) *Foundations of International Relations*. London: Bloomsbury.

McGrew, A. (2016). Globalisation and Global Politics. In Baylis, J., Smith, S. and Owens P. (Ed.). *The Globalization of World Politics: An Introduction to International Relations*. Seventh Edition. Oxford: Oxford University Press. pp. 15–31.

McLuhan, M. (1964). *Understanding Media: The Extensions of Man*. New York: Signet Books.

McNamara, K. (1999) *The Currency of Ideas: Monetary Politics in The European Union*. New York: Cornell University Press.

Mearsheimer, J.J. (1990). Back to The Future: Instability in Europe After the Cold War. *International Security*. 15(1): 5–56.

Mearsheimer, J.J. (1995). The False Promise of International Institutions. *International Security*. 19(3): 5-49.

Mearsheimer, J.J. (2001). *The Tragedy of Great Power Politics*. New York: W.W. Norton & Company.

Mearsheimer, J.J. (2014). Why the Ukraine Crisis Is the West's Fault: The Liberal Delusions That Provoked Putin. *Foreign Affairs*. 93(5): 77–89.

Mearsheimer, J.J. (2021). The Inevitable Rivalry: America, China, and the Tragedy of Great-Power Politics. *Foreign Affairs*. 100(6). Available at: https://www.foreignaffairs.com/articles/ china/2021-10-19/inevitable-rivalry-cold-war.

Meinecke, F. (1957). *Machiavellism: The Doctrine of Raison D'Etat and Its Place in Modern History*. Douglas Scott (Trans.). London: Routledge and Kegan Paul.

Monteiro, N.P. (2011). Unrest Assured: Why Unipolarity Is Not Peaceful. *International Security*. 36(3): 9–40.

Moravcsik, A. (2009). Europe: The Quiet Superpower. *French Politics*. 7(3-4): 403–22.

Moravcsik, A. (2010). Europe: The Second Superpower. *Current History*. 109(725): 91–8.

Morgenthau, H.J. (1948). *Politics Among Nations: The Struggle for Power and Peace*. New York: Alfred A. Knopf.

Morgenthau, H.J. (1965). *Vietnam and The United States*. New York: Public Affairs Press.

Mudde, C. (2019). *The Far Right Today*. Cambridge: Polity Press.

Müller, J.W. (2016). *What is Populism?*. London: Penguin Books.

Nature. (2020, Apr. 22). Coronavirus: the first three months as it happened. *nature.com*. Available at: https://www.nature.com/articles/d41586-020-00154-w.

Newlines Institute. (2021). *The Uyghur Genocide: An Examination of China's Breaches of the 1948 Genocide Convention*. Washington, DC: Newlines Institute for Strategy and Policy.

North Atlantic Treaty Organization. (2019). [1949]. The North Atlantic Treaty. *nato.int*. Available at: https://www.nato.int/cps/en/natohq/official_texts_17120. htm.

Nye, J. (2003). *The Paradox of American Power: Why the World's Only Superpower Can't Go It Alone*. Oxford: Oxford University Press.

Nye, J.S. (1990). *Bound To Lead: The Changing Nature of American Power*. New York: Basic Books.

Nye, J.S. (2004). *Soft Power: The Means to Success in World Politics*. New York: PublicAffairs Books.

Nye, J.S. (2006, Feb. 23). Think Again: Soft Power. *foreignpolicy.com*. Available at: https:// foreignpolicy.com/2006/02/23/think-again-soft-power/.

Nye, J.S. (2011). *The Future of Power*. New York: PublicAffairs.

Nye, J.S. (2012, May. 8). China's Soft Power Deficit. *wsj.com*. Available at: https://www.wsj. com/articles/SB10001424052702304451104577389923098678842.

O'Neill, A. (2021). Japan: National debt from 2016 to 2026 in relation to gross domestic product. *statista.com*. Available at: https://www.statista.com/ statistics/267226/japans-national -debt-in-relation-to-gross-domestic-product-gdp/.

Ohmae, K. (1995). *The End of The Nation-State: The Rise of Regional Economies*. New York: The Free Press.

OPHI. (2021). Global Multidimensional Poverty Index. *ophi.org.uk*. Available at: https://ophi.o rg.uk/multidimensional-poverty-index/.

Orsi, D. (Ed.). (2018). *The 'Clash of Civilizations' 25 Years On: A Multidisciplinary Appraisal*. Bristol: E-International Relations. Available at: https://www.e-ir.info/publication/the-clash-of-civilizations-25-years-on-a-multidisciplinary-appraisal/.

Ortega, V. (2021, May 17). Which countries are the world's biggest carbon polluters?. *climatetrade.com*. Available at: https://climatetrade.com/which-countries-are-the-worlds-bigg est-carbon-polluters/.

Panda, B.K., Mohanty, S.K., Nayak, I., Shastri, V.D. and Subramanian, S.V. (2020). 'Malnutrition and poverty in India: does the use of public distribution system matter?'. *BMC Nutrition*. 6(41). Available at: https://bmcnutr. biomedcentral.com/articles/10.1186/s40795-020 -00369-0#citeas.

Parashar, S. (2013). *Women and Militant Wars: The Politics of Injury*. London: Routledge.

Pearce, D. (2002). An Intellectual History of Environmental Economics. *Annual Review of Energy and the Environment*. 27(1): 57–81.

Pinker, S. (2011). *The Better Angels of Our Nature: A History of Violence and Humanity*. London: Allen Lane.

Placek, K. (2012). The Democratic Peace Theory. *e-ir.info*. Available at: https://www.e-ir.info/2012/02/18/the-democratic-peace-theory/.

Portland Communications. (2019). The Soft Power 30. *Softpower30.com*. Available at: https:// softpower30.com/.

Prebisch, R. (1950). *The Economic Development of Latin America and its Principal Problems*. New York: United Nations Department of Economic Affairs, Economic Commission for Latin America.

Quackenbush, S.L. and Rudy, M. (2009). Evaluating the Monadic Democratic Peace. *Conflict Management and Peace Science*. 26(3): 268–285.

Reiter, D. (2017). Is Democracy a Cause of Peace?. *Oxford Research Encyclopedia of Politics*. Available at: https://oxfordre.com/politics/ view/10.1093/acrefore/9780190228637.00 1.0001/acrefore-9780190228637-e-287.

Reiter, D. and Stam, A.C. (2003). Identifying the Culprit: Democracy, Dictatorship, and Dispute Initiation. *The American Political Science Review*. 97(2): 333–337.

Ricardo, D. (1817). *On The Principles of Political Economy and Taxation*. London: John Murray.

Roberts, A. and Zaum, D. (2008). *Selective Security: War and the United Nations Security Council since 1945*. London: Routledge.

Robinson, D. (2011). India's Rise as a Great Power, Part One: Regional and Global Implications. Associate Paper. *Future Directions International*. 1–7.

Rosenau, J. (1995). Governance in the Twenty-first Century. *Global Governance*. 1(1): 13–43.

Rosenberg, J. (2000). *The Follies of Globalisation Theory*. London: Verso.

Rostow, W.W. (1971). *Politics and the Stages of Growth*. Cambridge: Cambridge University Press.

Rummel, R. (1997). *Power Kills: Democracy as a Method of Nonviolence*. New Brunswick, NJ: Transaction Books.

Said, E. (1978). *Orientalism: Western Concepts of The Orient*. London: Routledge and Keegan Paul Ltd.

Seabrook, J. (2005). *Consuming Cultures: Globalization and Local Lives*. Oxford: New Internationalist Publications Ltd.

Sending, O.J. and Neumann, I.B. (2006). Governance to Governmentality: Analyzing NGOs, States, and Power. *International Studies Quarterly*. 50(3): 651-672.

Shah, A. (2013, Jan. 7). Poverty Facts and Stats. *globalissues.org*. Available at: https://www. globalissues.org/article/26/poverty-facts-and-stats#src1.

Shishlov, I., Morel, R., and Bellassen V. (2016). Compliance of the Parties to the Kyoto Protocol in the first commitment period. *Climate Policy*. 16(6): 768–782.

Sierra Club. (2018). *NAFTA 2.0: For People or Polluters?* Oakland, CA: Sierra Club. Available at: https://www.sierraclub.org/sites/www.sierraclub.org/files/uploads-wysiwig/NAFTA%20and %20Climate%20Report%202018.pdf.

Singer, H.W. (1998). *Growth, Development and Trade: Selected Essays of Hans W. Singer*. Cheltenham: Edward Elgar Publishing Ltd.

Skinner, Q. (2002). *Visions of Politics – Volume Three: Hobbes and Civil Science*. Cambridge: Cambridge University Press.

Sklair, L. (2002). Democracy and The Transnational Capitalist Class. *The Annals of the American Academy of Political and Social Science*. 581: 144–157.

Skolimowski, H.D. (2003). Cosmocracy: As the Next Stage in the Development in Democracy. *World Affairs: The Journal of International Issues*. 7(2): 133–151.

Smith, A. (1999) [1776]. The Wealth of Nations: Books I-III. London: Penguin Books.

Smith, A. (2009) [1759]. *The Theory of Modern Sentiments*. London: Penguin Books.

Smith-Windsor, B. A. (2000). Hard Power, Soft Power Reconsidered. *Canadian Military Journal*. 1(3): 51–56.

Snyder, G.H. (2007). *Alliance Politics*. Ithaca, NY: Cornell Paperbacks.

Statista Research Department. (2021, Jan. 27). Number of monthly active Twitter users worldwide from 1st quarter 2010 to 1st quarter 2019. *statista. com*. Available at: https://www. statista.com/statistics/282087/number-of-monthly-active-twitter-users/.

Sterio, M. (2013). *The Right to Self-Determination Under International Law: "selfistans", Secession and the Rule of the Great Powers*. Abingdon: Routledge.

Sterling-Folker, J. (2008). The Emperor Wore Cowboy Boots. *International Studies Perspectives*. 9(3): 319–330.

Stiglitz, J. (2002). *Globalization and Its Discontents*. London: Penguin Books.

Stiglitz, J. (2015). *The Great Divide*. London: Penguin Books.

Sun Tzu. (2010). *The Art of War*. Tom Butler-Bowdon (Trans.). Chichester: Capstone Publishing.

Szmigiera, M. (2021, May 7). Global military spending from 2001 to 2020. *statista.com*. Available at: https://www.statista.com/statistics/264434/trend-of-global-military-spending/.

Taylor, H. (2016, April 28). If social networks were countries, which would they be?. *weforum.com*. Available at: https://www.weforum.org/agenda/2016/04/fac ebook-is-bigger-than-the-worlds-largest-country/.

The Economist. (2019, Feb. 2). The paper Euro-army: France and Germany are pushing rival models for defence cooperation. *economist.com*. Available at: https://www.economist. com/ europe/2019/02/02/france-and-germany-are-pushing-rival-models-for-defence-cooperation.

The Fund for Peace. (2021). Fragile States Index. *fragilestatesindex.org*. Available at: https:// fragilestatesindex.org/global-data/.

Third World Network. (1999). Transparency, Participation and Legitimacy of the WTO. *twn.my*. Available at: https://twn.my/title/legit-cn.htm.

Union of Concerned Scientists. (2020). Each Country's Share of CO2 Emissions. *ucsusa.org*. Available at: https://www.ucsusa.org/resources/each-countrys-share-co2-emissions.

Union of European Federalists. (2019). The Ventotene Manifesto. *federalists. eu*. Available at: https://www.federalists.eu/uef/library/books/the-ventotene-manifesto/.

United Nations General Assembly. (1948). International Bill of Human Rights. A/RES/217(III). *undocs.org*. Available at: https://undocs.org/en/A/RES/217(III).

United Nations Peacekeeping. (2021). Our History. *peacekeeping.un.org*. Available at: https:// peacekeeping.un.org/en/our-history.

United Nations. (1945). Charter of The United Nations. *treaties.un.org*. Available at: https:// treaties.un.org/doc/publication/ctc/uncharter.pdf.

United Nations. (1948). Universal Declaration of Human Rights. *un.org*. Available at: https:// www.un.org/en/about-us/universal-declaration-of-human-rights.

United Nations. (1995). PAWSSD Chapter 2. *un.org*. Available at: https://www. un.org/devel   opment/desa/dspd/world-summit-for-social-development-1995/wssd-1995-agreements/paws sd-chapter-2.html.

United Nations. (2021). Sustainable Development Goals. *un.org.* Available at: https://www.un. org/sustainabledevelopment/sustainable-development-goals/.

United Nations Framework Convention on Climate Change. (2021). What is the United Nations Framework Convention on Climate Change?. *unfccc.info*. Available at: https://unfccc.int/proc ess-and-meetings/the-convention/what-is-the-united-nations-framework-convention-on-clima te-change.

Veltmeyer. H. (Ed.). (2016). *Antiglobalization: Prospects for a New World Order?*. Second Edition. London: Routledge.

Veseth, M. (2005). *Globaloney: Unraveling the Myths of Globalization*. Lanham, MD: Rowman & Littlefield Publishers, Inc.

Von Ranke, L. (2011). *The Theory and Practice of History*. Iggers, G.G. (Ed.), Iggers, W.A. (Trans.). Abingdon, Routledge.

Wallerstein, I. (1974). The Rise and Future Demise of the World Capitalist System: Concepts for Comparative Analysis. *Comparative Studies in Society and History*. 16(4): 387–415.

Wallerstein, I. (1979). *The Capitalist World Economy*. Cambridge: Cambridge University Press.

Waltz, K. N. (1959). *Man, the State and War: A Theoretical Analysis*. New York: Columbia University Press.

Waltz, K. N. (1979). *Theory of International Politics*. Reading, MA: Addison-Wesley Publishing Company.

Waltz, K.N. (1981). *The Spread of Nuclear Weapons: More May Be Better*. Washington, DC: International Institute for Strategic Studies.

Waltz, K. N. (1993). The Emerging Structure of International Politics. *International Security*. 18(2): 44–79.

Weber, M. (1994) [1919]. "The Profession and Vocation of Politics". In Lassman, P. and Speirs, R. (Eds.). *Max Weber: Political Writings*. Cambridge: Cambridge University Press. 309–369.

Wendt, A. (1992). Anarchy is What States Make of It: The Social Construction of Power Politics. *International Organization*. 46(2): 391–425.

Wheeler, N. and Booth, K. (2007). *The Security Dilemma: Fear, Cooperation and Trust in World Politics*. New York: Palgrave Macmillan.

Wheeler, N. J. (2000). *Saving Strangers: Humanitarian Intervention in International Society*. Oxford: Oxford University press.

Wight. M. (1977). *Systems of States*. Leicester: Leicester University Press.

Wilson, E.J. (2008). Hard Power, Soft Power, Smart Power. *The ANNALS of the American Academy of Political and Social Science*. 616(1): 110–124.

Wintle, M. (2020). *Eurocentrism: History, Identity, White Man's Burden*. London: Routledge.

Wintour, P. and Rankin, J. (2020, Mar. 26). G20 leaders issue pledge to do 'whatever it takes' on coronavirus. *theguardian.com*. Available at: https://www.theguardian.com/world/2020/mar/26/g20-leaders-issue-pledge-to-do-whatever-it-takes-on-coronavirus.

Wohlforth, W.C. (1999). The Stability of a Unipolar World. *International Security*. 24(1): 5–41.

Wolff, M. (2018). *Fire and Fury: Inside the Trump White House*. New York: Henry Holt and Company.

Woolf, L. (1916). *International Government*. New York: Brentano's.

Woolf, L. (1922). *International Cooperative Trade*. London: The Fabian Society.

World Bank. (2018, Sept. 19). Decline of Global Extreme Poverty Continues but Has Slowed. *worldbank.org*. Available at: https://www.worldbank.org/en/news/press-release/2018/09/19/decline-of-global-extreme-poverty-continues-but-has-slowed-world-bank.

World Bank. (2021a). Poverty Overview. *worldbank.org*. Available at: https://www.worldbank.org/en/topic/poverty/overview#1.

World Bank. (2021b). World Trade (% of GDP). *data.worldbank.com*. Available at: https://data.worldbank.org/indicator/NE.TRD.GNFS.ZS?end=2020&start=1960&view=chart

Note on Indexing

Our books do not have indexes due to the prohibitive cost of assembling them. If you are reading this book in paperback and want to find a particular word or phrase you can do so by downloading a free PDF version of this book from the E-International Relations website. View the e-book in any standard PDF reader and enter your search terms in the search box. You can then navigate through the search results and find what you are looking for. If you are using apps (or devices) to read our e-books, you should also find word search functionality in those.

You can find all of our books here: http://www.e-ir.info/publications

www.ingramcontent.com/pod-product-compliance
Lightning Source LLC
Chambersburg PA
CBHW060313030426
42336CB00011B/1027